Skills in the Age of Over-Qualification

Skills in the Age of Over-Qualification

Comparing Service Sector Work in Europe

Caroline Lloyd and Jonathan Payne

OXFORD
UNIVERSITY PRESS

Great Clarendon Street, Oxford, OX2 6DP,
United Kingdom

Oxford University Press is a department of the University of Oxford.
It furthers the University's objective of excellence in research, scholarship,
and education by publishing worldwide. Oxford is a registered trade mark of
Oxford University Press in the UK and in certain other countries

© Caroline Lloyd and Jonathan Payne 2016

The moral rights of the authors have been asserted

First Edition published in 2016

Impression: 1

All rights reserved. No part of this publication may be reproduced, stored in
a retrieval system, or transmitted, in any form or by any means, without the
prior permission in writing of Oxford University Press, or as expressly permitted
by law, by licence or under terms agreed with the appropriate reprographics
rights organization. Enquiries concerning reproduction outside the scope of the
above should be sent to the Rights Department, Oxford University Press, at the
address above

You must not circulate this work in any other form
and you must impose this same condition on any acquirer

Published in the United States of America by Oxford University Press
198 Madison Avenue, New York, NY 10016, United States of America

British Library Cataloguing in Publication Data
Data available

Library of Congress Control Number: 2016931574

ISBN 978–0–19–967235–6

Printed in Great Britain by
Clays Ltd, St Ives plc

Links to third party websites are provided by Oxford in good faith and
for information only. Oxford disclaims any responsibility for the materials
contained in any third party website referenced in this work.

Preface

A short preface can hardly do justice to the ambitious nature of the research project from which this book stemmed. The project, which began in 2009, and is only now, some six years later, drawing to a close, sought to compare three service sector jobs (vocational teacher, fitness instructor, and café worker) across three European economies (the United Kingdom, Norway, and France). The aim was equally ambitious, seeking to contribute to what we regard as one of the vital questions of our time: how to develop better jobs in an 'Age of Over-Qualification'? It is primarily a comparative book about the relationship between skills and the economy, and the role of institutions and power in shaping work organization and job quality. The research was funded by the Economic and Social Research Council's centre on Skills, Knowledge and Organisational Performance (SKOPE). Both authors were researchers with SKOPE between the late 1990s and 2013 and benefited greatly from the support and collegiality that the centre provided and, in particular, the time and freedom to develop our research on the political economy of skill. Those ideas have been central to both the research and writing of this book.

It goes without saying that we take full responsibility for the design of the research project and the writing of this book. While the project was developed and undertaken primarily by ourselves, in France we were assisted by Francoise Larré, an academic at the Université Toulouse Jean-Jaurès, who was involved in some of the fieldwork and also contributed to our understanding of developments in the vocational education system in France. In addition we would like to thank Mondher Belhadj and Karim Toumi for undertaking many of the café sector interviews in France, Michelle Alexis, Helen Marsden, Rebecca Moseley, Camille Toldre, and Jo Wilkes for transcribing many hours of interview tapes, and Joanne Blake for assistance with the bibliography. In Norway, Sveinung Skule helped us with a number of important research contacts. Thanks are also due to the many participants in the research who took time out of their busy working days to tell us about their work.

Several papers have been presented at conferences, including those held by Work Employment and Society, the British Universities Industrial Relations Association, the International Labour Process Conference, and the Society for the Advancement of Socio-Economics, and many participants have provided

Preface

valuable comments. We have incurred many debts of gratitude along the way, too many to mention in person. We do, however, owe a special note of thanks to SKOPE's Deputy Director, Ewart Keep, for his support and encouragement and the many stimulating conversations we have had down the years both at Warwick and Cardiff Universities. Our thanks also go to our colleagues in our respective departments for engaging us in ongoing discussions about the content and purpose of the book. Writing any book takes time away from other things and we owe special thanks to Mondher and Emma, our respective partners, for their support and patience as well as our children, Ryan, Yasmin, Ethan, and Anya, for putting up with our absences on our trips overseas.

Caroline Lloyd
Jonathan Payne

Contents

List of Figures ix
List of Tables xi

1. Skills, Jobs, and Services: A Challenge for Europe in the Age of Over-Qualification — 1
2. Work and Skills in Contemporary Capitalism — 14
3. National Institutions, Sectors, and Work Organization: A Theoretical Framework — 43
4. Industrial Relations, Skill Formation Systems, and Workplace Development: Continuity and Change in the UK, Norway, and France — 64
5. Professional Work, Autonomy, and Innovation: Vocational Teachers — 93
6. Regulating the Middle: Fitness Instructors — 125
7. Raising the Bottom: Café Workers — 155
8. Towards Better Jobs: Possibilities and Prospects in the Age of Over-Qualification — 188

Appendix 1 217
Bibliography 229
Index 255

List of Figures

2.1.	First time graduation rates for tertiary type A education	18
2.2.	Incidence of over-qualification	27
2.3.	Workers in high-skilled and unskilled jobs	27
3.1.	Employment by occupation, 2014	50
4.1.	Educational levels aged 25–64, 2014	79
8.1.	Differences in job design: vocational teachers	190
8.2.	Differences in job design: fitness instructors	191
8.3.	Differences in job design: café workers	191

List of Tables

3.1.	National differences in forms of work organization (%)	51
4.1.	Education and training features	78
4.2.	Pay and low-paid work (%)	86
4.3.	Measures of qualification demand	87
4.4.	Patterns of work organization 2010 (percentage of employees)	88
4.5.	Labour market data, 2014	91
4.6.	Support for childcare	91
4.7.	Measures of income inequality	92
4.8.	Measures of poverty (%)	92
5.1.	Public sector initial vocational education and vocational teachers	101
5.2.	Teacher education requirements in England, Wales, Norway, and France	104
5.3.	Characteristics of the case study workplaces	106
5.4.	Teacher contracts and programmes taught in the case study hairdressing departments	107
6.1.	Characteristics of case study gyms	128
6.2.	Key features of the fitness industry	129
6.3.	Industrial relations institutions and fitness instructor pay	133
6.4.	Qualification and training provision for fitness instructors	134
6.5.	Qualifications, job design, and pay in the case study gyms	138
7.1.	Food and beverage services industry	160
7.2.	Structure of the café market	161
7.3.	Employers' organizations and trade unions in the hotels and restaurant sector	164
7.4.	Café assistant pay and benefits in the case study workplaces	175
7.5.	Key features of the case study organizations	185

1

Skills, Jobs, and Services

A Challenge for Europe in the Age of Over-Qualification

Introduction

Across the developed world, a skilled workforce has long been viewed by governments and politicians as essential if countries are to compete successfully in a global, 'knowledge-based' economy. With advanced economies assumed to need more and better skills, investment in 'human capital' has come to be seen as increasingly important for international competitiveness, productivity growth, and social inclusion. It is skills, so the argument goes, which allow Western nations to withstand competition from low-wage countries, compete in high-value markets, attract quality foreign direct investment, sustain jobs with high wages, and equip individuals to cope in a fast-moving labour market (Reich 1991). This narrative has provided a rationale for policy intervention around education and training at a time when the ability of states to manage and regulate their national economies has often been questioned (e.g. Ohmae 1990; Gray 1998; Giddens 1998).

However, dark clouds have been gathering over this high skills vision for some years. The proportion of the workforce which can be described as 'knowledge workers', or even just highly skilled, remains a minority, while low-skilled jobs show few signs of disappearing as the number employed in areas such as cleaning, hospitality, retail, and care continues to expand. Over a decade ago, Crouch et al. (1999: 249) explicitly questioned the limits of the skills and learning agenda, asking what would happen if people who had been enjoined to invest in education and training to secure good job prospects subsequently found their expectations disappointed in the labour market. With rising graduate populations and pressure on individuals to gain more qualifications at all levels, there is increasing concern about the capacity of national economies to keep pace with the outputs of the education system, amid evidence of growing levels of over-qualification and skills wastage.

One of the most important questions for contemporary political economy is how can economies grow the number of jobs which require higher skills and, more broadly, what can be done to raise the skill content of jobs at different levels within the labour market? Progress is likely to be limited without addressing issues of work organization and job design. This means identifying the factors that impact upon how jobs are constructed and the possibilities that exist to *upskill jobs* as opposed to simply raising the skills of those who do them. An exploration of these possibilities may help us to assess how far problems of over-qualification and the under-utilization of skills can be 'solved'. This, in turn, may lead us to reflect upon the role and purpose of education itself.

Skills and work organization have been seen as central aspects of job quality not just because higher skilled work tends to be associated with better pay but for the intrinsic rewards of better designed jobs. Back in 2001, the European Union (EU) argued that the challenge confronting Europe was to develop 'more and better jobs' (European Commission 2001) and the issue of job quality began to move up the political agenda. However, the fallout from the 2008 financial crisis has seen a resurgence of a more aggressive form of neo-liberalism, with austerity policies openly championed by political elites in some countries, for example the UK, and imposed on others, such as Greece and Spain. The EU, once a symbol of European unity and a progressive 'social model', has itself become a champion of fiscal retrenchment and neo-liberal flexibility (Meardi 2014). These policies have compounded problems of sluggish growth, widening social inequalities, deepening poverty, and growing labour market insecurity. For some commentators, such responses are symptomatic of a shift towards a global financialized capitalism, which is eating away at the social and regulatory foundations required for its own stability (Streeck 2014a; Hyman 2015a).

Within this context the prospects for developing 'better jobs' appear bleak, to say the least. However, despite common pressures, national capitalisms come in a variety of forms with contrasting institutions and internal power relations between the state, capital, and labour (Jackson and Deeg 2012). There is also evidence to support the position that job quality outcomes, including aspects of work organization, vary between countries (Gallie 2007; Gautié and Schmitt 2010), although some of the comparative capitalism literature is increasingly stressing the internal diversity of 'national models' by sector or region (Crouch et al. 2009). Nevertheless, there are few studies that explore country-based differences and similarities in the way that particular jobs are designed and the role played by national institutions, sector dynamics, and individual organizations. Such research is central to exploring the extent to which it is possible to improve the organization of work and the skill content of jobs at different levels of the labour market.

This book seeks to compare jobs across countries with contrasting models of capitalism. At the same time, it is a book about the service economy, which accounts for the overwhelming majority of jobs in advanced capitalist countries, and specifically about those service jobs which are *rooted* in the national and, in many cases, local economy. A school teacher, a hospital cleaner, a cashier in the local supermarket, a physiotherapist, and a gardener, to name but a few, have a very different relationship with the internationalization forces that one sees in manufacturing or finance. These jobs have to be delivered close to the customer or user, thereby restricting the ability of organizations to move them across national borders in search of lower labour costs. Often marginalized in discussions around globalization, knowledge work, and convergence, jobs such as these make up a substantial proportion of national employment in all advanced economies.

The book draws upon detailed empirical research of three such service sector jobs, spanning both the private and public sector, located at different positions within the occupational ladder—vocational teacher, fitness instructor, and café worker. These jobs are compared across three European countries with contrasting institutional environments, namely Norway, France, and the UK. The aim is to shed light on theoretical issues surrounding the comparative study of work organization, the contribution of skills, the role and purpose of education, and the prospects for better jobs. This introductory chapter begins by outlining the central debates that inform the book in relation to skills, better jobs, and performance. The following sections elaborate on the rationale for a cross-country comparison of work organization in place-based service jobs before discussing the central aims of the research and the methods adopted. The final section provides a short outline of the chapters which follow.

Skill, Better Jobs, and Performance

The central question running through this book is what can be done to improve the skill content of service sector jobs that remain tied to national or local economies? This immediately raises important and contentious questions surrounding what is 'skill' and what constitutes 'skilled work' in services which involve direct interaction with a service user or customer (Bolton 2004; Payne 2009; Green 2011)? Underlying much recent debate is the issue of whether the so-called 'social skills' required in many lower end jobs typically undertaken by women are unrecognized and undervalued, owing to the gendered construction of skill or whether there is a danger of exaggerating the skill required within many of these jobs (Lloyd and Payne 2009 for a discussion). The question of whether 'emotional labour' (Hochschild 1983), or *managing emotions*, is a skill is a case in point and has been used by some authors to argue that even jobs with limited technical skills or knowledge requirements can still be skilled because of the complexity of interactions with customers (e.g. Bolton 2004).

This book does not attempt to compare workers' subjective experience of the relationship with the customer/user (Korczynski 2009) or the social or emotional requirements of jobs across countries. As we discuss in Chapter 2, these notions of skill are not only contested but are difficult to separate out from the qualities possessed by individual workers. To complicate matters further, understandings of skill and skilled worker differ across countries (Brockmann et al. 2011) and introducing the notion of 'social skill' renders any comparison extremely problematic, often serving to cloud rather than illuminate differences.[1] Instead the focus is explicitly on the design of the job, in terms of task complexity, knowledge requirements, and the scope and nature of the worker's ability to influence and make decisions about how work is carried out.

However, 'skill in the job' cannot be divorced from the way that skills are formed. Indeed, international comparative studies have often afforded particular significance to the skill formation system as an important element affecting national differences in the organization of work (see Daly et al. 1985; Maurice et al. 1986; Steedman and Wagner 1989; Streeck 1992; Hall and Soskice 2001). The evidence base on how the skills system helps to shape the design of jobs remains somewhat thin. Studies have tended to be based on developments in a single country, typically drawing on manufacturing industries (e.g. Culpepper and Finegold 1999). One of the aims of this book is to assess the contribution of the skill formation system to the way that jobs are designed within particular areas of the service sector.

Skill and autonomy have often provided a central focus for researchers looking at job quality. There is a substantial body of research pointing to the connections between low pay, poor health and lower life expectancy, and the damaging psychological effects which can result from jobs which are stressful, routinized, and allow workers little room for discretion and autonomy (e.g. Chandola 2010). However, the concept of 'job quality' is much broader than these elements alone (Green 2006). While our primary focus is work organization and skill, the book also explores their relationship with other aspects of job quality, such as pay and working conditions. As such, although the focus is

---

[1] This is not to suggest that exploring worker–customer relations across countries is unimportant, an area where there is scant research. For example, research might consider how social structure, 'class', and 'citizenship' impact on these relations or the role of national regulations or trade unions in offering protection to workers from 'customer abuse' (Korczynski and Evans 2013). However, these issues are not the focus here.

on the extent to which jobs can be upgraded in terms of work organization, the issue of improving other dimensions of work is also featured.

What role can skills play in delivering better jobs? Part of the argument for increasing a country's stock of skills or qualifications through education and training has been that it brings 'win–win outcomes', delivering both better performance and improved job quality. Human capital theory (Becker 1964) has often underlain policy assumptions that countries can boost productivity and international competitiveness through investment in skills and qualifications. For organizations, it has been claimed that benefits can be obtained from pursuing a 'high road' approach which emphasizes skilled and motivated workers producing 'quality' products and services. Research on interactive service work has emphasized the challenge all service sector organizations face in trying to reconcile competing logics of service quality and cost efficiency, with organizations positioned along a spectrum between the two (Korczynski 2002). Moving more organizations towards the 'service quality' end, it has been argued, would require workers to have higher levels of knowledge, expertise, and autonomy, enabling both improved performance and better jobs (e.g. Batt 2000).

However, these claims about the links between investment in skills and qualifications and performance are far from being substantiated, in part because of the difficulty of disaggregating skills from other factors in explaining outcomes, for example capital investment, the economic cycle, or new market entrants (see, for example, Keep et al. 2002). This problem applies when assessing the contribution to performance, be it at the level of the nation, sector, region, or organization. At the same time, there is the longstanding issue of obtaining, and agreeing on, comparable performance data. Indicators such as productivity are highly contentious in the service sector because of the difficulties in identifying common measures (Grugulis and Stoyanova 2011: 518). For the public sector, there are few comparable measures of performance making it problematic to draw any meaningful conclusions at either national or international level (O'Mahony and Stevens 2005).

Furthermore, performance can be defined in multiple ways; for the organization it could be productivity, profit level, market share, or growth, whereas for the worker job quality and sustainability of employment may be seen as more important. Perspectives on performance are also likely to vary between shareholders, managers, government, and communities, and from interests based at local or national level. In the public sector, what constitutes 'good' performance or 'quality' is, if anything, even more contentious than in the private sector, not least in areas such as education where purposes are contested. In many neo-liberal economies, the adoption of New Public Management (NPM) has involved importing a range of practices from the private sector as part of a drive to shift the meaning and measurement of public sector performance and to exert more control over professional workers. NPM may have become something of a globalizing discourse as the best (or only) route to public sector efficiency and quality, but its impact across countries is highly variable (Bach and Bordogna 2011). Public sector jobs are, therefore, likely to be subject to different governance regimes, face various country-based constraints, and operate within different understandings of performance, quality, or success.

For each of the jobs included in the study, consideration is given to exploring the different ways in which performance can be understood. Part of this process involves assessing whether there is any evidence of performance implications at organizational and/or sector level of different approaches to work organization and management. Is it possible to draw any conclusions about whether better jobs are consistent or at odds with, what might be defined as, better performance and how far does this depend on the job, the sector, or the broader national institutional environment?

A Cross-National Perspective

In examining what can be done to develop better service sector jobs, this book takes as its starting point the view that cross-national comparative research on work organization and job quality has much to offer. Of prime importance is to uncover whether there are differences both in the relevant institutions and the way that they might affect work and skills in a specified job. At one level, there is an established body of theoretical work which has focused on understanding how and why work organization varies between countries and the role played by institutions. From the path-breaking French 'societal effects' approach to Streeck's social institutionalism and the more firm-centred 'varieties of capitalism' (Maurice et al. 1986; Streeck 1992; Hall and Soskice 2001), claims have been made about the strong links between national institutions, not least the education and training system, and the organization of work. However, these approaches were drawn from studies and research predominantly undertaken within manufacturing, and often very narrowly defined in terms of engineering. Germany was consistently held up as the high skills beacon compared to the less regulated and more market-based systems of the UK and USA.

The evidence that has emerged more recently from European surveys suggests it is the Nordic countries of Sweden, Denmark, and Norway that have the largest proportion of their workforce in jobs combining higher levels of discretion and learning intensity (see Gallie 2007; Lorenz 2015). Dobbin and Boychuk (1999) refer to different national 'employment logics' in Nordic and neo-liberal economies which result in the former having higher levels of job autonomy across a wide range of occupations. The few qualitative studies of 'matched plants' and jobs, stretching back several decades and involving various European countries, have uncovered some differences in work organization and skills across countries (for example, Quack et al. 1995; Thompson et al. 1995; Mason et al. 1996; Gautié and Schmitt 2010). Germany, the Scandinavian countries, and in some cases France, tend to offer 'better jobs', particularly when compared with those in the UK.

In recent years, progress has been made in developing revised frameworks for exploring the impact of national institutions on *service* sector work which build on some of the aforementioned studies, and which are discussed at greater length in the book (see Bosch and Lehndorff 2005; Carré and Tilly 2012). These are helpful in drawing attention to institutions which are likely to have a stronger influence on service sector work, and in particular lower level jobs, for example the role of pay-setting institutions, the welfare state, caring roles in the domestic sphere, the affordability of childcare, and the availability of student and migrant labour. However, the focus is predominantly on employment conditions rather than on the outcomes for skills and work organization. With research in this area still in its infancy and the empirical evidence base remaining limited, there may be other factors which have yet to figure within these theoretical frameworks.

At the same time, commentators have stressed the need to come to terms with the internally variegated nature of national capitalisms (Crouch 2005) and to appreciate differences between sectors in terms of industrial relations and approaches to skill formation as well as the organization of work and job quality (Grimshaw and Lehndorff 2010; Bechter et al. 2012). Indeed, one of the problems with macro-level accounts based upon theory (Hall and Soskice 2001) is that, as Carré and Tilly (2012: 80) note, 'Their typical mode of argument is to identify key institutional differences and then draw out their consequences in terms of national averages or of some set of jobs viewed as typical or archetypical.' Research drawing upon surveys faces similar issues. Micro-level studies, comparing selected case organizations across countries, also struggle to deal with internal country variation, whether by sector or by workplace within a sector. A comparison of a given sector across countries at the 'meso-level' has the advantage of allowing researchers to examine the impact of national institutions, sector dynamics, and organizational approach (Carré and Tilly 2012).

This trails many questions in its wake. How far does the dominant national model impact across an economy, and which elements of the national institutional framework apply in the case of *particular* sectors, not least new sectors within the service economy that have emerged relatively recently (Bosch and Lehndorff 2005)? Are there sector dynamics or logics which apply across countries and which have implications for the organization of work? Alternatively, can we still speak of national 'employment logics' which cut across sectors and influence a broad range of jobs and in what sense (Dobbin and Boychuk 1999)?

Central to the approach taken in this book is the need to more fully comprehend the role of organized labour. One of the many criticisms levelled at the varieties of capitalism literature is that it has tended to overlook, or downplay, power relations between capital, labour, and the state in explaining the origins of national institutions and subsequent change and transformation (see Streeck 2010). Other theories, by contrast, have explicitly adopted a 'power resource' perspective in explaining why jobs are designed differently across countries. Gallie (2007) has argued that the Nordic countries have higher levels of task discretion owing to the influence wielded by trade unions in national policy formation and within the workplace through their ability to constrain employer actions in ways which improve the quality of working life.

There are a number of case studies which have attributed more broadly designed service jobs in the Nordic countries or Germany to the relative strength and influence wielded by unions over work organization decisions within organizations (Gautié and Schmitt 2010; Doellgast 2010). In these studies, unions are found to act in *combination* with other elements within the national institutional and regulatory framework. However, for sectors where unions may be weak and which are also more detached from the national institutional framework, there is a lack of evidence on whether differences in work organization still exist (and if so why) or whether jobs resemble more closely those in neo-liberal economies. The weakening of organized labour and the resurgence of neo-liberalism following the 2008 financial crisis also raise serious questions about the continuing ability of unions to undertake this type of role, even in countries with a more supportive institutional structure.

Understanding broad country patterns may help us to grasp the role played by national institutions in developing proportionally more jobs of higher quality. However, such studies do not tell us much about how jobs vary within countries and the extent to which there is cross-national variation in the case of particular jobs, not least in new areas of the service sector which may not fit neatly with the prevailing national institutional model. If substantive differences can be shown to exist, this can help to challenge assumptions that jobs have to be the way they are and that there is simply no alternative, assumptions which are more likely if analysis is confined within a national perspective. Equally, where differences do not exist or remain slight, it may suggest that there are more formidable barriers to upskilling jobs and improving work organization. Again, that would have significant implications in terms of the extent to which problems such as over-qualification might be fully resolvable. In both cases, comparative studies can provide clues as to *what is possible* and the *conditions* required for progress. Inevitably this raises further questions about what countries might learn from others that are different to themselves.

Aims and Methods

This book seeks to contribute to this emerging and important area of research by comparing three service sector jobs across three European countries. The three countries chosen reflect contrasting institutional regimes. The UK is typically described as 'neo-liberal' or a 'liberal-market' economy, characterized by less regulated product, capital, and labour markets, weak trade unions and employer organizations, and a shareholder model of corporate governance (Hall and Soskice 2001). Norway is an oil-rich, social democratic welfare state (Esping-Andersen 1990) or 'coordinated economy' (Hall and Soskice 2001), with strong trade unions, extensive multi-level collective bargaining, and strong coordinating mechanisms involving the state, capital, and labour in managing the economy. France, by comparison, rarely features in theoretical framings of institutional regimes and is often treated as a somewhat 'special case' with a more 'state-led' or 'state-regulated' political economy, featuring low union density, extensive collective bargaining coverage, and a highly regulated labour market. Norway was selected as it is among those countries which cluster at the top of surveys of 'better' forms of work organization, while the UK is at the opposite end with relatively low levels of skill and discretion. France offers a more complex pattern, with surveys suggesting it sits somewhere in between.

It might be argued that choosing countries that are so different to one another is itself problematic in terms of what lessons can be learnt. There is some truth in this if one takes a narrow technocratic view that focuses on issues of policy transfer. However, if we are concerned with the broader perspective of what is actually possible and why it is possible, then exploring seemingly very different countries is essential. Each country is constrained by its institutions, traditions, and internal power relationships and has to start from where it is in terms of forging mechanisms for progress. But this should not lead us to assume that radical change is simply impossible or that countries are locked into particular trajectories, a view which tends to obscure the 'centrality of struggle', the 'battle of ideas', and the scope for political choice (Harvey 2010; Stuart et al. 2013: 391).

The particular jobs that have been included for comparative study are vocational teachers in the public education system, fitness instructors working in the leisure sector, and café workers in hospitality. These three jobs roughly correspond to professional-level, intermediate-level, and routine-level in occupational classifications, and are all found in areas of the service sector that are not internationally tradable. In all three job categories (including catering assistant rather than the specific job of café worker), there is a fairly even balance between male and female workers. However, as detailed in Appendix 1, the empirical research focused on hairdressing teachers, who were all women in the case study organizations, while many cafés predominantly employed women. As detailed in the forthcoming chapters, the influence of broader national-based differences in gender relations was more apparent for café workers than for teachers and fitness instructors.

Vocational teachers in the public education sector are a key group of professionals who are subject to contrasting national approaches to the management of their work. Fitness instructors are a relatively new group of workers in an industry that has only really developed over the last twenty-five years. Countries have adopted very different approaches to qualification standards within the sector. Café workers form part of a growing area of lower-end jobs in hospitality, with major questions over the level of skills required and the quality of work. With the partial exception of vocational teachers, these jobs have hitherto attracted relatively little research attention and have yet to be the subject of cross-country comparisons.

Are there significant differences in the way that skills are developed and work is organized in respect of the above jobs across the three countries? Does the national institutional and regulatory environment make a difference to skill, work organization, and broader aspects of job quality or is this overwhelmed by specific sector dynamics? Are we able to say anything about changes over time? How much variation is there *between* organizations *within* a sector, and how does the institutional environment shape organizational choices? Are there policies, practices, or approaches that can be shown to improve the experience of work? What role does power play at national, sector, and workplace level? What are the broader implications in terms of 'performance' and job quality?

The aim was to examine a clearly defined job category, while at the same time exploring the national, sector, and organizational context within which the job was located. Cross-national comparative studies of jobs based on qualitative case studies have sought to compare jobs in closely matched organizations as discussed earlier. While extremely valuable, this approach raises a number of methodological issues. One is to what extent it is possible to obtain a good match; the other is that by seeking such a match one may end up selecting organizations that are not typical or representative of the sector. As Carré and Tilly (2012: 80) note, such an approach is apt to 'omit within-country variation and varied employer strategies'. The combination of multiple case studies and interviews with key actors at sector level can help in this respect.

In order to compare jobs across countries, there is a balance to be made between seeking out similar types of workplaces in each country and attempting to reflect in the research the national make-up of the sector. The structure of a given sector may vary substantially between different countries, with one dominated by upmarket, quality services and the other by standardization and low prices. While there may be some advantages in only selecting organizations that match up, such an approach would exclude the role of different sector structures in any explanation and potentially focus on atypical jobs. The selection of workplaces was, therefore, aimed at broadly reflecting the sector in each country. Interviews with key industry stakeholders, including employer organizations, trade unions, and training organizations, alongside reviews of industry reports and analyses, were used to provide a general picture of the sector and to identify key issues affecting skills and training in the target job.

The bulk of the data was derived from multiple workplace case studies for each sector in each country, using semi-structured interviews with those doing the job as well as their direct supervisors and managers. The aim was to probe in detail the nature and experience of work (see Appendix 1). Crucial were accounts of day-to-day tasks, the type of knowledge, training, and experience required to undertake these tasks, and questions around the scope for discretion on specified activities and the way that managers monitored, intervened, or directed workers. In this way, differences and similarities between countries as well as between organizations within a national sector could be examined.

The research was funded through the UK Economic and Social Research Council's core grant to its then research centre on Skills, Knowledge and Organisational Performance (SKOPE). This was not an international collaborative project which drew upon the expertise of national teams of researchers; rather it was conducted primarily by the two UK-based authors, with some additional support in France. Such an approach can be seen to have certain advantages and disadvantages. The authors could not claim to have the in-depth knowledge of Norway and France that might accrue from nationally based research teams, although one had previously conducted research in France and the other in Norway. This limitation was seen to be outweighed by what was viewed as the primary advantage of the project, namely that the research data for each job in each country were collected, as far as possible, by the same researchers. This allowed for an effective comparative methodology where seeing and feeling how organizations operate were a key part of the research process, and the authors had direct knowledge of the research sites across the countries from which to make comparisons.

That said, only one of the authors (Lloyd) speaks French, which effectively precluded the other from being involved in the collection of the data. In addition, fieldwork in France proved more problematic in terms of access to research sites. In the case of vocational teachers, we were able to draw on the expertise of French academic Françoise Larré, who assisted with the site visits, as well as helping to organize access in the fitness industry, and provided an invaluable contribution in understanding the nature of the education system and in interpreting the data (see Larré et al. 2013). For café workers, difficulties of access meant some interviews were undertaken by two research assistants—Mondher Belhadj and Karim Toumi. While this process was far from ideal, the recording of all interviews and the use of standard interview schedules ensured that the data collected were of a good quality and could be analysed effectively. All but three interviews across the sectors were conducted in French and all quotes included in this book were translated by Lloyd. In Norway, language problems were limited as only a few of those interviewed were not fluent in English. These were typically older vocational teachers and in a few cases help was provided by their fellow workers who agreed to act as interpreters. In total, the book includes 245 interviews undertaken between 2009 and 2012; the details of the selection process and the workplaces and interviewees covered for each of the jobs are included in Appendix 1.

Structure of the Book

The book is structured broadly into two parts. The first deals with debates and controversies as well as providing some background context to the three countries. Chapter 2, 'Work and Skills in Contemporary Capitalism', reviews contemporary debates on the future of work, interrogates the rhetoric surrounding the knowledge economy and arguments for universal upskilling, and discusses the challenges surrounding the measurement and meaning of skill. Chapter 3, 'National Institutions, Sectors, and Work Organization', examines the theoretical frameworks which have been used to explain how and why jobs differ between countries, reviews the empirical evidence base, and sets out the approach adopted in the book. Chapter 4, 'Industrial Relations, Skill Formation Systems, and Workplace Development', outlines the national institutional context of the UK, Norway, and France, focusing on key domains or spheres identified in the preceding chapter as likely to be particularly salient for work organization and job quality. It also reviews efforts made by policy-makers and social actors in the three countries to improve work organization.

The second part of the book is devoted to the sector studies, each of which can, if chosen, be read as a stand-alone chapter. In each case, a brief background to the sector in the three countries is provided along with the key challenges it confronts. The rest of the chapter compares the job itself using the data from the workplace interviews. Chapter 5, 'Professional Work, Autonomy, and Innovation', deals with vocational teachers and explores different national approaches to sector governance and management, the way in which teachers are educated, the influence teachers exert over what they teach (the curriculum) and how they teach (pedagogy), and the extent to which their work is monitored and controlled. Chapter 6, 'Regulating the Middle', focuses upon fitness instructors. It explores different national approaches to the regulation of fitness instructor qualifications and the way that competitive pressures are impacting on the knowledge and skill requirements of the job. Chapter 7, 'Raising the Bottom', turns to the hospitality sector and the job of café worker, and addresses debates about the scope to raise the skill content of jobs at the lower end of the labour market. Chapter 8, 'Towards Better Jobs', brings together the findings from the three data chapters and discusses their implications for current debates around skills and work organization, the role and purpose of education, and the challenge of developing better jobs.

2

Work and Skills in Contemporary Capitalism

Introduction

Over recent decades education and training have come to be seen as increasingly important for the success of national economies, organizations, and individuals. Central has been the idea of a shift towards globalized, knowledge-based economies and associated innovations in computerized technologies, which are claimed to be raising employer demand for skills. The suggestion that *higher* levels of skill are needed across the entire workforce has been challenged by commentators who highlight problems of labour market polarization and the growth in low-skilled work. While policy initiatives in many countries and in international bodies, such as the OECD, have over-emphasized the importance of supplying more and better skills, evidence of increasing levels of over-qualification has led to some shift, at least in rhetoric, towards a recognition that: '[m]aking optimal use of existing skills...and encouraging employers to demand higher level of skill...are equally important elements of skills policies' (OECD 2011: 19).

The chapter reviews these debates by raising a number of empirical and conceptual issues, including the limitations of human capital theory (HCT), evidence on the changing nature of work and skills in the workplace, and the complex relationship between an organization's product or service and the skills of its workforce. The question of whether contemporary economies are generating enough jobs to keep pace with the outputs of the education system is addressed through exploring the evidence on over-qualification and the under-utilization of skills. While there are many difficulties involved in quantifying skill and qualification use, a central issue is the meaning of 'skill' itself. The chapter contextualizes the discussion of skill through an examination of some of the arguments around the specificity of the service sector, before outlining how skill is conceptualized within this book. It is argued that skill is a complex and essentially contested concept and that there are multiple factors which shape the way work is organized and the skills required in a job.

The Upskilling Narrative

Across the advanced capitalist world a near-universal policy consensus has emerged which argues that a fundamental shift is taking place in the nature of contemporary capitalism that has increased the demand for skilled workers (see Brown et al. 2010). Academic and policy discourses around the 'new' economy, described under multifarious titles as the 'knowledge economy', 'the information age', or 'the network society', see rapid technological advances, not least in information and communication technologies, as shifting the source of economic competitiveness increasingly towards high-value and productivity-enhancing knowledge-intensive services (OECD 1996; World Bank 2002). Ideas, creativity, and innovation are said to have replaced land and physical capital as the main drivers of productivity and wealth creation (Drucker 1993; Castells 1996). This is where the new world of 'symbolic analysts' (Reich 1991), high-tech 'knowledge workers', and the 'creative class' (Florida 2004) meets that of professionals, managers, and skilled manufacturing work.

The changes are often seen to be giving rise to new organizational forms where 'old' bureaucratic structures, based upon command and control, are replaced by 'flatter', less hierarchical ones, and teams of workers exercise high levels of creativity, control, and 'authorship' over their work. Similarly, narratives around 'high commitment human resource management' (HRM) and 'high performance working' also promise a workplace where workers have greater responsibilities and discretion in their work and where they are managed in ways which are aimed at eliciting high levels of commitment and motivation (for a discussion, see Becker and Huselid 1998; Godard 2004).

The heightened importance attached to skills is also linked to arguments around globalization, intensifying international competition, and the mobility of capital across national borders. Faced with competition from low-cost producers in the developing world, wealthy countries, it is argued, have little option but to seek comparative advantage in high value-added, high productivity goods and services, and leave labour-intensive commodity production to those countries where wage costs are substantially lower. 'You can't beat Beijing on price', as one German regional initiative put it (Schilling and Vanselow 2011). This is said to be forging a new international division of labour in which knowledge and skills become the sole remaining and sustainable source of competitive advantage for developed economies. In this view, the global economy neatly divides into what Rosecrance (1999) calls 'head' and 'body' nations.

In 2008, José Manuel Barroso, the then President of the European Commission remarked that, 'While we don't yet know what the jobs of the future will be, we do know that more and more jobs will demand high skills' (Barroso 2008: 2). His comments speak to a widespread belief that the demand for skills is rising thereby rendering a skilled workforce increasingly important for national economic success. The European Commission continues to insist on the need for 'a more skilled workforce, capable of contributing and adjusting to technological change with new patterns of work organisation' (2010: 2). The assumption is that economic changes require a more skilled workforce and that these skills will enable organizations to embrace new and better ways of working. Boosting skills supply can thereby 'raise productivity, competitiveness, economic growth and ultimately employment' (European Commission 2010: 2). While there remains a generalized position across many individual governments and international policy bodies that the new environment requires ever rising levels of workforce skill, there has also been a gradual acceptance that the existing skills of some workers may be under-used. Nevertheless, policy intervention has, in most cases, remained focused on improving the supply of skills, reflecting the enduring influence of human capital theory.

The view that there is a relatively simple relationship between the skills of the workforce and outcomes in terms of productivity and performance draws principally on HCT (Becker 1964). Essentially, 'human capital' is defined as *any* capacity (knowledge, skills, and behaviours) that makes a worker more productive and which adds to their present and future earnings. In theory, rationally calculating individuals make decisions to invest in their human capital, through education or training, in anticipation of expected wage returns in the labour market. From here, it is but a short step to the view that investment in a better educated and skilled labour force can deliver generalized productivity growth, improved international competitiveness, and rising living standards.

In policy terms, the economic case for investment in skills has also been allied to a broader social inclusion agenda. For the individual, skills, reskilling, and learning throughout life are highlighted as providing the means to obtain employment, change jobs, and secure higher wages in the context of what are claimed to be rapidly changing labour market conditions. Those with low or outdated skills are seen to be at risk of being left behind and will struggle to access employment (European Parliament 2000). These arguments have often provided the underpinning rationale for government policies that rely on the expansion of skills supply as a source of economic and social well-being. International skills tests and benchmarking exercises have also served to fuel policy-makers' obsession with how the nation is performing in terms of its stocks of qualifications or the skill levels of its young people relative to competitors. The concern that the USA was being out-competed internationally led US President Barack Obama to set a goal of having the highest proportion of college graduates in the world by 2020 (Obama 2009). Former UK Prime Minister Gordon Brown even spoke of a 'global skills race' where economic success went to the nation which developed the talents of all its citizens (Brown 2008). While neo-liberal austerity policies, adopted by some countries, have meant that national education and training budgets have come under severe pressure, the skills discourse remains prominent.

The emphasis afforded to education and training in some national contexts as constituting the *primary* policy lever for economic and social well-being is consistent with neo-liberal arguments which eschew other more direct forms of interventions in the economy (Crouch et al. 1999; Coates 2000). Cutler (1992: 181) argued that in Europe the increasing importance attached to training from the 1980s onwards reflected an ideological and political shift whereby interventions against the market, such as industrial policy and labour market regulations, were precluded. Training policies were politically expedient because they were seen as enabling 'the market to work more effectively'. This approach has been particularly apparent in the UK, where skills policy under both Conservative and New Labour governments was allied to a neo-liberal growth model centred on a lubricating role for the state that relied heavily upon the market, limited employment regulations, and widespread cuts to out-of-work benefits designed to incentivize work (Lloyd and Payne 2002). While the increased emphasis on education and skills is a common theme of national policy documents, the narrative has nevertheless played out differently in different contexts. In Scandinavia, the emphasis upon education and training went alongside a continued commitment to a 'social model' which included strong unions, well-regulated labour markets, a generous welfare state, and high unemployment benefits.

This knowledge economy discourse has led to widespread increases in publicly funded training initiatives and attempts to increase the supply of qualified workers through the education system, with a particular focus on graduates (European Commission 2013). The UK increased the proportion of the age cohort with a higher education qualification from around 16 per cent in 1988 to 55 per cent in 2011. Many other countries have adopted similar approaches with particularly high rates of graduation in Iceland (60 per cent), Poland (58 per cent), Australia (50 per cent), and Denmark (50 per cent) (Figure 2.1). Not all countries, however, have followed the path of mass higher education. Austria and Germany, with their strong work-based apprenticeship routes, have increased graduate numbers but remain below the average at around 30 per cent. Alongside the growth in higher education, many governments have sought to expand apprenticeships, raise 'staying-on' rates in post-compulsory education, and improve basic skills, particularly in areas such as numeracy and literacy.

Skills in the Age of Over-Qualification

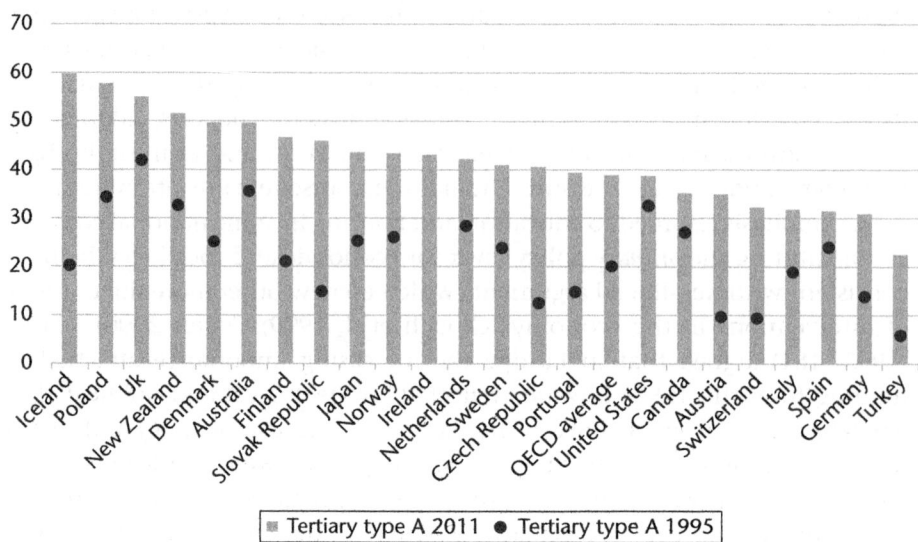

Figure 2.1. First time graduation rates for tertiary type A education

Notes: UK 2000 not 1995; Australia 2000 and 2010; Iceland 2010; Poland 2000; Canada 2000; Italy 2010.

Source: OECD, *Education at a Glance 2013*, Table A32a. Tertiary type A are academically oriented studies.

Interrogating the Skills Narrative

Human Capital Theory

As noted earlier, HCT (Becker 1964) has provided much of the intellectual grounding for the skills narrative. HCT has often been read in such a way as to support the view that there is a simple and direct link between skills supply and productivity. Put simply, the more human capital acquired by individual workers (usually proxied by qualifications or length of education and training), the more they add to the organization's output and hence the higher their productivity. In perfectly competitive markets, workers are then paid according to their productivity, and 'priced' in the same way as other factors of production, such as physical capital. While this is a very simplified version of the theory, it is nevertheless widely adopted as an explanation of the benefits that are assumed to derive from raising skills and qualification levels and is often used as an explanation for differences in pay.

Notwithstanding its influence, the theory has been widely criticized (see Green 2011). A key assumption is that organizations buy human capital, or labour, which is then put to productive use at the relevant skill level. The question of whether skills are actually used within the job is largely viewed as unproblematic. Skill mismatches, that is the difference between the skills workers possess and what employers want, are assumed to apply only in the short run while individuals and firms adjust to new market conditions or they are deemed to result from 'market failure', such as imperfect information. By treating labour as just another factor input, like physical capital, approaches based on HCT ignore the issue of how to convert 'labour power' (the capacity to work) into labour, i.e. actual work. The way in which jobs are designed or the manner by which workers are controlled and motivated at work can then be disregarded (see Ashton and Green 1996; Fine 1998). Other criticisms focus on the ability of individuals to make decisions around their investments in education and training, which go beyond simply lack of information on wage returns to particular qualifications. Structural factors, such as class, ethnicity, and gender, have long been recognized as shaping people's access, engagement, and orientation towards education at various levels (see, for example, Fevre et al. 1999).

The other important critique relates to the argument that individual wages necessarily reflect a worker's productivity. Those with higher levels of human capital are said to receive higher wages because they are more productive. Increased wage inequality in many countries since the 1980s has been claimed to be an outcome of differential changes in productivity growth caused by, what has been termed, 'skill-biased technical change' (SBTC) (e.g. Autor et al. 2003). Computer technology is said to have disproportionately increased the productivity of the more educated, thereby enabling them to receive higher wage growth than less educated workers. However, these ideas are based on suppositions with little empirical evidence to support claims about productivity changes. As Maglen (1990: 288) explains, rather than attempt to measure productivity and the *actual* relationship with wages, it is *presumed* that 'as more-educated workers are generally paid more than less-educated workers... then clearly they must be more productive'. Identifying individual productivity (or even labour productivity more generally) is undoubtedly difficult if not impossible, particularly in much of the service sector and the public sector.

There is also a substantial body of research evidence accumulated over many years which shows that employers have a degree of latitude when it comes to setting pay rates (Nolan and Brown 1983; Groshen 1991; Bryson and Forth 2006). A brief look at the remuneration packages of senior executives in the USA and UK, which in many cases bear little association with company performance, raises the broader issue of power within the labour market (Mishel and Davis 2014). Approaches based on HCT tend to exclude the ways institutions and social norms shape and structure labour markets, including government regulations, employers' associations, trade unions, and elite groups. Instead, institutions are viewed as an aberration, or at best an obstruction, that hinder the efficient operation of the market. There are also long-standing critiques related to the undervaluing of what has been seen as 'women's work' (Grimshaw and Rubery 2007), alongside widespread evidence of pay discrimination in the labour market (e.g. Metcalf 2009; see Fine 1998 for a detailed critique of more sophisticated forms of HCT).

Trends in Skills

The promise of an economy transformed by competition and technology that requires increasing levels of knowledge and skill is not new and can be traced back to a long line of similar arguments advanced in the 1960s and 1970s which spoke of a new 'post-industrial' society (Kerr et al. 1960; Blauner 1964; Drucker 1969; Bell 1973). Responding to such arguments, Braverman (1974) presented an alternative thesis of the degradation of work, which examined the deskilling of jobs through the use of automation and assembly-line production. He argued that this was the *main* tendency within capitalism, with workers increasingly subject to preset routines, tight supervision, and a detailed subdivision of labour. His research provided a detailed, evidence-based refutation of arguments for *generalized* upskilling through education that were in wide circulation at the time (see Tinker 2002). Although much of his analysis focused on manufacturing in the USA, he also explored how these processes were being applied within the growing service sector, with a specific focus on changes in clerical work.

Although widely influential among academics, Braverman's work has not escaped criticism (Friedman 1977; Wood 1982; Cockburn 1983; Thompson 1983). Part of the critique has been theoretical, in particular around the concept of generalized deskilling. A nuanced reading of Braverman, however, reveals that he regarded deskilling as the *dominant tendency* under capitalism rather than an absolute or iron law. Others have questioned the deskilling hypothesis through empirical studies of occupational change, surveys of workers' skills, and examples of complex skilled work. Throughout the 1980s, concepts such as 'flexible specialization' (Piore and Sabel 1984), a variant of 'post-Fordism', were used to claim that examples of new industrial districts with small-batch production methods, using highly skilled and functionally flexible labour, would become the dominant form of organization. Again, these were met with both theoretical critique and a barrage of counter-examples of 'neo-Fordism' characterized by numerical flexibility, deskilling, and the intensification of work (Hyman 1988; Pollert 1988).

Post-Fordist arguments would be carried forwards into debates around the knowledge economy. As with SBTC, computer technology is viewed as having a generally positive impact on skill requirements. Workplace case studies, however, have shown that the choice and use of new computer technologies, together with their impact on skills, depend on a variety of factors (see Lloyd and Steedman 1999 for a review). These include the national industrial relations system, labour market and corporate strategic choices (Thompson et al. 1995), wider political and social factors (Senker and Senker 1994), and the power of trade unions in the workplace (McLoughlin and Clark 1994), thereby questioning a simple functionalist view of the relationship between technology and skill. Rather than attempt to assess all the literature within the field on trends in skill, the next two sections focus upon services, beginning with the arguments around deskilling at the lower end of the labour market, before discussing evidence about changes affecting high-skilled jobs.

Deskilling and Low-Skilled Work in the Service Sector

Finding contemporary examples of deskilling and evidence of sustained numbers of low-skill jobs in services has not proven to be difficult. A generalized account of deskilling can be found in the work of Ritzer (1993). Taking US-headquartered burger chain, McDonald's, as the modern archetype of Taylorism and the Fordist assembly line, he argues that many aspects of life are subject to cost-reducing processes of routinization and standardization. These processes are said to encompass a whole range of service sector work from professional jobs, such as university lecturers using ready-made textbooks and associated packages in teaching, to interactive service workers reading a script in a call centre, swiping a barcode in a supermarket, or serving a coffee with a cake. In this way, the learning process, the consumption of food, and patterns of living are subject to, what Ritzer refers to as, 'McDonaldization'.

'Mass' service work is replete with examples of jobs which are highly Taylorized, tightly controlled, and rely on restricted skill sets. Call centres are often cited as 'emblematic' or 'good exemplars' (Thompson 2013: 479), with many relying upon work fragmentation, standardized scripts, and a range of bureaucratic, technical, and normative controls (Taylor and Bain 1999). As Adam Smith (1776) noted over two centuries ago in his classic description of pin manufacturing, a more detailed division of labour can significantly increase output per worker. At the same time, fragmenting work and stripping out skills enables the use of easily replaceable, cheaper workers who require only minimal training (Braverman 1974). Debates have raged, particularly in the USA and UK, over how generalized these developments are and how they are to be weighed against counter-evidence of the upskilling of specific jobs.

Indeed, many commentators have argued that trends in work and skill are best captured through the idea of skills polarization, which leaves this question open. Gallie (1994) drew upon individuals' perceptions of their own skills. He concluded that upskilling was widespread and that deskilling was rare. The causes of these changes were primarily due to a shift from manufacturing to the service sector and the implementation of new technology. He argued that there was a 'deep fissure within the service sector' (Gallie 1994: 59), however, due to growth in higher skilled positions, particularly in the public sector, and in low-skilled jobs in private services. Those using automated technology were identified as being more likely to say their skills were rising, while women disproportionately experienced stagnant skill movements largely due to their employment in part-time work in the service sector.

Studies of growing pay inequality and occupational change have also been used to support the idea of a polarization of skill. As discussed earlier, SBTC has become an increasingly popular concept used by economists to explain growing wage inequality. This theory has been extended beyond its initial focus, on the use of technology to enhance productivity at the higher end of the labour market, to explain developments lower down. Many workers in the 'middle' (e.g. craft and clerical occupations), it is claimed, were undertaking predominantly 'routine', if precise, activities which have been progressively replaced by technology. Those at the bottom, such as cleaners or retail workers, are engaged in 'non-routine' jobs. These jobs are difficult to automate in that they require a worker to undertake non-standardized tasks or involve customer-facing interaction, but they still remain relatively low skilled and have seen their numbers increase. These changes are said to have resulted in the 'hollowing out' of the middle and a growth of both 'lovely' and 'lousy' jobs (Goos and Manning 2007). While initially considered a feature of neo-liberal economies, such as the UK and USA, Goos et al. (2009) subsequently found evidence of polarization across a range of European countries.

This polarization thesis draws upon shifts in the occupational structure of most countries whereby the numbers of managers, professionals and associate professionals, and technicians have been increasing, alongside the rise in more routine, lower skilled jobs (e.g. Nolan and Slater 2010). Indeed, one of the simplest ways to map broad trends in skill has been to rely upon changes in occupational categories. The assumption within much of the literature is that if managerial and professional jobs are expanding then this is taken to denote an increase in skill demands, while if the number of cleaners and supermarket workers increases then the converse applies.

Such an approach, however, is unable to distinguish the variable skills required within a job title and the changes that may be taking place within an occupation over time. A chef may be creating *cordon bleu* food for a Michelin star restaurant or could be heating up pre-prepared meals in a microwave in a local pub. In strict occupational terms, both would be categorized as being at the same skill level. Similarly, at the lower end of the labour market, a retail worker's job may consist of scanning items on a supermarket checkout or it could include responsibility for selecting products, ordering, displaying items, and providing in-depth advice to customers. It is also very difficult to pick up changes in occupations over time. An IT programming job might have started out as cutting-edge design only to be transformed over the years into simply writing standardized programs that require little creative input. Occupational categories also struggle to deal with the possibility of title inflation. A good example is the use in the UK of the job title 'manager'. Revisions to the Standard Occupational Classification (SOC) codes in 2010 reduced the proportion of managers in the UK from 15 per cent to 10 per cent. As the Office for National Statistics reported, 'The title "manager"...is frequently used in the UK to denote what would be regarded as supervisory or administrative positions in many other countries.'[1]

Knowledge Work and High-Skilled Jobs

As evidence points to growth at the top of the occupational ladder, many commentators have questioned the size and penetration of the knowledge economy and whether knowledge work, or even high-skilled work more generally, is ever likely to constitute more than a minority of jobs in any advanced economy (Crouch et al. 1999; Thompson et al. 2001). A study by the Work Foundation estimates that no more than 30 per cent of jobs in the UK can be described as having a 'high knowledge content', and that within this 'core' knowledge group only around 11 per cent of the workforce are in 'high knowledge intensity jobs' that combine 'high level cognitive activity with high level management tasks' (Brinkley et al. 2009: 4). Even one of the most prominent writers on the knowledge economy, Robert Reich (2002), concedes that what he calls 'creative workers' in the USA make up no more than a quarter of the workforce. Indeed, for all the talk of skills as a source of individual labour market power, as Thompson (2013: 480) notes, 'The labour market is not being flooded by armies of mobile, high powered knowledge workers whose ownership of their own assets has companies at their mercy'. For those whose skills and qualifications lack scarcity, their ability to confer labour market power by enabling them to escape 'bad' jobs and trade up to a better one with another employer is far more limited.

Even the more rosy images of work at the higher end of the labour market have been questioned. Research on 'knowledge workers', 'professionals', and 'creative labour' suggests that while such work is more likely to involve higher levels of skill, autonomy, and learning compared with other jobs, here too there are constraints along with pressures intensifying work (Konzelmann et al. 2007). Studies of the creative industries find that celebratory accounts of worker autonomy and creative freedom can be somewhat exaggerated (McKinlay and Smith 2009). Professional and managerial jobs may also have 'expansive work demands' and can become '"extreme" jobs', with long hours

---

[1] <http://www.ons.gov.uk/ons/guide-method/classifications/current-standard-classifications/soc2010/soc2010-volume-1-structure-and-descriptions-of-unit-groups/index.html#7>, section 4.4.

and high levels of stress (Pocock and Skinner 2012: 73). Public services in a number of countries have faced the importation of private sector management practices under the banner of new public management (NPM) (Hood 2006). It is claimed that there has been a shift in 'the locus of control and decision making' away from professionals (Ferlie and Geraghty 2005: 432), as professional autonomy is subordinated to a managerial discourse of 'accountability', 'efficiency', and 'quality'.

Arguments around the shift towards a more inclusive knowledge-based economy involving rising demand for skill have also had to confront evidence of declining task discretion, generally seen as central to skilled work (Holm and Lorenz 2015). However, there is evidence of some variation across countries, with the European Working Conditions Survey indicating some southern European countries experiencing increases in task discretion and Sweden, France, and Ireland suffering from decreases between 2005 and 2010. Using the same survey but starting from 1995 and using a broader indicator of work autonomy, Lopes et al. (2014: 311) report that of fifteen countries only Denmark, Finland, the Netherlands, and Sweden did not experience a fall in autonomy. They also found that autonomy at work for higher skilled workers saw a small decrease. In the UK during the 1990s, national surveys revealed that while task discretion declined for all groups of workers, it was professional workers who experienced the most dramatic fall (Felstead et al. 2004; Green 2006: 105).

Looking specifically at the strategies of 'global companies', Brown et al. (2010) argue that digital technologies have unrecognized potential to deskill many professional and knowledge jobs in Western nations. Drawing upon interviews with senior executives, they refer to a process of 'Digital Taylorism' whereby information technology allows organizations to translate '*knowledge work* into *working knowledge* through the extraction, codification and digitalisation of knowledge into software prescripts that can be transmitted and manipulated by others regardless of location' (Brown et al. 2008: 139). The argument is that multinational companies are increasingly looking to segment their higher skilled service workers, deskill many of them and shift this 'grunt' work to lower cost locations.

Brown et al. (2008) question the depiction of a world neatly divided between 'head' and 'body' nations (Rosecrance 1999), explaining how emerging economies such as China and India are expanding their education systems apace and increasingly seeking to compete for a share of higher value-added, 'brain work'. High-skill workers in the West, it is claimed, are likely to find themselves caught in a pincer movement between Taylorized deskilling and intensifying overseas competition which will render it increasingly difficult for them to translate their educational investments into high-skill, high-paying jobs. Brown et al. (2008) argue that these developments cast further doubt on a policy agenda which sees improvements in the supply of higher-level skills as a route to a high-skill, high-wage economy. However, it is unclear how extensive Digital Taylorism is, or might become, to what extent 'expert labour' can be deskilled, and how far the developments they identify apply beyond a few key industries and large multinational organizations.

Over-Qualification and Under-Utilization of Skill

The rapid expansion of the education and training system in many countries, aimed at boosting skills supply, has increasingly led to questions about whether economies are capable of producing enough jobs that can utilize existing skills (see Buchanan et al. 2010; OECD 2012). Over-qualification is where the worker holds a *qualification* at a higher level than that required to carry out a job, although as discussed in Box 1, it is often referred to in terms of qualifications required to obtain a job. Under-utilization of skill relates more specifically to the situation where the *actual skills* possessed by a worker are not being fully or substantially used. There is a range of evidence that over-qualification and the under-utilization of skill, which may overlap, can have a negative impact on job satisfaction (e.g. Cabral Vieira 2005; Maynard et al. 2006; Green and Zhu 2010), and is often associated with a desire to leave the organization (Giret et al. 2006). Okay-Somervill and Scholarios (2013) emphasize the importance of intrinsic work characteristics as crucial to job satisfaction, in particular skill use and opportunities for development. Belfield (2010) reports over-qualification as having a negative impact on industrial relations with lower rates of workplace harmony and diminished worker morale.

What is the evidence on trends in over-qualification and the under-utilization of skill? To begin with over-qualification, the first problem is one of measurement. There are a number of different ways of measuring the mismatch between the qualification required to do a job and the qualifications of the job holder. While measuring an individual's qualification level is fairly straightforward, identifying the qualification demands of a job is much more difficult. The normative and subjective methods (see Box 1 for further details) are arguably more robust and generally have fairly similar outcomes. Groot and van den Brink's (2000) review of a range of studies from a number of European countries and the USA found an average incidence of over-qualification of around 26 per cent that had not changed significantly over time. More recent evidence indicates that this rate has subsequently increased (see Rohrbach-Schmidt and Tiemann 2011; Lemistre 2013).[2] While these studies show some

---

[2] Brynin et al. (2006), using an individual subjective assessment, reported rates of 33 per cent in the UK, 19 per cent in Italy, 28 per cent in Germany, and 22 per cent in Norway. In Britain and

> **Box 1** METHODS FOR MEASURING OVER-QUALIFICATION AMONG THE WORKFORCE
>
> *Normative approaches* aim to identify job level qualification requirements through job analysis or are generalizations about the qualifications required for broad occupational groups, e.g. professionals require higher education, while routine workers require only compulsory schooling. The *subjective method* asks individuals doing the job to assess the qualifications required for entry into the job or to carry out the job. The *statistical method* is probably the most widely used measure of over-qualification (see Quintini 2011) due to the ease of data collection, yet it has the greatest problems. The method defines the requirements of a job as the mean or median qualifications possessed by those doing the job. Take the following hypothetical example. Ten years ago, bar workers may have comprised a relatively small proportion of graduates, with the remainder made up of those with lower level or no qualifications. Ten years later, with changes to tuition fees, the impact of economic recession, and the inability of many graduates to obtain graduate level jobs, the number of graduates working in bars has increased to 80 per cent. Under the statistical method, a bar worker is now a graduate level job and the figure for over-qualification has declined from 20 per cent to zero, while those without a degree become under-qualified.[3]

evidence of under-qualification (where workers lack the qualifications required to do or obtain the job), these tend to be fairly limited and often concern older workers who do not meet new job requirements.

The OECD Adult Skills Survey (PIACC) found that reported levels of over-qualification ranged from a low of 13 per cent of workers in Italy to a high of 31 per cent in France and Japan (see Figure 2.2). The UK (which only looked at England and Northern Ireland) also ranked towards the higher end, with 30 per cent, and Norway was towards the middle at 20 per cent (OECD 2013: 171). In terms of the level of education required for the job, 9 per cent of jobs across these countries were stated to require primary education or less, and 35 per cent required tertiary qualifications. Spain and the UK were characterized by a highly polarized distribution, with 25 per cent and 23 per cent of jobs respectively asking for only low levels of education, the worst position of twenty OECD countries (Figure 2.3). Unfortunately, this survey is not able to tell us anything about the direction of change.

One of the most detailed surveys of skills is the UK Skills Survey, which is a longitudinal representative survey of employees (Felstead et al. 2013a). It

---

Germany, they report over-qualification as being found predominantly among the mid and lower qualified, while in Italy it is fairly evenly spread and in Norway it is concentrated among graduates. In France, a study found that three years after leaving education, around one quarter of young people were considered to be over-qualified in 2001 (Giret et al. 2006). Over-qualification is estimated at 27 per cent in Australia (Linsley 2005), affecting roughly the same proportion of the working population as in Canada (Wald 2004).

[3] Thanks to Ken Mayhew for drawing our attention to this problem.

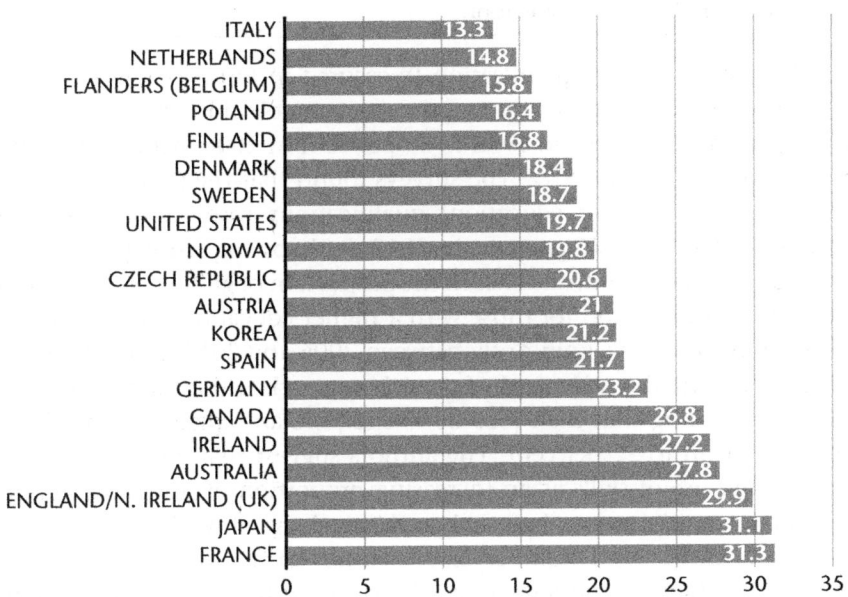

Figure 2.2. Incidence of over-qualification

Note: Percentage of workers who report that their highest qualification is higher than that deemed necessary to obtain the job today.

Source: OECD (2013: Table A4.25) <http://www.oecd.org/site/piaac/chapter4howskillsareusedintheworkplace.htm>.

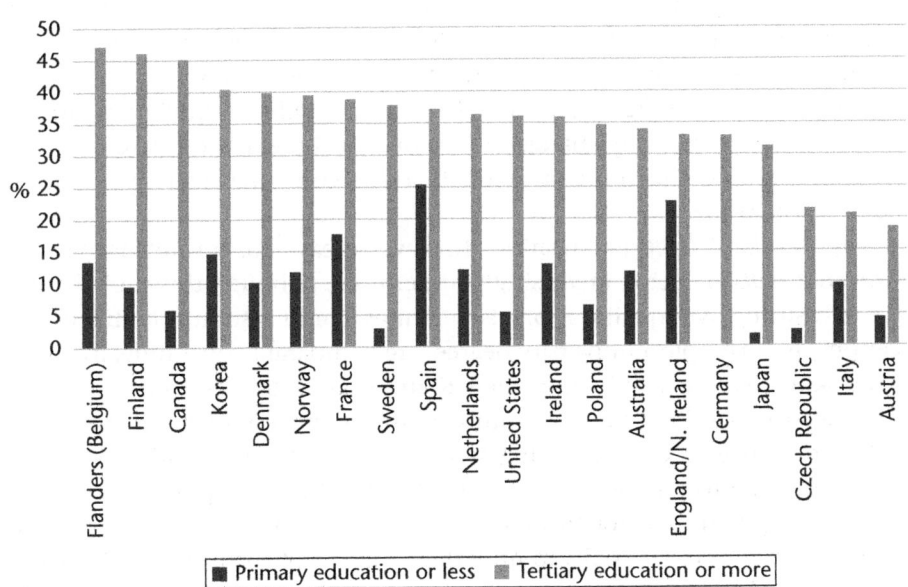

Figure 2.3. Workers in high-skilled and unskilled jobs

Note: Percentage of workers in jobs requiring primary education or less and in jobs requiring tertiary education or more.

Source: OECD (2013: Table A4.24) <http://www.oecd.org/site/piaac/chapter4howskillsareusedintheworkplace.htm>.

shows that levels of over-qualification (measured in terms of the employee's qualification as compared to the requirements to obtain that job) increased markedly from 28 per cent in 1986 to 39 per cent in 2006, before falling back slightly to 37 per cent in 2012. The surveys found that the proportion of jobs requiring level 4 (higher education) qualifications rose substantially from 10 per cent in 1986 to 26 per cent in 2012. Perhaps surprisingly, given both the recession and the continued rise in the proportion of graduates in the labour market, over-qualification for those with a higher education qualification was reported to have fallen significantly between 2006 and 2012, from 28 per cent to 22 per cent. At the other end of the labour market, the proportion of the workforce reporting that their jobs do not require any qualifications also fell from 27 per cent to 22 per cent. The authors suggest that employers may be making better use of skills as an increasing proportion of respondents report having opportunities to use their skills and knowledge at work.

There are, however, a number of difficulties in assessing levels of over-qualification when the measure used is based upon the qualification required to obtain a job and the supply of qualified labour is rising rapidly. Studies have long noted how employers can use qualifications to 'screen' applicants for jobs (Spence 1973), using credentials to allocate individuals to a 'job queue' (Thurow 1975). In Thurow's 'job competition' model, a process of credentialism may arise as employers respond to an increased supply of qualified applicants by raising entry requirements to jobs but without making corresponding changes to their actual skill content. Studies from the USA and UK have shown that many jobs which previously required upper secondary education or a high school diploma are increasingly becoming 'graduate-only' occupations with little evidence of any change in job content (Brown and Hesketh 2004). Determining what constitutes a 'graduate job' becomes particularly problematic (see Box 2).

Rising levels of over-qualification, however measured, do not necessarily mean that *skills* are being increasingly under-used, although this could be the case. Measuring over-qualification also requires a prior assumption that qualifications, for example a university degree, are comparable over time, in terms of the skills that are acquired. In the UK and USA, higher education systems have faced expanding student numbers and a process of 'marketization', leading to concerns over declining study time (as students undertake more paid employment) and 'grade inflation' (Côté 2014). One possibility is that the skills acquired by graduates have diminished over time, such that some graduates only have the skills to undertake 'non-graduate' jobs. In this case, rising levels of over-qualification need not imply the under-utilization of skills any more than rising qualification requirements necessarily indicates that jobs are becoming more skilled. In this scenario, more graduates might report holding

> **Box 2** WHAT IS A GRADUATE JOB?
>
> Purcell et al. (2004) used an occupational classification to assess whether graduates in the UK are over-qualified. They expanded the notion of a 'graduate job' to include areas that have typically been 'non-graduate', for example retail and hotel managers. Their view, at the time, was that the:
>
>> labour market has been changing in a way which has largely absorbed the expanded supply of graduates and that they are doing work that, in terms of our classification job requirements, is likely to require people with their skills and qualifications. (Purcell et al. 2004: 7)
>
> As a result, they estimated that around 15 per cent of graduates were in 'non-graduate' jobs in the UK six years after graduation. Briscoe et al. (2011), using the same classification, found that for those born in the devolved regions of the UK, i.e. Scotland, Wales, and Northern Ireland, 25 per cent were in 'non-graduate' jobs five years later, although for those fifteen years out of graduation that figure was 15 per cent. Following reflection (and criticism) of their initial classification, Elias and Purcell (2013) developed a new approach in which they evaluated each occupational group in relation to job content to classify them as either 'graduate' or 'non-graduate'. The outcome was the removal of some of the previous 'graduate' jobs from their calculations, noting:
>
>> We have recent evidence of graduate 'crowding' into a variety of jobs and sectors where it would appear unlikely that the constituent tasks demand the skills and knowledge associated with higher education. (Elias and Purcell 2013: 1)
>
> On this new calculation, Purcell et al. (2013) found that over-qualification had *increased* in the UK. Thirty per cent of graduates were in 'non-graduate' jobs either one and a half or two and a half years after graduation (2009/10) and this figure had increased compared to ten years earlier.

a qualification higher than needed to obtain the job, yet not report their skills as being under-used.

Measuring the under-utilization of skills is, if anything, trickier than measuring over-qualification as it requires some subjective assessment either by the researcher, the employer, or the employee concerned. The respondent is usually asked whether or to what extent the skills of the worker are being used in the job. There is less evidence available on these measures. Wright and Sissons' analysis of the 2001 UK Skill Survey indicated that 35 per cent of respondents were under-using their skills in work, with considerable variations according to industry and occupation. Overall, those in lower end jobs reported substantially higher levels of skill under-utilization than those in managerial and professional jobs. The highest rates were found in hotel and catering (55 per cent) and elementary jobs (60 per cent) (Wright and Sissons 2012: 9).

The 2011 Workplace Employment Relations Survey (WERS) indicated that 22 per cent of employee respondents thought they had skills which were much higher than those required for the job, while 32 per cent felt they were a bit higher, with little change from the 2006 survey (Kersley et al. 2006; van Wanrooy et al. 2013). Reported under-utilization of skills was found to be highest among workers with the highest qualifications. There is also some evidence that employers thought that the under-utilization of workers' skills was widespread. The UK Employer Skills Survey (UKCES 2014: 11) noted that, 'Half of UK employers (48 per cent) report skills under-use, and 4.3 million workers (16 per cent of the total UK workforce) are reported as being over-skilled and over-qualified for the jobs that they are currently doing.' The opposite outcome of workers being under-skilled is generally fairly small. For example, the survey found that only one in twenty employees were not fully proficient in their jobs.

The lack of surveys in other countries makes international comparisons difficult, but there are indications that the problem is not confined to the UK. Studies from Australia have found that 37 per cent of employers feel that their employees possess skill levels above those required for the role, with only 5 per cent indicating they were less (Watson 2008). Watson's analysis of surveys of Australian employees suggests that 15 to 20 per cent do not consider their skills are being put to effective use at work. While there are widespread difficulties with the data and measurement, overall there would appear to be a substantial group of workers across many OECD countries who are over-qualified and under-using their skills within their current jobs, with little evidence of widespread skill shortages (OECD 2013).

Skill Utilization and High Performance Working

As evidence of over-qualification and under-utilization of skills has mounted, bodies such as the OECD (2012) have begun to recognize that attention needs to be given to raising employer demand for, and usage of, skills. In neo-liberal countries such as the UK (most notably Scotland and Wales), Australia, and New Zealand, a few small-scale experiments have taken place to encourage organizations to enhance levels of skills utilization. Alongside initiatives such as the 'skills ecosystems pilots' in Australia and 'skills utilization projects' in Scotland (Payne 2008a, 2012), Nordic countries have a longer legacy of workplace innovation programmes aimed at helping organizations to adopt new and better ways of working (for an overview, see Buchanan et al. 2010). For the most part, neo-liberal countries have relied mainly on *exhorting* organizations to make greater use of what are variously labelled 'high commitment', 'high performance', or 'high involvement' work/management practices, hereafter referred to as 'high performance work practices' (HPWP) (Appelbaum et al. 2000; UKCES 2009).

There is an extensive literature which explores the potential performance benefits that may flow to organizations that adopt integrated 'bundles' of work organization and HR practices. These models imply more autonomous job design, the acquisition and deployment of new process skills, such as team working, problem solving and communication, increased training and development opportunities, and associated HR policies and practices designed to secure employees' motivation, commitment, and 'discretionary effort' (Appelbaum et al. 2000). The implicit *promise* is one of 'mutual gains' for both the organization and its employees (Osterman 2000).

In policy terms, it is often assumed that more firms will be adopting these practices given changes in the external environment and that their ability to do so will depend in part upon the supply of workforce skills. Persuading firms to adopt such an approach, alongside a policy agenda around education and training, is seen to offer a route to improved productivity and competitiveness through better jobs which afford workers more opportunity to deploy their skills (Wood et al. 2013). There are, however, a number of well-documented problems with HPWP that will not be rehearsed here (see Godard 2004 for a review). These include inconsistencies in defining HPWP, establishing a causal link with performance, contradictory evidence as to the impact on workers, and limited 'take-up' by organizations. It should be emphasized that despite claims that these practices impact positively on *skill*, there is very little supportive evidence to substantiate such a view (see Lloyd and Payne 2006).

Skill and Competitive Strategy

A further issue which runs throughout the debates on the link between skills and performance, including high performance working, is the role played by the competitive strategy of the organization. It is widely assumed that the skills demanded by employers reflect the organization's product market positioning (Keep and Mayhew 1999). Put simply, the more an organization competes through complex, differentiated, or 'high-spec' products and services, the more the organization will require a higher skilled workforce with the discretion to respond to variation in customer requirements. Conversely, where organizations compete primarily upon the basis of 'low-spec', standardized goods and services, they are likely to require relatively limited skills from the bulk of their workforce.

These ideas draw on the work of Porter (1980) who differentiated between three types of competitive strategy for the firm, namely cost minimization, quality, and innovation. The role of product market positioning is central to 'best-fit' approaches to 'strategic HRM' which draw a direct link to HR approaches and skill use (Schuler and Jackson 1987). The influence of the product market, however, is also consistent with perspectives which seek to understand the role of national political economy in shaping firms' choices around how they compete in the market place (see Chapter 3). Finegold and Soskice's (1988) influential analysis of the UK's 'low skills equilibrium' centred on low-skilled workers producing low-quality goods and services, and was contrasted with Germany's 'high skills equilibrium', where high-skilled workers were producing for high-quality, innovative markets (Finegold 1991).

While evidence supports the view that there can be a relationship between market positioning and skill (see, for example, Mason 2004), these links are neither simple nor automatic. High value-added strategies can be pursued without the need for a high-skilled workforce. A company such as Nike, for example, uses branding and marketing to command a high price premium for its sportswear, which is nevertheless produced using mass production techniques and low-skilled labour in the developing world (see Wensley 1999). In services, the relationship may be even less straightforward than in manufacturing. While some research does find a link between a quality-driven, high value-added product market strategy and more skilled work (Batt 2000), others have questioned whether this is necessarily the case (Bailey and Bernhardt 1997; Lloyd 2005; Lloyd et al. 2013).

One attempt to theorize this more complex relationship between competitive strategy and HR strategy, from a skills perspective, is provided by Sung and Ashton (2015). They draw a distinction between 'technical relationships', which refer to where an organization sits on the continuum between product and service standardization at one end and differentiation at the other, and 'interpersonal relationships'. It is the 'interpersonal relations', the way people are managed, which offers more scope for managerial choices over the use of skills. Employers can pursue a 'task-focused' or cost-minimization approach, where there is a high level of control over delivery of specified tasks and skills are minimized. Alternatively, they may opt for a 'people development' focus, where the aim is to maximize individual employee contributions, and where skills, along with employees' motivation and commitment, are seen as important for competitive advantage. The latter approach, in this view, is not restricted to those organizations focused on high value-added or more complex products or services. Employers producing standardized products can also adopt a competitive approach based on quality, by adopting 'high involvement' work practices that enhance workers' skills and encourage commitment and motivation (Ashton and Sung 2006: 20; see also Appelbaum et al. 2000).

This argument echoes much of the literature around 'high performance working' and 'best practice' HRM, as discussed earlier, but seeks to tie this to discussions within the skills area. The key point for Sung and Ashton (2015) is that organizations are not as restricted in terms of their people approaches as 'best-fit' implies and there is greater scope to achieve 'HR advantage' which can benefit both workers and their employers even in those organizations competing in predominantly cost-based markets and where workers undertake less complex tasks. For example, a 'high involvement' approach could be applied to a supermarket where workers' skills are enhanced via training and policies are directed at eliciting their motivation, as well as affording them greater opportunities to make decisions about how the work is done and service is delivered. While providing a more nuanced approach to the relationship between skills and competitive strategy, little is said about the *level of skills* and how far they are being enhanced or, critically, whether there might be more scope to reshape work organization (the 'technical relations') to raise more substantially the skill content of the job.

What is not in doubt is that a narrow focus on improving the supply of skills through expanding higher education or raising the skills of the existing workforce is problematic if it fails to address factors which shape the demand for skill (Keep and Mayhew 1999). First, it cannot necessarily be assumed that if organizations have available to them a more educated and skilled workforce they will necessarily respond by shifting upmarket. Some firms may be perfectly profitable competing as they are through a cost-minimization strategy or 'low road' approach, with a low-skilled, low-waged workforce (Wilson and Hogarth 2003; Royle 2004; Holzer et al. 2011). Second, for those organizations that are unable or unwilling to shift their market position (whether low/mid/high), one possibility is that they may undertake incremental changes in the way that jobs are designed in response to recruiting more skilled/qualified workers. However, research suggests that, on the whole, workers fit into the jobs on offer, rather than jobs being designed to fit with worker capabilities. There is little evidence to suggest that employers automatically upgrade jobs to match the qualifications or skills profile of those they recruit (see Mason 2002). The response to this lack of supply-side effect on organizations' 'demand for skill' has led to a number of commentators pushing for a more integrated approach that includes business support to help firms move upmarket (Keep and Mayhew 2010; Ashton and Sung 2011; Froy 2013). Yet, as some of the studies cited earlier indicated, there is no guarantee that such a move would necessarily lead to organizations adjusting their technology, management approach, and work organization to upskill jobs.

What's so Different about the Service Sector?

The transition to a service-dominated economy has been central to debates about the changing nature of work and skill. For some commentators, the growth of services is seen as synonymous with the shift towards a more knowledge-based economy with global competition based around knowledge, ideas, and creativity. For others, it goes hand in hand with an expansion of low-skilled, low-wage employment (Frenkel 2005). Many studies of employment have also highlighted how there has been a decline in the model of standard employment, often linked to the shift towards services (Standing 2011; Kalleberg 2011). The loss of semi-skilled jobs in large, unionized manufacturing workplaces has been replaced by the growth of jobs in parts of the service economy, such as retail and hospitality, where unions are absent or weak. It has been argued that while these jobs are often 'low autonomy' and 'low skill', similar to many of those they replaced, they are more likely to be low waged (Vidal 2013: 589).

Many service sector jobs have a different relationship to the forces of internationalization than one finds in manufacturing, remaining embedded within national and local economies. Bentham et al. (2013: 2) describe these jobs as forming part of the 'foundational economy', which in the UK employs around 40 per cent of the workforce and provides goods and services that are 'territorially distributed', such as care and food retailing. Global competitive forces that might push firms in internationally exposed parts of the economy to move up the value chain and into more specialized niche markets are less likely to apply in these areas, with some firms able to bed down as 'bottom' feeders in low-cost, profitable markets (Warhurst and Findlay 2012: 5). Such jobs can be found in both private and public services. Research on the public sector indicates the importance of long-standing national traditions and institutional legacies in shaping the nature of public provision and employment (e.g. Bevir et al. 2003).

In focusing on the service sector, it is essential to emphasize the heterogeneity of organizations and work, with jobs ranging from brain surgeon to fast food worker. Looking more specifically at 'interactive' or 'front-line' service work, a burgeoning literature has emerged that has sought to distinguish the character of services as well as categorize the differences between various types of service work. Services are said to differ from manufactured products in that they are *intangible, perishable,* and *variable* and often cannot be separated from the worker and the customer in their production (Cowell 1988). A useful discussion is provided by Korczynski's (2002) theory of the 'customer-oriented bureaucracy' which argues that *all* service organizations need to balance tensions between cost efficiency and service quality, with both employees and customers caught within these tensions.

Korczynski (2002: 11–12) identifies three broad categories that have been used in the literature to differentiate this type of service work: a mass service organization, such as fast food, where work organization has the most similarities with assembly lines in manufacturing; an intermediate group where the service experience is an important part of the product; and an upper end of professional and knowledge-intensive services where the service is the product. The assumption is that mass services equate with Taylorism and intense managerial controls, while upper end services are characterized by high levels of complexity and autonomy. The middle group, where most organizations are said to reside, are likely to experience the most acute contradictions between cost efficiency and service quality. Organizations must strive to balance the imposition of controls over the worker and customer with the need to ensure that employees deliver acceptable levels of service required for customer retention (Korczynski 2002; Boxall and Purcell 2007). Even at the low end, such as budget hotels or fast food, organizations cannot afford to neglect the customer experience of the service provided to them.

Many of the typologies that are used to differentiate service work can be rather broad brush and contain many anomalies. There are certainly difficulties in seeking to integrate market positioning within these classifications. Hotels may be in high or low value-added markets but would be considered either mass services or as lying within the middle group in Korczynski's typology. For professional workers, there is often considerable variation in the way work is organized and skills are used. In industries such as software, research has uncovered substantial differences in the types of jobs available to developers and engineers for example (see Marks and Scholarios 2008).

A central focus of research on the service sector is often the relationship with the customer and the implications for the organization of work (Korczynski 2013). With the customer present within the labour process, employees are said to be required to manage their emotions as well as those of the customer in order to achieve a successful service interaction, what Hochschild (1983) terms 'emotional labour'. However, this process is shot through with tensions and contradictions as management seeks to exert a degree of control and predictability over these exchanges, while balancing quality with cost efficiency. Bélanger and Edwards (2013: 446–7) acknowledge that service work has some distinctive features, noting that the 'proximity with an individual whom the employee seeks to serve, to help or to care for' makes employees 'feel' more the conflicts between the demands of management and the needs of those they serve. Even so, they argue that the differences to other forms of labour can be overplayed. In addition, many service sector workers are not directly engaging with customers, clients, or patients, while in other cases these exchanges may account for only a small part of their daily routine.

What is Skill?

The discussion so far around what is happening to skills in work has bypassed the extremely complex question of 'what is skill?' (Attewell 1990). This topic has prompted considerable debate and controversy in recent years as the use of the term 'skill' has expanded to accommodate the shift from manufacturing to services, the emergence of new forms of work organization and management practices, and policy concerns to address issues such as unemployment and social exclusion. Fifty years ago in the UK and USA, 'skilled' was a term reserved mainly for the manual craft worker who tended to be unionized and predominantly male. It implied a combination of technical 'know-how', spatial awareness, and manual dexterity (Keep and Mayhew 1999; Payne 2000). Skill was also bound up with the ability of unions to control entry to the job through lengthy apprenticeship programmes that limited the supply of labour in support of higher wages; practices which have all but disappeared in these countries.

It has long been recognized that the ability to ensure work is defined and rewarded as 'skilled' is bound up with complex social and political processes which involve issues of power. A particular focus has been the *gendered* construction of skill, with skilled work often defined as 'work that women don't do' (Phillips and Taylor 1980: 86; Cockburn 1983). Indeed, many historical examples can be found of where women had to struggle against both their employer and even their own union to gain recognition that their work was as skilled and complex as that of their male counterparts. Jobs that have been seen as typically 'for women', such as a hairdresser, which requires a two- or three-year training period, are normally classified as lower skilled and are typically low paid. Even at the higher end, gendered definitions of jobs can be observed. It took equal pay for equal value legislation and the intervention of the European Court of Justice for speech therapists in the UK to obtain pay grades that were commensurate with those of clinical psychologists and hospital pharmacists who were predominantly male.

The idea then that skill can be understood through a narrow technical lens, as originally applied to skilled manual work, is now widely recognized as being too analytically restrictive to deal with developments in the modern economy. A trend observed across much of the service sector is the emphasis placed by employers on what are variously labelled 'soft', 'social', or 'people' skills, required for customer interaction. Research suggests that recruitment and selection processes in many call centres and across large tracts of retailing and hospitality often place little store on technical skills or formal qualifications (Callaghan and Thompson 2002; Lloyd and Mayhew 2010). A new academic, policy, and practitioner discourse has emerged which encompasses, what are variously labelled, 'generic', 'transferable', 'employability', 'basic', 'soft', and 'social' skills. As a result, a technical view of skill has *already given way* to a much broader notion that includes behaviours, attitudes, dispositions, emotions, and even physical characteristics. The widening application of the term 'skill' to include elements as diverse as reading, writing, and numeracy, team working, problem solving, customer handling, motivation, leadership, and a positive attitude to change has nevertheless sparked considerable debate (Keep and Payne 2004; Hurrell et al. 2013).

While some of these 'soft' or 'social' skills apply to those at the higher end of the labour market, for example 'team working' and 'communication skills' for IT workers and 'leadership skills' for senior managers, it is the application of some of these new 'skills' to those at the lower end that has been most contentious. Lafer (2004) argues that motivation, loyalty, a flexible attitude to change, and punctuality when applied to jobs that are dull, monotonous, and low paid, ends up effectively defining skill as 'discipline', stripping the term of any real meaning. In this way, the skills discourse can end up shifting blame for unemployment and poor quality jobs onto the individual and the education system for failing to acquire, or impart, the 'right' skills, behaviours, or attitudes.

Other commentators, while acknowledging some of these problems argue that there is a danger of dismissing many *routine* interactive service jobs as being 'low skilled' as the skilled component of 'emotion work' or 'emotion management' involved in dealing with the customer is overlooked (Bolton 2004; Korczynski 2005; Gatta et al. 2009). These 'skills' are said to be a complex 'social accomplishment' (Bolton 2004: 33), with their deployment and use remaining partly at the discretion of the worker. They are also not readily captured by conventional measures of skilled work, such as qualification requirements, training, and learning times. Because they are performed mainly by women, these 'real' skills are said to be denied due recognition and reward through the gendered construction of skill. Such arguments challenge conventional understandings of routine interactive service jobs as being low skilled. Nevertheless, they have courted controversy (see Box 3), with critics arguing that they are prone to *exaggerating* the complexity of skills required in what remain highly routinized jobs (see Lloyd and Payne 2009; Hurrell et al. 2013). One important conclusion that emerges from these debates is that there is a need to come to terms with the *heterogeneity* of interactive service work that is sensitive to context, which addresses the scope for discretion, complexity, and knowledge within the *job*, and avoids 'the tendency to lump all emotion workers and all jobs involving emotion work together' as examples of skilled work (Payne 2009: 359).

It is not just the broadening definition of skill and its application to routine service work that makes analysing skill trends problematic. Any discussion of skill also needs to recognize that notions of skill, competence, and what it

> **Box 3** EMOTION WORK AS SKILLED WORK?
>
> Much of the discussion around skill in interactive service work derives from Hochschild's (1983) concept of 'emotional labour', as originally applied to flight attendants and debt-collectors. Emotional labour is used to describe how service workers use their own emotions to produce a particular emotional state in the customer that is of commercial benefit to the organization. Even in routinized work environments, service organizations may require employees to perform emotional labour, and, in some cases, will go to considerable lengths to mould, shape, and control workers' 'emotional displays' through induction and training programmes and the imposition of prescribed 'feeling rules' (Leidner 1993; Callaghan and Thompson 2002). Bolton (2004: 32) contends that 'emotion work is indeed skilled work which contains recognisable elements of discretionary content, task variety and employee control'. Given the unpredictability and variability of service encounters, managerial control can never be absolute, such that even 'the lowest order of emotion workers' (2004: 28) must learn to adapt their emotional displays to the demands of different customers and situations.
>
> There is no denying that service organizations often seek disciplined displays of 'feeling' for those interacting with customers, and that they may be increasingly intent upon exercising control over employees' voice, appearance, and demeanour, as the recent literature on 'aesthetic labour' suggests (see Warhurst and Nickson 2007). Neither is there any dispute that employees may retain *some* degree of discretion over the way they use their emotions in the workplace. Still, it is hard to overlook the evidence that in many call centres, hospitality and mass retail outlets, jobs have been *designed* in ways that ensure employees require little product knowledge, while their interactions with customers, as Bolton (2004: 33) notes, are often fleeting, perfunctory, and may involve little more than 'routinised "niceness"'. Defining skill as being able to deal calmly and politely with customers in such work environments is to view skill in terms of abilities which most people are likely to develop through early socialization and everyday life. Moreover, applying the label 'skilled' to jobs which are poorly designed, highly routinized, and stressful is intensely problematic (Payne 2009; Hurrell et al. 2013).
>
> There is a danger that describing 'emotion work' as a 'social accomplishment', with emotion workers said to be in need of a 'never before required...high level of skill' (Bolton 2004: 33, 25), inadvertently ends up supporting assumptions about generalized rising skill demands. Research in the UK confirms that 'soft skills' rarely command any wage premium unless combined with technical skills (Felstead et al. 2007). As Grugulis et al. (2004: 12) note, 'This is skill as a rhetorical device that carries no material benefits...[and] may even damage the currency of "skill" itself.' This does not mean, however, that jobs involving 'emotion work' cannot be 'skilled work'. What matters is *context* and the need to address issues of job complexity, technical skill, knowledge components, and the degree of autonomy permitted to the employee before applying the label 'skilled work'.

means to be a 'skilled worker' can mean very different things in different countries (Brockmann et al. 2011). In the UK, for example, 'skilled' and 'qualified' often remain distinct, and vocational qualifications bear little relation to wage structures and collective agreements. As Clarke and Winch (2006: 262) note, 'In Britain...a "skilled worker" is someone whose operational ability to carry out particular tasks is recognised by the immediate employer but who is not necessarily formally trained or "qualified" with the potential to carry out a wider range of tasks than those immediately confronted.' In contrast, a 'skilled worker' in Germany, for example, is someone who has undergone an apprenticeship and who has acquired, through an extensive learning programme, a high but broad base of knowledge and skills required to operate and progress within an *occupational field*. This model is embedded within an institutional context, where apprenticeship training is regulated through tripartite arrangements and the value of skilled, *qualified* labour is negotiated and recognized through collective agreements. This serves as a reminder that 'skill' is embedded within societal and institutional frameworks that have developed historically through processes of social and political struggle, particularly those relating to industrial relations (for a useful discussion, see Streeck 2011a; Busemeyer and Trampusch 2012).

A Contested View of Skill

Skill is difficult to measure and quantify, and qualifications or occupational categories are far from perfect indicators. Rising qualification levels may be taken to imply rising skill levels, but much caution is needed. Furthermore, there is no guarantee that skills, once formed or acquired, will be put to effective use within the workplace. Matters become even more complex given the intensely slippery nature of 'skill' itself which together with its broadening meaning and application may again serve to *imply* rising skill demand. Employers may place more emphasis upon 'soft' or 'social skills' as knowledge and technical skill is stripped out. Grugulis et al. (2004: 11) give the example of UK supermarket checkout operatives where demands are for customer service and interpersonal skills, while the mental arithmetic skills, required prior to the introduction of the electronic till, have been removed.

Cockburn's (1983) three dimensions of skill—the skills possessed by the individual, the skill requirements in the job itself, and the 'social construction' of skill—are useful in understanding why we often end up with very different accounts of changes in skill. However, this does not put pay to the definitional controversies raised earlier. Given these conceptual ambiguities, skill is perhaps best viewed as an 'essentially contested concept' (Gallie 1956), where agreement and consensus are unlikely to emerge. However, commentators can at least be clear on how they are using and defining skill.

Thompson's (1989: 92) definition of skill as 'knowledgeable practice within elements of control' focuses attention on the way work is organized and jobs are designed, and the extent to which they allow employees the scope to both develop and use knowledge and skill within the job. However, it is also somewhat limited in that it does not provide a sufficiently clear basis upon which to define 'knowledgeable' or the nature of control. The depth and level of knowledge or skill is central, not least because most workers can in one sense be said to be 'knowledgeable' about their jobs (Thompson et al. 2001). As we have noted elsewhere, 'If service workers had *substantive* knowledge of a sophisticated product, process or technique and considerable autonomy in terms of how they did their job and interacted with customers and clients, one may be much closer to a workable definition of skilled service work' (Lloyd and Payne 2009: 630, emphasis added). The key question is not just whether workers have slightly more discretion or opportunity to contribute ideas, as referred to in much of the literature on HPWP, but what is the scope to redesign the job to improve skill levels and how might this be achieved?

In this book, skill is explored as a relative and socially constructed concept in terms of the knowledge requirements of a job—typically the length of prior education and training needed to acquire that knowledge, the amount of additional learning that takes place on the job that allows an individual to be competent in the task, and the new knowledge that is needed over time. Deciding whether a job requires two, three, or four years of training or a specified qualification and what knowledge goes into that qualification is not an objective measure of skill but reflects a combination of actual needs within a job and the way that interest groups have defined the development of that knowledge. Skill is not just about knowledge, it is also about application through learning techniques, for example the ability to cut hair, teach, operate a cash machine, or communicate effectively to others. These techniques are not learnt in isolation but are related to knowledge within a job. Teaching involves a subject and a particular group of learners, while cutting hair requires knowledge of styles, hair texture, and so on.

Although it can be difficult to define 'complex' work (see Green 2011), it remains central to any understanding of what is a 'skilled job' as does the degree of autonomy and discretion available to the job holders (Braverman 1974; Littler 1982). While discretion and autonomy are often used interchangeably, this book refers to discretion as the ability of individuals or work groups to use their own judgement and make choices within their work at the level of the task, in terms of how to do the job, in what order, and to what quality standards. All jobs afford some degree of discretion so it is important to probe its extent, alongside the depth of knowledge and techniques required. Autonomy is used in a broader sense and refers to the extent of decision-making power available to the worker or work group to work independently from management and their influence on higher-level decisions, such as government policy in the public sector or an organization's restructuring plans. It is these components which are the focus of this book, examining how they vary both within and across countries.

Conclusion

Skill is a complex and contested concept, having both objective and subjective properties. Disagreements as to what is a skilled job are clearly evident in contemporary debates around 'employability skills', 'soft skills', and 'skilled emotion work'. Skill is also difficult to quantify and measure, with a tendency to rely upon proxies including qualifications, training and learning times, occupational categories and job titles, and subjective assessments of the skills required or used within the role, all of which come with problems. At the same time, the notion of a 'skilled worker' has different meanings in different countries. All of this makes skill one of the most challenging topics to research within the social sciences. It is also one of the most important as it is central to the way in which capitalist societies are structured and rewards are distributed between social groups.

HCT is ill-equipped to deal with such complexity. It is based on a purely individualized notion of skill, sees investment in education and training as an essentially rational calculus, and has little to say about the factors which affect the extent to which skills are utilized or not. It has often served to fuel policymakers' belief that there are simple linkages between the outputs of the education and training system and the performance of the economy in terms of productivity and competitiveness. In this chapter, we have argued that skill needs to be understood holistically as encompassing the skill of the job holder, the skill required within the job itself, and the social construction of skill. However, the key point to emphasize is that the way work is organized and jobs are designed is central to the level of skill required and the ability of workers to deploy the skills they bring to the job.

There are many factors which shape work organization and skill requirements, such as the nature and complexity of the product or service and the extent of differentiation. Existing research, however, indicates that 'there is no necessary congruence between markets, technologies and particular forms of work design' (Thompson et al. 1995: 721). The relationships and linkages are more complex and contingent as power relations within the organization, in conjunction with wider institutional constraints, play a key role in the development of forms of work organization and skill levels (Lloyd and Payne 2002). While employers have some degree of choice over their approach, it is important to acknowledge the structuring effects of the sector and the institutional environment, aspects that are explored in the next chapter.

Given the complexity of these debates, it is not surprising to find a lack of agreement over whether contemporary capitalism is predominantly characterized by upskilling, deskilling, or a combination of both. The Braverman view of deskilling as the dominant tendency has been largely replaced by labour market polarization as the standard, critical riposte to arguments that the dominant trend within contemporary capitalism is upskilling. While the complex and contested nature of skill makes it difficult to prove any general trend, it is hard to deny that the search for lower costs through technology, the fragmentation of work, and the cheapening of labour (via replacement, increasing control, and deskilling) remain central to the dynamics of capitalist competition. Furthermore, there is widespread evidence that many economies are failing to generate enough skilled jobs to keep pace with the expansion of the education system.

In recent years, the debate has also shifted away from theorizing generalized patterns of change towards exploring factors at the organizational level (e.g. product market and labour management strategies) and the impact of the national institutional environment and societal context on work organization and skill (Grugulis and Lloyd 2010; Gallie 2011). As we shall see, there is some evidence to suggest that the diffusion of jobs which combine high levels of learning, skill, and autonomy in a country may depend upon the power of organized labour both within the workplace and at the political-societal level. In other words, the upskilling of jobs rests not upon proclaimed paradigmatic shifts in the nature of advanced capitalism or simply changes in the supply of skills but upon institutions and the ability to *regulate* capital. The latter strikes at the heart of neo-liberal arguments around the need for greater labour flexibility and deregulation that have been resurgent within Europe since the 2008 financial crisis (see Chapter 1). These debates form the subject of the next chapter.

3

National Institutions, Sectors, and Work Organization

A Theoretical Framework

Introduction

Over the last thirty years, researchers have become increasingly concerned to explore national differences among advanced capitalist countries and the impact of political economy on economic performance, job quality, and other social outcomes. Some of these approaches specifically focused on distinctive patterns of skill and work organization, while for others these issues were of marginal interest. The most relevant for this book are 'societal effects', 'skills equilibria', 'varieties of capitalism', and 'employment systems' approaches. These studies present various interpretations of the role of national institutions, class relations, and different forms of competition and inter-firm organization in creating distinctive national regimes. This chapter examines what these approaches can tell us about differences in work organization and skill across countries, assesses the evidence provided, and considers the role of the sector in accounting for within-country variation.

The chapter begins by critically appraising these theoretical perspectives which drew evidence largely from manufacturing sectors. It then examines key findings from major surveys which indicate that the Scandinavian countries, on the whole, have 'better' forms of work organization. Although the surveys indicate broad national differences, there is evidence that these differences do not apply consistently across sectors. This raises important research questions. Do national institutions make themselves felt in a given sector resulting in cross-country differences or are there sector dynamics which shape similar outcomes in work organization and skills, irrespective of national context? What can existing studies tell us about the key factors which explain why jobs may vary? In exploring these questions, the chapter assesses the qualitative comparative research from the service sector and identifies gaps in the evidence. Finally, the chapter draws together the findings from existing research and uses these to put forward an analytical framework that guides the remainder of the book.

National Institutions

From the late 1970s to the early 1990s, researchers conducted a number of industry case studies, mainly in the engineering and automotive sectors, which identified distinct national differences in work organization. Germany was consistently highlighted as offering jobs with higher levels of skill and autonomy, particularly when compared with the UK and, less frequently, with France. The path-breaking 'societal effects' approach, associated with the LEST group in France, drew on detailed empirical studies of 'comparable' firms, and argued that there was an 'institutional logic that is particular to a society' which brings about 'nationally different shapes of organization', with firms adopting 'different solutions to similar challenges' (Maurice et al. 1980: 59, 61). The research showed how the same manufacturing goods could be produced with contrasting country-based occupational hierarchies, division of labour, and work organization. Focusing on France and Germany, they concluded that firms 'are organized quite differently and that the worker hierarchy in the two countries is not the same' (Maurice et al. 1986: 161). In Germany, work was organized in ways that encouraged polyvalence, with workers having a greater span of control and less managerial supervision. In France, hierarchical authority was prominent, with work organized on the basis of a more detailed division of labour. There was no one dominant factor to explain these differences; rather they were an outcome of long-standing, interconnected 'social spheres' that had developed in 'manufacturing, industrial relations, education and training' (Maurice et al. 1980: 61), and which were closely linked to class relations and power in the wider society.

While the education and training system was a central 'sphere' for the 'societal effects' group, other approaches implied that it was the *core* explanation for differences in skills and work organization. Driven by a UK policy concern about low productivity, the National Institute of Economic and Social Research (NIESR) sought to explore the contribution of vocational education and training (VET) to under-performance. A series of 'matched-plant' studies were conducted in the 1980s and 1990s which compared UK workplaces in a number of sectors with those in Germany, France, and the Netherlands. The outcome was a collection of detailed workplace and sector comparisons of technology, work organization, training, and performance. UK workers were typically found to be undertaking less training, performing lower skilled work with greater supervision, and to be less productive than their continental European counterparts (e.g. Daly et al. 1985; Prais et al. 1989; Steedman and Wagner 1989; Mason at al. 1994).

The authors prioritized the role of VET as the main causal factor, pointing for example to the impact of Germany's high quality dual apprenticeship system. However, the evidence to single out this one factor was, for some critics, unconvincing as many other elements were also in play (see Cutler 1992). A different reading of their data indicated that organizations in the UK had lower levels of capital investment, targeted 'mass' as opposed to 'differentiated' high-quality markets, and were faced with more intense short-term financial pressures. While the aim was to focus on comparable plants, in many cases it was the very problems involved in obtaining good matches that was itself illuminating. Nevertheless, the idea that the education and training system was the main driver of differences in skill outcomes in the workplace would have an enduring appeal for many UK academics and policy-makers alike.

While the differences in the way countries were specializing in particular product markets had been downplayed, other studies were focusing on the distinction between mass markets and differentiated products, and their implications for skills and work organization. Streeck (1992: 7) emphasized the 'thick institutional structures' in Germany that included, but went beyond, the apprenticeship system, and which provided a series of 'beneficial constraints' that pushed employers onto 'high road' accumulation strategies centred around 'diversified quality production', high skills, and high wages. German 'institutional rigidities', such as sectoral wage bargaining, employment protection, training requirements, and legally-backed systems of co-determination and works councils, largely 'foreclosed price based competition'. This distinctive set of socio-economic institutions, which also included systems of bank-based finance delivering 'patient capital', encouraged firms to seek competitive advantage in markets focusing on high-quality, differentiated products (Sorge and Streeck 1988: 26–7). This environment was seen to be associated with higher skilled and more autonomous forms of working than in 'institutionally impoverished settings' such as the UK and USA (Streeck 1992: 10).

The German system reflected a 'complex historical compromise' between the state, capital, and labour (Streeck 1997a: 34), which emerged when organized labour was relatively powerful. A similar argument about power, but linked to different institutional features, was also used to explain Swedish distinctiveness as regards work organization. Writing around the same time, Berggren (1992) argued that features such as strongly coordinated bargaining systems and low wage differentials, a generous welfare state, strong workplace trade unions, and a period of full employment (and therefore recruitment difficulties) had led Swedish companies to adopt more autonomous forms of team-based work organization, notably in the automotive industry. In the Nordic context, commentators like Esping-Andersen (1990) emphasized the power of unions and social democracy in the development of an inclusive welfare state model which provided constraints on employer choices and helped push them towards 'high road' strategies (see also Korpi 2006).

Writing in the 1980s, Finegold and Soskice (1988) also focused on the role of institutions to explain why the UK had such a poor training record and relatively low levels of qualification among school leavers. Rather than a cultural or class-structure problem of ingrained 'anti-industry' or 'anti-education' attitudes undermining investment in skills (see Wiener 1981), the problem was one of system failure (Finegold 1999: 60). Britain was seen to be 'trapped in a low-skills equilibrium', defined as 'a self-reinforcing network of societal and state institutions which interact to stifle the demand for improvements in skill levels' (Finegold and Soskice 1988: 22). Many UK firms were said to be competing in 'mass markets' for standardized goods with forms of work organization and job design that required only low levels of skill. Short-term shareholder pressures, the weak coordination capacity of employers and trade unions within an 'adversarial' and decentralized industrial relations system, the lack of sectoral coordination, and the low quality of vocational training were all implicated. While the education and training system had evolved to meet the needs of an economy based primarily upon large, mass production manufacturing, this system was seen as ill-equipped to meet the changing nature of international competition which placed a premium on new industries and flexible, batch production methods, echoing debates around 'flexible specialization' prominent at the time (Piore and Sabel 1984) (see Chapter 2). Finegold (1991) drew an explicit comparison with the German 'high skills equilibrium', where interlocking institutions created a 'virtuous circle' of product and skills upgrading (see also Culpepper 1999).

The varieties of capitalism (VOC) literature (Hall and Soskice 2001), which has come to dominate comparative industrial relations, drew upon these theories of skills equilibria, and emerged as an academic defence of the viability of German capitalism at a time when the US economy was widely viewed to be forging ahead. Responding to arguments that globalization was leading to a process of 'Anglo-Saxonization', the theory distinguished between 'liberal market economies' (LMEs), such as the UK and USA, and 'coordinated market economies' (CMEs), which included Germany, Japan, and the Nordic countries. It located *firms* as 'the crucial actors in a capitalist economy', focusing attention on how they *coordinate* their economic activities to develop 'core competencies' that can deliver comparative advantage (Hall and Soskice 2001: 6). In LMEs, firms seek to resolve their coordination problems through markets and hierarchies, while in CMEs they rely more on non-market relations and strategic collaborations between firms and other actors (Hall and

Soskice 2001: 8). These different processes of coordination were seen as being shaped by interlocking and complementary institutional 'spheres' encompassing industrial relations, VET, corporate governance, inter-firm relations, and intra-firm relations, the last of which concerned labour utilization and management of the 'wage–effort bargain'.

These different institutional settings were said to provide firms with advantages which allowed them to compete successfully in particular types of markets. In CMEs, firms tend to adopt production strategies characterized by 'incremental innovation', requiring long-term cooperation with a skilled and functionally flexible workforce. Incentives to compete on the basis of quality and product differentiation were provided by access to patient capital, labour market regulations which restricted the use of redundancies, an education and training system that ensured high levels of firm-specific and industry-specific skill, and industrial relations and corporate structures (e.g. codetermination/works councils) designed to provide collective voice and elicit cooperation.

For LMEs, a numerically flexible ('hire-and-fire') labour market, a highly developed stock market, hierarchical corporate management, and an education system providing 'general skills', created different incentives. Quick and easy access to start-up capital, rapid decision-making, and the ability to restructure with limited costs were seen to provide advantages for firms competing in sectors where the emphasis was upon 'rapid innovation' in new products (e.g. biotech in the USA). At the same time, a high level of labour market flexibility enabled many firms to compete via low-cost, low value-added strategies, with a less skilled, lower-cost workforce (Hall and Soskice 2001). The UK emerges as an economy with some advanced innovative sectors (e.g. finance, pharmaceuticals, and aerospace) but which is also heavily reliant upon mass-produced services (Crouch et al. 1999). A high level of tertiary education was seen to support innovative sectors, with the broader education system providing entrants to the workforce with 'general skills' needed to adjust and adapt to rapidly changing job demands.

VOC took a particular view on the role of product market strategy and the centrality of the skill formation system. On the former, it suggested that there was a direct link between the product market strategy of the firm and its skills requirements. In CMEs, firms 'employ production strategies that rely on a highly skilled labor force given substantial work autonomy and encouraged to share the information it acquires in order to generate continuous improvements in product lines and production processes' (Hall and Soskice 2001: 24). Beyond this general assumption, however, they left it to later contributors to explore work organization in detail.

Although the theory acknowledges the role of interconnected 'institutional complementarities', the skill formation system, as with the NIESR studies, was afforded particular attention in relation to job design decisions (Estevez-Abe et al. 2001: 146; Busemeyer and Trampusch 2012). Institutional practices make a difference because they encourage and discourage particular types of skill formation approaches from both workers and employers, i.e. firm/industry 'specific skills' in Germany and 'general skills' in the UK. The skills created are assumed to align closely with their use within the workplace; issues of over- or under-qualification or skills wastage, therefore, do not enter the analysis. In addition, the distinction drawn between specific and general skills is not unproblematic. German apprentice-trained workers have broad-based transferable skills, with Streeck (2011a: 24) giving the example of skilled bakers who are sufficiently knowledgeable about chemistry to be employed by chemicals firms! Furthermore, it cannot be assumed, as is the tendency within the VOC literature, that tertiary-level education necessarily represents higher level general skills, with questions surrounding the quality of many degree programmes in the UK and USA and the level of cognitive skill acquired (Streeck 2011a; Côté 2014).

It is important to reiterate that while VOC was partly a defence of the viability of coordinated capitalisms, Hall and Soskice (2001) nevertheless insisted that both LMEs and CMEs could be economically successful, although their implications for social and distributional issues would be very different. There was also a strong implication that countries were locked into particular trajectories, or path dependencies, by virtue of their interlocking institutional complementarities. Little was said about processes of change and transformation (Streeck and Thelen 2005). It was claimed, for example, that the UK could never hope to emulate Germany's high quality apprenticeship system, required for success in differentiated product markets, because it lacked strong employer organizations. Instead, it should focus on the mass expansion of higher education (Soskice 1993; Finegold 1999) and compete on labour market flexibility. Despite developments in Germany challenging these assumptions about the locked-in nature of country trajectories, there remains an enduring argument that as LMEs struggle to develop strong forms of coordination, they are, therefore, destined to pursue further deregulatory measures.

While both the 'societal approach' and VOC explore the role of interlocking institutions, a key difference is that the first draws on *power* to explain the development of institutions and accompanying social norms. As Streeck (2010) has argued, the VOC approach reflects a functionalist perspective based on rational decision-making in response to institutional incentives. The approach is technocratic and tends to neglect politics, specifically the power resources at the disposal of employers and trade unions which, together with the role of the state, are central factors in shaping how systems emerge historically as well as change over time. There is, for example, no recognition of the power of organized labour and class conflict in explaining the development of labour market and welfare institutions. Rather, Hall and

Soskice (2001) consider issues like welfare provision or employment protection as rational choices, 'consensually created devices to facilitate cooperation between employers and workers and thereby increase productivity and competitiveness' (Streeck 2011a: 13).

Both these type of approaches have focused predominantly on identifying institutions that lead to specific forms of production strategies and the skills and types of work organization assumed to be associated with them. As seen in the previous chapter, the relationship between product markets, technology, and skills/work organization may be far more complex than these accounts imply, not least when applied to the service sector. Indeed, attempts at theorizing comparative differences in work organization have been based on a very limited number of workplace studies, predominantly in the automotive and engineering sectors. Whether these theories were intended to be applied beyond manufacturing to the private service sector or the public sector is far from clear. Commentators were certainly concerned to identify country-level differences and distinct national models, and these theoretical approaches have since provided conceptual shorthand for those seeking to frame cross-national comparative studies, including those in the public and private service sector. Given some of the difficulties specifically with conceptualizing the nature of the product, quality, and skills within the service sector, the question arises as to the applicability of these theoretical frameworks. How far does the evidence from these studies of often well-organized sectors in manufacturing reflect broader patterns of work organization across an economy?

A National System?

In order to establish a more representative picture of differences in skills and work organization across countries, attempts have been made to use broad brush national data and international surveys. There are major difficulties in measuring skills, as discussed in the last chapter, even within countries, and these problems intensify when making international comparisons. Broad occupational data have been used to indicate differences across countries. Figure 3.1 shows that the UK has a high proportion of managers, Germany has more associate technical, clerical, and craft positions, and the UK and the Scandinavian countries a higher proportion of professionals and relatively few associate professionals. The problem for comparative purposes is that each occupational group consists of a wide range of jobs with extremely varied levels of skill. A classic case is that of managers; the UK apparently needs 10 per cent of the workforce to be managers, whereas Germany makes do with 4 per cent and Denmark with 2 per cent. While one reading might be that Germany and Denmark require fewer managers as work is organized in such a

Skills in the Age of Over-Qualification

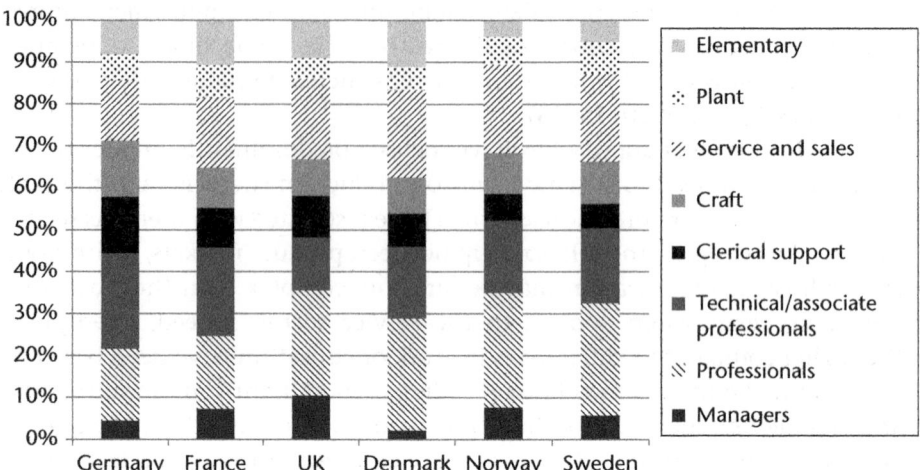

Figure 3.1. Employment by occupation, 2014
Note: Excludes agriculture, forestry and fishery and armed forces.
Source: Eurostat LFS series lfsa_egais.

way that there is greater use of self-management, it could also be that the UK is subject to 'job title' inflation as discussed in the previous chapter (see Lloyd and Payne 2014). In addition, whether a job is defined as management, professional or associate professional, or technical may relate more to the job title or the bargaining power of the relevant occupational group than to the content of the job itself.

Unfortunately, there is a lack of survey data attempting to measure skill levels across countries, reflecting the methodological and conceptual problems identified in the last chapter. There are, however, a number of comparative surveys that provide evidence in relation to job autonomy, control, and learning at work. There are still methodological difficulties when it comes to the different ways in which questions are interpreted in different national contexts[1] but they may offer some indication of national patterns. From the surveys that have been conducted, the generalized conclusions are that Scandinavian countries consistently stand out as having better forms of work organization.

Dobbin and Boychuk (1999), drawing on comparative surveys of individuals, found that workers in Denmark, Finland, Norway, and Sweden experienced higher levels of autonomy than those in the USA, Canada, and Australia, and

---

[1] A worker in Germany might report that they are not involved in decisions affecting their work but this may neglect involvement through institutions such as works councils. Workers in the UK might report that they have involvement but lack these legally backed voice mechanisms. As a result, it may not be clear what surveys are telling us about *substantive* worker influence, relying merely on individual worker *perceptions*.

National Institutions, Sectors, and Work Organization

that this was the case for both managers and non-managers. Using the European surveys on working conditions, Gallie (2007: 99) questioned the accepted model of Germany as a beacon of high autonomy work, and instead argued that it was the Scandinavian countries which had 'exceptionally high levels of individual task discretion, job variety and opportunities for self-development in the job'. Germany is seen as having a 'dualistic' employment regime (Gallie 2011) as higher skilled jobs involving more autonomous forms of working are concentrated within 'core firms' in the export-oriented manufacturing sector. Lorenz (2015), using the same surveys but adopting a cluster analysis, also found support for the view that the Nordic countries (and the Netherlands) are characterized by the relatively high use of 'discretionary learning' forms of work organization and low levels of Taylorism, as shown in Table 3.1. By contrast, the UK and Ireland emerge with proportionally fewer employees in work characterized by 'discretionary learning', along with a relatively high incidence of 'lean production' (as does Finland) and jobs described as 'Taylorist' (see also Holm et al. 2010; Esser and Olsen 2012).

Some of these commentators have contended that these differences may reflect national employment regimes or 'logics' which affect a broad range of jobs across an economy. Dobbin and Boychuk (1999) argue that market-based countries, such as the UK and USA, orient towards systems which are 'rule-based', with the Nordic countries typified by a more 'skill-based' approach. These systems have different 'logics of work control' whose influence extends across a 'whole spectrum of jobs' and occupational levels (Dobbin and Boychuk 1999: 261–2). Rule-based systems entail more direct control and less autonomy; skill-based systems offer more autonomy and higher skilled work to both managerial and non-managerial groups. While not elaborating on their historical origins, they stress that high-skill employment systems in the Nordic case have been sustained through corporatist traditions 'because unions have lobbied not only in firms but also in parliaments, to enhance skill levels' (Dobbin and Boychuk 1999: 262). The national employment logic is

Table 3.1. National differences in forms of work organization (%)

	Discretionary learning	Lean organization	Taylorist	Simple organization
Denmark	61.9	16.9	8.3	16.9
Finland	42.2	36.5	9.8	11.6
France	30.6	27.7	19.7	22.1
Germany	44.4	22.6	16.0	17.1
Ireland	25.1	41.4	21.8	11.8
Netherlands	59.8	12.6	13.0	14.6
Norway	54.7	27.8	11.7	5.8
Sweden	61.9	20.1	8.6	9.5
UK	28.4	36.6	19.6	15.5

Source: Lorenz (2015: selected data from Table 3, based on 5th European Working Conditions Survey).

seen as having become entrenched through systems of management, training, bargaining, and welfare that affect 'how actors conceive of problems and solutions' (Dobbin and Boychuk 1999: 282).

Gallie (2003: 77), using a similar argument, suggests there 'may be significant societal effects' taking place in the Scandinavian countries due to the policy orientations of government and the social partners towards improving the quality of working life. He emphasizes the centrality of organized labour to explain differences in the 'employment regime' (see also Fligstein and Byrkjeflot 1996). The relatively advanced position of the Scandinavian countries is attributed to the inclusive nature of the regime 'where organized labour has a strong institutionalized participation in decision making and where policies are designed to extend both employment and employee rights as widely as possible through the population of working age' (Gallie 2011: 8–9). This ability reflects 'the capacity of governments and organized labor to constrain the actions of employers in the interests of improving the quality of work life of employees' (Gallie 2007: 100).

Hollingworth and Streeck (1994: 272–3) draw on empirical findings from a range of sectors to identify ways in which the national context 'makes itself felt' and is able to 'modify the impact of sectoral contingencies'. In relation to work organization, this context can include national laws on job security which affect all workers regardless of sector, the national system of education and training, and the dominant role played by the social partners within society which may engender a level of trust and socially imposed obligations on all actors (see also Gustavsen 2007). This type of analysis suggests that national effects on work organization are not just transmitted through dominant institutions but may also permeate the *attitudes* of managers as well as workers' expectations.

Other commentators have argued that the relatively advanced position of the Nordic countries in terms of work organization cannot simply be explained by macro-institutional and societal conditions but also reflects a long history of workplace development programmes, whereby action researchers help organizations to adopt better ways of working with the support of the social partners and the state (Gustavsen 2007; Lorenz 2015). The impact of these programmes in the Norwegian case is discussed in the next chapter.

It is certainly difficult to ignore the evidence of significant cross-country variation when it comes to patterns of work organization and levels of job autonomy, in particular the progress that has been made in Scandinavia. Nevertheless, these surveys present a broad overview and tend to be used to highlight the differences that exist across countries rather than the similarities. For example, there are still substantial numbers of workers in Norway who are in jobs with low autonomy and little learning; they are just proportionately fewer than in Germany and the UK. Whether their experience of work is substantially different across these countries is a question this book seeks to address.

Bringing the Sector 'Back In'

In recent years, writers within the field of industrial relations have argued that there is a need to bring the sector 'back in', partly as a corrective to what is often referred to as the 'methodological nationalism' inherent in the comparative capitalisms approach as typified by VOC (see Crouch et al. 2009; Grimshaw and Lehndorff 2010; Bechter et al. 2012). What applies to core firms in the German manufacturing export sector, for example, may be very different in retailing or IT. In some ways, this shift back towards the sector should come as no great surprise as industrial relations scholarship traditionally afforded considerable attention to sectors as exerting an important influence on employment relations, managerial practice, and work organization (Bechter et al. 2012).

Sectors differ considerably in terms of the degree of product market regulation, the public/private mix, the range of technologies and skills, the composition of the workforce, approaches to skill formation, the nature of inter-firm networks and employer organization, and levels of trade union representation (see Hollingsworth and Streeck 1994; Grimshaw and Lehndorff 2010). While this does not mean that all organizations in a sector will adopt the same strategy or managerial approaches, there are nevertheless powerful sector dynamics, which mean that employers will tend to 'face similar pressures and options in the organization of work and labour relations by virtue of common activities and constraints' (Arrowsmith 2010: 181). For example, supermarkets compete predominantly for local consumers, offer a similar range of products, and face high levels of price competition. Companies have to ensure that products are stacked on shelves and that customers can select and pay for them, use fairly similar technology, and require workers to deliver acceptable standards of service. Customer demand varies throughout the day and week, leading to considerable emphasis on matching staffing levels to sales. These commonalities help to frame the approach that employers take in relation to staffing, skill profiles, and the organization of working time.

Within any national model, it has long been recognized that key institutions are not necessarily closely coupled, nor are they evenly spread. For example, in Germany and the Nordic countries works councils only apply to firms above a certain size and both have 'co-determination free zones' (Streeck 1997a; Ferner and Hyman 1998). Studies suggest that collective bargaining institutions are becoming more internally differentiated, particularly within the hitherto more homogeneous coordinated economies like Germany. Coverage of collective bargaining declined from 90 per cent in West Germany in 1990 to just over 60 per cent in 2011, and the traditional system of labour representation through works councils has receded (Bosch and Kalina 2008; Hassel 2012). The rapid growth in the low-wage sector, now estimated at 23 per cent of the workforce, is a stark indicator of the lack of inclusiveness of Germany's dense institutional structures (Gautié and Schmitt 2010). As Lane and Wood (2014: 161) argue, there now exist 'side by side totally different institutional arrangements, seemingly insulated one from the other by sectoral boundaries'. Even within sectors, there are differences; for example German telecoms call centres have works councils and levels of employment protection very different to those of call centre subcontractors (Weinkopf 2008; Doellgast 2010).

Some evidence indicates that other countries may be more homogeneous, at least in relation to institutional structures. Bechter et al. (2012) examined key collective bargaining and social partner indicators in nine sectors across twenty-seven European countries. They found that the Nordic countries and France displayed 'strong cross-sectoral similarity' (2012: 194), indicating that only in these countries 'does it appear legitimate to speak of national models'. The UK and Germany were presented as particularly differentiated by sector, while across a range of countries the sectoral effect was much stronger in some industries than others. Strong sectors, where the structures of industrial relations were very similar irrespective of country, were those dominated by large multinational companies, such as steel and telecommunications, and the public sector, i.e. hospitals. Weaker sectors, where institutions varied both across and within countries, comprised those with smaller companies and those delivering localized services. These findings illustrate the potentially complex interrelationships between the sector and the national employment regime. However, the study did not explore how these formal structures relate to outcomes, including work organization and skills.

This relationship between the national system and sectoral dynamics has rarely been the explicit focus of studies on comparative patterns of work organization. More recently, Grimshaw and Lehndorff (2010: 24) have argued that addressing such complexity offers the scope to develop a fuller and more sophisticated understanding of the 'interaction between the character of national models and the particularities of sectoral systems operating within and across countries'. Of particular importance is the experience of newly emerging sectors (see also Crouch et al. 2009), and how they are integrated (or not) with more traditional institutional forms. Whether national actors, such as trade unions, are able to ensure integration takes place is seen as central to the sustainability of these national institutions (and, therefore, the national system) in the longer term (see also Fligstein and Byrkjeflot 1996;

Bosch and Lehndorff 2005: 24; Berribi-Hoffman et al. 2010). The available evidence on the existence and causes of national differences in work organization in specific service sector jobs (new or well-established) has rarely been explored. Some of the recent key studies in the field are briefly examined in the following section.

Comparing Service Sector Work Organization and Skills

When it comes to cross-country comparisons of work organization in the service sector, there are few studies and many gaps. The studies that have been undertaken differ in their focus, depending upon whether they are looking at high-skilled jobs or low-skilled jobs. In the former case, rather than comparing the tasks undertaken and levels of knowledge and skill, the focus tends to be on qualification requirements and levels of autonomy and control, particularly in the public sector. At lower skill levels, there is more interest in actual skill levels and task content, along with systems of management and supervision.

The area that has attracted the least attention is higher skilled *private* sector service work. An EU-funded project on the impact of restructuring on work organization included qualitative studies of R&D workers in the ICT sector and IT professionals in software services (see Valenduc et al. 2007). These two IT-related jobs were among those occupational groups described as 'rather homogenous' both across and within countries (Krings et al. 2007). It was claimed that 'their occupational profile and individual identities at work can be characterised independently from national contexts or company features' (Krings et al. 2007: 169). National differences, however, were apparent in broader areas of job quality and were linked to countries' institutional settings, although the impact was not consistent across the two jobs. Norway, for example, provided R&D workers with better working conditions (work–life balance, job security) than were available in Austria, France, and Germany. In contrast, for those working in software companies, there was found to be little evidence 'of formal structures of social dialogue' in any of the countries under study (Valenduc 2007: 96).

There has been more interest in comparing the work of public sector professionals reflecting concerns about the impact of different governance and institutional regimes. Again, however, studies are limited and work organization and skills are generally not the main focus. Nevertheless, the few studies that have been undertaken point towards country-level variation in levels of autonomy and forms of accountability. Central has been the way in which jobs have been changing as a result of a variety of public sector reforms and, in particular, the uneven patterns of liberalization and marketization (see Chapter 5).

One EC-funded project, for example, examined the impact of welfare state restructuring on nurses and primary school teachers (see Goodson and Lindblad 2011) across seven European countries (Müller et al. 2007). Nurses experienced common trends in restructuring, including the shift towards a contracting model of employment and increased demands for cost efficiency, throughput, and results obtained through guidelines, standardization, evaluation, and rewards (Kosonen and Houtsonen 2007). In most countries, nurses reported increased workloads and stress, insufficient time to care for patients, and being unable to work according to their professional ethos. However, experiences are far from uniform. In England, where the use of controls was particularly pronounced, the picture is one of instability, fear of redundancy, low morale, deteriorating work–life balance, heightened stress, and concerns about 'burn-out'. In Sweden and Finland, what stands out is 'the relative autonomy the nurses enjoy' in each context (Kosonen and Houtsonen 2007: 11). Indeed, Finland presents a largely

> trouble-free picture of its consultancy nurses' work. They have enough opportunities to participate in decision-making concerning their unit. Further, they are able to train and educate themselves relatively independently. They are also quite satisfied with their conditions of work, excluding perhaps salary. (Kosonen and Houtsonen 2007: 11)

Research on teachers also shows variation across countries and over time in levels of teacher autonomy. In Portugal, Spain, and Finland, teachers reported no noticeable pressures from official inspections or monitoring, while in England there was an increasingly tight regime of evaluation and accountability that limited teachers' autonomy (Müller et al. 2007). In Scandinavia, there is evidence of variation in the organization of teachers' work according to the particular country concerned. Helgøy and Homme (2007) found that teachers in Sweden tend to have a higher degree of individual classroom autonomy, whereas Norwegian teachers had more autonomy and influence at the collective level, i.e. in relation to the national policy-making process. Another study indicates that teachers in Finland experience higher levels of autonomy when compared to those working in Sweden (Houtsonen et al. 2010). Across these studies of public sector professionals, national differences are linked to the structure of public sector institutions, i.e. the health and education systems, the direction of reforms, and the ways in which the occupational group has responded. For teachers, their response is seen to be a reflection of their relative power in different countries to shape reforms and their implementation, alongside national conceptions of professionalism and status (see also Osborn 2006).

The most extensive comparative evidence on work organization at the lower end of the labour market is a study of low-wage work sponsored by the US-based Russell Sage Foundation which looked at the USA, Germany, France, Demark, Netherlands, and the UK (Gautié and Schmitt 2010). Five service sector jobs were examined and in four cases (call centre worker, hospital cleaner, hospital nursing assistant, and retail assistant), sustained national differences were found in the skill levels and organization of work. In the UK and the USA, these jobs were found to be generally lower skilled, with narrower tasks and less autonomy.

For the other countries, there is more variability across the sectors. For example, in Germany, four-fifths of retail workers have completed a two- or three-year retail apprenticeship and many are employed in jobs where they are responsible for a particular product area. In these jobs, there is a requirement for substantial product knowledge in order to undertake a broad range of activities, including product selection, ordering, and display work (Voss-Dahm 2008). These tasks in other countries are typically undertaken by supervisors or managers (see Carré et al. 2010). In contrast, German hospital cleaners experience very narrow, low-skilled jobs, while in France and Denmark hospitals were found to have introduced a broader range of job tasks with some elements of upskilling (Méhaut et al. 2010). The job of hotel cleaner, however, showed little variation within or across countries (Vanselow et al. 2010). Nevertheless, evidence from another study found that office cleaners in Norway were seeing moves towards more team working, with higher levels of worker autonomy (see Holtgrewe and Sardadvar 2012).

Both case study and survey evidence indicates that call centre jobs are likely to be more skilled, with higher levels of discretion in Germany, Denmark, and, to a lesser extent, France than in the UK, USA, and the Netherlands (Lloyd et al. 2010). Doellgast (2010) also found that German telecoms call centre agents had broader job design and experienced less monitoring than those operating in similar markets in the USA. Factors that appear to be important in pushing firms to adopt less fragmented forms of work organization include employment regulations that require companies to retain existing (often well-qualified and relative well-paid) workers, the strength and activism of trade unions and works councils, and, in some cases, recruitment difficulties (Lloyd et al. 2010; see also Doellgast et al. 2009).

While these studies of lower end jobs and, to a much lesser extent, high-skilled jobs indicate that country-based differences exist, the picture is complex and variable. National institutions matter, but so does the sector. The explanation as to why there is variation within and across countries in the way that lower skilled jobs are designed is under-developed. For those in professional and managerial jobs, there is a dearth of comparative studies. We may know something of their education and broader working conditions, but little about the way that the job of say a research scientist in the pharmaceuticals industry compares across countries in terms of skill demands and levels of discretion and autonomy. Overall, the evidence base for examining the effects of national institutions, sector dynamics, and organizational approach on skills and work organization is limited, while there has been a lack of comprehensive attempts to develop an explanation for the relationship between these different elements. The following section draws upon existing research to develop an analytical framework for the research undertaken in this book.

Developing an Analytical Framework

A comprehensive analytical framework for the comparative study of work organization and skills must be sensitive to the interplay of national institutions, sectors, and organizations, and must be able to deal adequately with the service sector. Some commentators have already put forward frameworks in relation to job quality which draw upon the societal approach literature (Maurice et al. 1986) and move beyond manufacturing to address services (Bosch and Lehndorff 2005), including lower level jobs (Carré and Tilly 2012). Bosch and Lehndorff (2005) emphasize interrelated domains of influence which include product and consumers, management strategies, labour market conditions and institutions, the welfare state, and gender relations. Carré and Tilly (2012) place particular emphasis upon the role of labour market regulations, trade unions, and the welfare state for those in lower paid jobs. However, none of the studies specifically address work organization and skills, being concerned more with issues of working time and pay. There is, therefore, a need to consider more carefully what matters for work organization and to integrate these analyses with power-based perspectives discussed earlier.

Drawing upon existing studies on the impact of national institutions on work organization and skills, a number of key factors emerge: the role of product markets, the skill formation system, the impact of employment regulations and welfare institutions, and the influence wielded by trade unions at national, sector, and workplace level. Each of these is dealt with in turn.

First, in terms of product markets, countries produce different products and services from each other, reflecting the structure and composition of the economy, and they may pursue different market segments in a given industry. National institutional configurations, such as long-term finance, a strong VET system, and higher wages, appear to help push more firms to adopt strategies based on higher quality products and services. These complex offerings are *more likely* to require higher skilled workers, while short differentiated production runs or personalized services encourage the use of a less detailed division of labour and higher levels of discretion. However, as seen in the last chapter, there is no necessary or direct relationship between high-quality/high-value product markets and skills, and such connections may be particularly problematic in interactive service work.

Second, the design of work may be influenced to some extent by the supply of particular forms of skilled labour (Regini 1995). The relative balance in a country between higher education and intermediate vocational qualifications may influence how employers structure their workforce (Mason and Wagner 1994). The German dual apprenticeship system was said to develop a strong sense of 'practical professionality' among workers and managers who had followed the same vocational path (Maurice et al. 1980: 81). This shared identity, coupled with the quality of skills that workers possessed, was claimed to influence work; not only were there fewer managers but relationships were less hierarchical with workers experiencing higher levels of discretion and autonomy (Streeck 1992). Skilled workers, with strong collective organization, may also offer resistance to managerial attempts to fragment and deskill work (Gallie 2007; Grimshaw and Lehndorff 2010).

Both Regini (1995) and Streeck (2011a: 5) also identified the advantages to German firms of an over-supply of skilled labour in competing successfully in more customized, quality products markets. However, while this may have been the case in the 1980s in core manufacturing firms, it is unclear about how far it extended to other employers and whether there were detrimental effects for workers. For example, an over-supply implies that some individuals were unable to obtain jobs at their skill level, and may also serve to reduce union power and depress wages. As discussed in Chapter 2, while high-skilled work requires a supply of appropriately skilled labour, it does not follow that supplying high-level skills, in itself, means that work will be organized in ways which ensure their use in the workplace.

Third, higher average levels of job autonomy and influence in work have been linked to strong trade union movements that have been able to ensure that gains are more evenly distributed across the economy. Union power operates through a wide range of interrelated elements, such as high collective bargaining coverage, a policy focus on full employment and quality of working life programmes, employment security, a generous welfare state, co-determination rights in the workplace, and a direct role for organized labour in VET provision. Coverage of collective bargaining and high union density can also ensure that unions have an influence across a wider range of sectors and workplaces. How these different aspects influence skills and job autonomy across varied workplaces is less clear, but we might expect these constraints imposed on employers, alongside higher income standards at the bottom, to be associated with more quality-based products and services. Where unions are strong, sectoral collective bargaining, which creates high wages and limits differentials between workers, may encourage employers to reduce the number of low-skilled (low-productivity) jobs.

Strong trade unions and/or works councils can help to limit the monitoring of workers in the workplace as well as encourage more participatory forms of management, even in jobs such as call centres where other institutional supports for quality-based strategies are being undermined (Doellgast 2010: 376).

Fourth, employment and industrial relations regulations may also have an influence on job design. Trade union strength is likely to be assisted by the existence of national legal rights that support organizational capacity and co-determination or weakened by restrictive legislation, as in the UK. High national minimum wages, working time regulations, and legal supports for collective bargaining may all play a part. Strong constraints on the ability of employers to 'hire and fire' through national employment regulations can also assist in union organization, and may encourage employers to train more, while removing the option of deskilling through redundancy and relocation (Lloyd 1999; Lloyd et al. 2010).

Fifth, welfare systems which are inclusive and provide a high reservation wage require employers to pay more for labour, as do policies that are successful in delivering full employment, thereby adding to labour scarcity. Together these constraints may encourage organizations to use workers' skills more productively and to consider issues of job quality as part of recruitment and retention (Gautié and Schmitt 2010). The role of the welfare state may have a more profound influence across the service sector than in manufacturing due to the large numbers of women working in areas such as health and education (Gadrey 2000; Bosch and Lehndorff 2005; Carré and Tilly 2012). The labour market participation of women is much more closely linked to the organization of child/elderly care provision and the tax and benefits system. For example, in some countries (e.g. the UK and Germany), employers have been more able to obtain (cheap) working time flexibility through the use of part-time working mothers. In addition, the size of the welfare state directly relates to the number of service sector workers, while its policies and approaches help structure the types of workers required, for example, in terms of qualification levels, contract status and working time, and the ways in which they are managed.

Rather than adopt a functionalist account of the relationship between national institutions and outcomes, the approach adopted in this book stresses the role of social relations and power struggles as central to an understanding of how institutions emerge, change, and operate over time. In focusing upon power, we draw upon our earlier work on the political economy of skills, which sought to address what would be required to move a country, specifically the UK, onto a more inclusive higher skills trajectory (Lloyd and Payne 2002). Included were elements that have been identified in Germany and Scandinavia but which, to varying degrees, are now coming under pressure, such as patient capital, a strongly regulated labour market, inclusive collective bargaining institutions, and an active industrial policy. Part of the analysis stressed the necessity of blocking-off 'low road' approaches and developing more ambitious employer strategies focused on higher quality products and services across the wider economy and not just high-skill sectors. However, without a strengthening of union presence within the workplace, there could be no guarantee that shifts in market positioning would be associated with improvements in work organization. This approach shares certain analytical affinities with those presenting a 'power-based' explanation, outlined in this chapter, who see positive work organization outcomes contingent upon the 'societal power' of labour. It also foregrounds the role of agency and conflict as a counterweight to the structural constraints of institutional path dependencies, implied by VOC.

In applying this approach, it is important to explore the interplay between institutions at the national, sector and workplace level, alongside the way that workers are able to shape and use institutions to improve skills and work organization. These include actions with an explicit aim of improving work organization as well as those that impact indirectly. For example, work councils may directly restrict the use of individual performance monitoring, while union success in gaining higher wages may have an indirect effect of encouraging employers to raise the skill demands of jobs. The way in which different elements of the national institutional context *coalesce* in a given sector as well as the power wielded by labour at sector level will, inevitably, vary.

Following on from Bechter et al. (2012), public sector organizations and large well-resourced employers, such as in the financial sector, are more likely to have formalized systems of collective bargaining and union organization regardless of country. Although the impression may be of a 'strong sector effect' with similarities across countries, the nature of these institutions, the level of union strength, and the rules they operate under vary substantially. If union power is a key factor in shaping differences in job design, it may be in these sectors where we uncover more profound national variation in work organization, despite the similarity in formal institutional structures.

Sector and workplace institutional structures may appear to have more country-based distinctiveness in those sectors which are generally seen as 'hard to organise' (Arrowsmith 2012). Sectoral collective bargaining still takes place in hospitality and retailing in countries like Sweden and Norway, with tripartite bodies in areas such as training, while similar institutions are absent in the USA and UK. However, if unions have been unable to organize successfully at workplace level in any of these countries, there may be less cross-national variability in actual outcomes (see Bosch and Lehndorff 2005; Berrebi-Hoffmann et al. 2010). For these jobs, certain factors may be of particular importance. Carré and Tilly (2012) note that for low-wage jobs employment legislation and social security systems are highly significant for securing improvement in wages and working conditions. These factors may also have an indirect impact in terms of work organization at this level, but less so among professional workers. Sectors that are relatively new, such as IT, and which have emerged in periods where unions' capacity to extend their influence has been substantially weakened, may lack the institutional structures typically associated with, say, the German or Swedish model, for example collective agreements or works councils. Again, this may limit the differences between countries.

Although power is central to the analytical framework used in this book, there is also the question of how power relations translate over time into a set of social norms and behaviours. While difficult to research their origins, as Dobbin and Boychuk (1999) argued, the idea of a 'national employment logic' is that it not only works through institutional and regulatory constraints on employers but also permeates managers' thinking as well as employees' expectations and social norms around how relationships should be conducted at work. If there is some sort of broader socialization effect, then there might still exist some distinctive country-based approaches to work organization even in sectors where unions are weak and formal institutions, like works councils, are absent.

Conclusion

There is evidence of significant variation in work organization and levels of autonomy across nations, with the Nordic countries appearing to perform relatively well in terms of the proportion of the workforce in jobs which combine high levels of discretion and learning demands, along with relatively few jobs characterized by Taylorism. This has been attributed by some commentators to the power of organized labour in these societies, its links with social democracy, and their ability to shape an inclusive employment regime. While the evidence base is not extensive, cross-national comparative studies of work organization at the macro- and micro-level, involving a small range of jobs in different countries, appear to indicate that national institutions do matter.

Increasingly, attention has been drawn towards exploring internal variation *within* countries, in particular by sector. To what extent, for example, do 'new' sectors and occupations, not least those in the service economy, follow or depart from the experience of those which, historically, came to shape the dominant national employment regime? Does the national institutional environment still make itself felt; if so, in what ways and through what mechanisms, and, if not, why not? How does professional work fit in to this picture? The question can be approached in terms of the organization of work (the level of autonomy and knowledge/skill demands within the job) but also must be set within the context of broader dimensions of job quality. The evidence base to date, while limited and fragmented, suggests that the picture is likely to be complex.

A number of themes emerge from existing studies. One issue, which warrants further exploration, concerns the power of organized labour at different levels—the ability to shape the national employment regime and public policy as well as the influence that unions can wield at sector and workplace level. Another is around how different institutions may matter disproportionately in different circumstances. Job quality in lower end, service work seems to depend heavily upon employment legislation, the institutions of the welfare state, and gender relations outside of work. A further question concerns the scope for strategic choice on the part of organizations (discussed in Chapter 2), given existing institutional conditions. How do national institutions, sectoral dynamics, and organizational strategies interact to shape outcomes for workers? What can such studies tell us about how to progress better designed jobs and what is possible within particular national contexts? The following chapter sets the scene by outlining key features of the national institutional contexts of France, Norway, and the UK.

4

Industrial Relations, Skill Formation Systems, and Workplace Development

Continuity and Change in the UK, Norway, and France

Introduction

This chapter outlines key features of the institutional environments of the UK, Norway, and France, providing a context for the sector studies that follow. However, it is also concerned to explore how and in what ways these countries may be changing. The question of whether national capitalisms are converging, or remain on divergent paths, has been a recurrent theme within the comparative capitalisms literature (Kerr 1983; Streeck 1997a; Gray 1998; Katz and Darbishire 2000). More recently, the voices on the side of convergence have grown louder as levels of social inequality have risen and trade unions have faced substantial decline. Many commentators suggest that while European capitalisms remain different *institutionally*, the way in which institutions *function* is changing as a process of creeping 'liberalization' takes place linked to economies that are increasingly global, interconnected, and financialized (Coates 2000; Streeck 2011b; Baccaro and Howell 2011; Jackson and Deeg 2012). As a result, employers are often seen to be acquiring greater power and scope to determine terms and conditions of employment as all capitalisms become less organized, more liberalized, and increasingly subject to the market. However, the process is recognized to be complex and uneven, taking different forms in different countries, reflecting their institutional histories and power relations between state, capital, and labour. Such discussions belie any simple notion of convergence, but raise issues about the nature of capitalism and what is possible at the current time.

Industrial Relations, Skill Formation Systems, and Workplace Development

If national differences in work organization and skill reflect the societal power of organized labour to shape constraining institutions that push employers to develop better forms of work organization, as well as union influence within the sector and workplace (see Chapter 3), then any weakening of 'beneficial constraints' (Streeck 1997b) on employer action clearly matters. The direction of travel is important as comparative snapshots at any one time may otherwise overlook whether existing differences between countries will be sustainable as well as what progress can be made within particular national contexts. In differentiating the UK, Norway, and France, the chapter concentrates on institutions which research suggests are important for work organization (see Chapter 3). The opening section focuses on industrial relations, labour market regulation, and welfare, before discussing education and training systems. The chapter moves on to consider the efforts that have been made by policy and social actors, in particular trade unions, to develop initiatives specifically aimed at improving work organization. The three countries are then compared in relation to a range of employment and work organization outcomes. The conclusion returns to the question of whether the countries are converging and, if so, in what ways and to what extent, and considers the potential implications.

Industrial Relations, Labour Market Regulation, and Welfare

United Kingdom

The UK is typically identified as a 'liberal-market' or 'neo-liberal' economy, with historically limited state regulation and weakly coordinated capital and labour organizations. Throughout the post-war years, the dominance of finance capital, industrial decline, strikes, low productivity, and weakness in vocational training figured prominently in accounts of British capitalism (Coates 2000). This period saw an extension of the welfare state, the nationalization of key industries, and a British version of 'neo-corporatism' that was much weaker than that which emerged in Northern Europe.

Historically, the British industrial relations tradition was one of 'voluntarism', with relatively limited state regulation, few employment rights, and weak central organizations of employers and labour (Hyman 2003). Even at the height of 'corporatism' in the 1970s, the Confederation of British Industry (CBI) and the Trades Unions Congress (TUC)—the peak employer and union confederations—were never able to concert their members to deliver on incomes policy agreements or 'social pacts'. Nevertheless, by the late 1970s over half of the workforce was unionized and more than three-quarters were covered by collective bargaining. Unions were typically strongest at workplace level and generally rejected the state's involvement in 'free collective bargaining'.

The major hiatus came in 1979 with the election of an avowedly neo-liberal Conservative government, hostile to trade unions and determined to dismantle the post-war settlement (MacInnes 1987). Against the backdrop of high inflation and industrial relations turmoil, the new government embraced privatization, labour and capital market deregulation, and welfare retrenchment. Over time, there was a gradual introduction of marketization and quasi-competition across the public sector under the auspices of new public management (NPM), which aimed to shift the emphasis away from an ethos of public service towards performance-based monitoring, auditing, and targets. In a break with voluntarism, successive Conservative administrations used the law to weaken trade unions by severely restricting their ability to take industrial action, removed wage controls at the bottom of the labour market, and weakened individual employment rights (Marsh 1992). Unions found themselves out in the political cold, denied any involvement in policy, and facing a frontal assault from the state, graphically demonstrated by the 1984–5 coal dispute (Howell 2005; McIlroy 2011). The collapse of manufacturing industry, accelerated by monetarist policies, weakened trade unions in their traditional heartlands as the economy became increasingly service-based and inequality grew.

The election of a New Labour government in 1997 ushered in a less hostile political climate for unions. The signing of the EU Social Chapter, the introduction of a weak statutory union recognition procedure and low-level national minimum wage, along with a minimum platform of mainly individual employment rights (most of which came via the EU), represented points of departure from the Conservatives. There was a willingness to engage with unions publicly, to encourage dialogue between the TUC and CBI on productivity for example, and to provide unions with a limited role on bodies such as the Low Pay Commission and Sector Skills Councils[1] (Payne 2008b).

Overall, however, the picture was one of continuity rather than change (Smith 2009; Howell and Givan 2011). The Conservatives' anti-trade union laws were retained, with New Labour committed to maintaining 'the most lightly regulated labour market of any leading economy in the world' (Blair 1998: 3). Trade union membership and the coverage of collective bargaining continued to fall. While public expenditure on health and education increased, NPM evolved towards a stronger focus on centralized targets and marketization as part of a drive to 'modernize' public services. In the area

---

[1] The Low Pay Commission was a public body set up to advise the government about the national minimum wage; Sector Skills Councils were established as state-funded, ostensibly 'employer-led', organizations with responsibility for skills and workforce development.

of welfare, there was a growing focus upon means-tested and conditional provision, alongside 'workfare' policies aimed at the long-term unemployed. The numbers of working poor and children in poverty had soared during the previous eighteen years. Rather than directly tackle low wages, the response was to introduce in-work tax credits, a form of in-work benefits paid to eligible workers which also acted as a subsidy for low-paying employers and childcare providers. By the time the Labour government had left office in 2010, although poverty rates had fallen, the UK still had one of the highest levels of low-wage work within the advanced industrial world and inequality, already high by European standards, had risen further (Lloyd et al. 2008).

Throughout the New Labour years, the City of London had continued to grow as a world financial centre, and remained the main focus of economic policy. A weakly regulated banking system, however, left the UK fully exposed to the 2008 financial crisis with a series of bank failures and subsequent 'bailouts' that left a gaping hole in public finances. The subsequent elections of a Conservative–Liberal Democrat Coalition government in 2010 and a Conservative government in 2015 led to a focus on austerity policies, aimed at tackling the rising budget deficit, and a 'rolling back' of the state. Major cuts in public expenditure and welfare provision have followed, alongside a heightened commitment to reduce the regulatory 'burden' on employers. High levels of unemployment intensified a trend towards more flexible work contracts, such as zero hours and unpaid 'work experience' ('internships'), as well as part-time work. The creation of large numbers of low-wage, part-time jobs saw steady falls in unemployment alongside declining productivity levels and average real wages (Keep and Mayhew 2014).

In industrial relations, the story has been one of continuing *decollectivization*, involving a major shift in the balance of power towards employers (Howell and Givan 2011). By 2014, union density stood at 25 per cent, with 28 per cent of the workforce covered by collective bargaining (DBIS 2015). There remain significant differences between the private sector, where union density was 14 per cent and 15 per cent of workers were covered by collective bargaining, and the public sector, where the corresponding figures were 54 per cent and 61 per cent respectively. However, it is the public sector that has borne the brunt of austerity, jobs cuts, and pay freezes, and it is here where unions have also been most active. Recent moves by the Conservative government have included proposals to apply extensive restrictions to industrial action in the public sector which would make it extremely difficult for unions to take strike action.

Norway

Norway is often described as a 'coordinated market economy' (Hall and Soskice 2001) or social democratic welfare state regime (Esping-Andersen

1990), which was shaped during the post-war years by social democracy and a strong labour movement. Its origins go back to the 1920s and 1930s and a history of bloody industrial relations conflict at a time when 'communism seemed to offer a real alternative' (Bieler 2012: 226). A small, open economy, with a population of around five million, Norway built its economy around abundant natural resources, chemicals, and semi-finished metals, before the discovery of North Sea oil in the 1970s transformed it into one of the world's richest countries. The private financial sector remains relatively weak, and there is an extensive public sector and generous welfare state. Productivity is higher than in the USA, although, as Kasvio et al. (2012) note, the size of the public sector in Scandinavia makes measurement and comparison difficult.

Norway is characterized by powerful collective actors and a highly centralized, multi-level system of collective bargaining which allows for extensive policy mediation between the state, capital, and labour. The main peak-level confederations of capital (NHO) and labour (LO)—the social partners—remain the dominant players, despite industrial relations becoming more complex and differentiated as new actors have entered the arena. Employers are strongly organized, with around 65 per cent in the private sector belonging to an employers' association (Løken et al. 2013). Trade union density is stable at over half of the workforce, although lower than in other Scandinavian countries which operate Ghent systems of unemployment insurance linked to union membership. As Baccaro and Howell (2011: 529) note, Norway is one of only two countries in Europe, along with Belgium, to buck the trend of generalized union decline.

The basic agreement between NHO and LO sets the framework for collective bargaining, including rules on industrial action, detailed requirements for union-based information and consultation arrangements in the workplace, and the establishment of works councils. The industry or sector is the main level of collective bargaining where agreements reinforce, and usually build upon, minimum standards set by legislation. Collective bargaining extends beyond pay and conditions, often embracing social policy areas such as pension rights, sickness absence, and training. In 2013, around two-thirds of the Norwegian workforce were covered, including all employees in the public sector (Nergaard 2014a). In the private sector, the figure drops to around half, with a union density rate of 38 per cent compared to 81 per cent in the public sector (Nergaard 2014a). Lower rates are found among smaller firms, business services (28 per cent), and sectors such as hotels, restaurants, and retailing (23 per cent) (Nergaard 2014b).

There is no statutory minimum wage in Norway; the introduction of such a measure is generally supported by employer organizations but opposed by unions who favour collective agreements. The use of the law to extend collective agreements to all firms and employees in a sector (as is the case in France)

Industrial Relations, Skill Formation Systems, and Workplace Development

is only available if there is evidence of widespread use of foreign workers paid at substandard rates. This extension has occurred in only a few sectors, following submissions by unions (in some cases with the employer association), notably in construction, agriculture, cleaning, and freight transport (Arbeidstilsynet 2015). Overall, pay rates are relatively high, not least for those at the lower end, with collective agreements usually setting the norm for wage levels including in many unorganized companies. As noted earlier, however, collective regulation remains weak in some sectors.

While the state has traditionally allowed the social partners to regulate employment through collective bargaining, the law plays an important role in working life, in particular the 1977 Work Environment Act (including subsequent amendments) which covers areas of employment protection, equality, and health and safety. Co-determination legislation provides employees with a right to board-level representation in private companies with more than thirty employees. Similar arrangements cover the public sector. The Work Environment Act makes 'work environment committees', with equal employer/employee representation, compulsory in organizations with fifty or more staff, and available at the request of one of the parties in companies with over twenty staff.

Norway has a long tradition of tripartite policy mediation between the state, capital, and labour. Unlike in Sweden, there has been no employer withdrawal from tripartite arrangements (Kjellberg 1998; Howell and Givan 2011). The system of centralized incomes policies, whereby unions exchange wage moderation in return for social rights and influence over labour market and welfare reforms, has played an important role in containing inflationary pressures within Norway's oil-rich economy (Dølvik and Stokke 1998; Løken and Stokke 2009). Strikes are rare, and are used mainly as symbolic displays of labour strength during national bargaining rounds. The model of tripartite consultation is reflected in a tradition of involving the social partners in public committees and forums designed to agree the future direction of social and labour market policies.

Norway is renowned for its generous welfare provision, including its high level of unemployment benefits. The low cost of state-subsidized pre-school education also helps to support a high level of female participation in the labour market. While the Norwegian model bears the heavy imprint of social democracy and powerful union influence, the political context is more complex today, with the Labour Party facing competition from the centre-right as well as new right-wing populist parties. In the public sector, NPM has been used by both Conservative-led and Labour-led governments, but the latter have encountered strong opposition from unions who have threatened to withdraw political support (see Bieler 2012). Despite evidence of some tensions within the labour movement between those unions in export sectors and those in the public sector about the size of the welfare state, unions have managed to maintain a 'united front' (Bieler 2012: 238).

A strong economy, coupled with a powerful labour movement and a consensus-oriented polity, geared to coalition-building, also militate against radical political swings, lending considerable longevity to 'the Norwegian model'. Løken and Stokke (2009: 8) refer to a 'relatively stable balance of power between labour and capital, a balance deeply anchored in a class compromise connected to historical and political developments'. There are, however, concerns that new social divisions are opening up in the labour market with immigrants and those with low levels of education said to be concentrated in low-end jobs in sectors such as hospitality (Heiret 2012).

France

France has been variously labelled as 'state coordinated' or 'state-regulated' reflecting the central role of the state in economic development, education, welfare, and industrial relations (Gallie 2011; Howell and Givan 2011). Shaped by its republican and statist traditions, France's economic model, as it developed during the post-war period, was characterized by *dirigisme*, with a high level of state economic planning (Hall 1986; Goetschy 1998). The French state was instrumental in developing 'national champions', which included private companies such as Renault, alongside a number of large public enterprises that acted as a model for employment practices (Palier and Thelen 2010). Extensive Fordist rationalization and capital investment contributed to a relatively high level of productivity which currently remains above that of the USA but below Norway.

Alongside the economic model is France's 'social model' summed up by Gautié (2015: 123) in terms of the 'strong involvement of social partners...a highly regulated labour market; a generous welfare state and the key role of public services'. In the 1990s and 2000s, a spate of privatizations took place as part of a wave of 'liberalization', which also encouraged greater financialization of the economy, along with increased foreign investment. The result was a shift in corporate governance away from a more stakeholder model to one based on maximizing shareholder value (Palpacuer et al. 2011; Alvarez 2015). At the same time, there has been considerable pressure to reform and cut the costs of the welfare state, which has one of the highest levels of expenditure in Europe (Hassenteufel and Palier 2015).

France is unusual in that it has one of the lowest levels of trade union density in Europe as well as the highest collective bargaining coverage. Historically, French trade unions have been deeply fractured along ideological lines, reflecting the strong influence of the Communist Party, and have been characterized by organizational weakness at workplace level. Employers are, as

Howell (2009: 234) notes, 'every bit as weak, divided, and unrepresentative as their trade union counterparts', with a history of aggressive and authoritarian practice within the workplace. Conflict and adversarialism on the part of both trade unions and employers are enduring features. The failure to develop orderly systems of industrial relations has led the French state to step in and create institutions and laws in an attempt to institutionalize labour–capital relations (Goetschy 1998; Parsons 2005).

The main level of collective bargaining is the sector where agreements are in place covering the whole range of employment terms and conditions as well as setting minimum pay rates related to grading structures. These agreements are normally extended by law to all companies within the sector, leading to near universal coverage. Placing a floor to these agreements is a dense legal web of detailed collective and individual employment rights. For wages, the most significant is the national minimum wage (the SMIC), first introduced in the 1950s. In 2014, the SMIC was equivalent to 62 per cent of the full-time median wage, compared to 47 per cent in the case of the UK's national minimum wage, and is central in accounting for the low proportion of low-wage workers in France. It also sets the pace for minimum pay rates within the sector collective agreements in lower paying industries.

Trade union density has never been high in France, partly due to the institutionalized role of unions, whereby membership has little relevance to recognition, resources, or the representation of individuals. Estimated at around 22 per cent in 1970 (Hancké 1993), union density has fallen steadily to an historical low of under 8 per cent today. The decline in union support in workplace elections, the lack of members, and an ageing union hierarchy have fuelled the recurrent theme of French trade unions in crisis (Andolfatto and Labbé 2012). However, others have pointed to the emergence of new forms of unionism and the ability of traditional unions to bring large numbers of people out onto the streets, particularly in opposition to cuts to France's social model (Connolly 2010; Milner and Mathers 2013).

Over the years, governments of the left have sought to strengthen the position of unions in the workplace through processes of bargaining decentralization. The Auroux laws in 1982 included an obligation on companies to negotiate annually (financial penalties were introduced in 2009), the right of group 'direct expression', and a strengthening of the role of union representatives, *délégués du personnel* (employee representatives), and the *conseil d'entreprise* (works councils). The greatest impetus to local bargaining was the introduction of the 35-hour week in 1998 which required implementation in the workplace. While employers were initially hostile, it allowed many to achieve increased working time flexibility, particularly for manual and lower skilled workers (Hayden 2006). At company level, works councils have been in operation since 1945 but remain weak by German standards, with rights to be informed and/or consulted on a range of issues and to be involved in organizing the company's social activities.

Centre-right governments have typically attempted to increase numerical flexibility in the labour market and have enabled some 'derogations', that is exemptions from national and sector collective agreements, although not in relation to pay. Early evidence indicated little use of company level derogations on a systematic basis (Keune 2010). However, a weak economy and persistently high unemployment prompted legal changes in 2013, based upon a social partner agreement to enhance labour market flexibility. This allows for temporary (up to two years) company agreements to derogate from the sector agreement, including pay levels, in order to avoid redundancies (Schulze-Marmeling 2014). Those unions that did not sign the agreement are concerned about the threat of social dumping, while some commentators argue that in the context of weak trade unions at workplace level, pay and conditions may be eroded as part of job-saving compromises (Jany-Catrice and Lallement 2015).

While France has some of the strictest employment regulation in Europe when it comes to job security and the regulation of temporary work, there are increasing concerns about growing divisions within the labour market in the context of persistently high levels of unemployment (Caroli and Gautié 2008). There has been a steady rise in the use of fixed-term and casual contracts, accounting for 14 per cent of the workforce in 2014, which disproportionately affect the young. During the financial crisis, temporary employees bore the brunt of jobs losses reconfirming the divisions within the labour market (Jany-Catrice and Lallement 2015: 185). While bodies such as the OECD and EU have consistently advised France to deregulate its labour market, new laws continue to be introduced, for example restricting part-time work (in most cases) to a minimum of twenty-four hours per week.

Despite adversarial relations between employers and unions, there are various public committees for 'social dialogue' on employment, training, and social policy, although they are much weaker than those in Norway. Welfare provision, including pensions, is generally high in France and related to a system of occupational and contributions-based benefits for the core workforce. For the young and those without regular employment, however, benefits are relatively low. Prior to the economic crisis, various attempts had been made by a succession of governments to cut public spending through reducing entitlements and to increase flexibility in the labour market. These were for the most part successfully resisted by trade union mobilization. However, the economic crisis that began in 2008 has seen public spending squeezed, unemployment rise, a slow growth of social benefits and the SMIC, and an increase in levels of poverty and inequality (ONPES 2014). Even with the pressures to reduce public debt, cuts in budgets, and changes to employment regulations, it is questionable as to whether labour market policy and the social security system have changed substantially, highlighting the resilience of the French model (Gautié 2015; Noram and Uba 2015).

A Comparative View

What is clear from looking at these three countries is that there is continuing diversity in their economic and social models. In the UK, Conservative governments after 1979 undertook a frontal assault on trade unions, while the New Labour years saw a further entrenchment of a neo-liberal accumulation model, centred on deregulated capital and labour markets. By contrast, Norway is very much a story of continuity in a country where organized labour remains strong, the national system of centralized negotiations and political exchange has survived, and there has been little in the way of deregulation. France has certainly experienced some changes. Some commentators have argued that financialization, shifts towards bargaining decentralization, and the increased scope for derogations have substantially increased employer power to determine terms and conditions (Baccaro and Howell 2011). However, it is important not to overplay matters. The organizational weakness of French unions has meant that employers have always had considerable control over the organization of work, while the framework of sectoral collective bargaining and a tightly regulated labour market remain in place. The next section outlines the major features and changes in the skill formation systems in each country.

Skill Formation Systems

United Kingdom

The UK[2] can be characterized by moderate levels of participation in post-16 education and training, a sharp divide between academic and vocational routes, and weak employer engagement in, and coordination of, initial VET (Wolf 2011). Educational inequalities, particularly related to social class, are extremely high at all levels. A major policy focus over the last twenty years has been on raising post-16 participation and qualification levels, including the shift towards a 'mass' higher education system, albeit one of variable quality with participation patterns linked to social class (Keep and Mayhew 2004). The costs of higher education have shifted to the individual student or

[2] Education and training are the responsibilities of the devolved governments of Northern Ireland, Scotland, and Wales. Policies and the policy-making process are increasingly divergent but the main features across the nations are relatively consistent.

'consumer', most notably in England,[3] where a system of student loans has been established to cover tuition fees and provide help with subsistence costs.

The UK has traditionally operated a 'voluntarist' training system with training decisions left at the discretion of individual employers and where the law plays a limited role (Keep and Rainbird 2003).[4] Licence-to-practise arrangements, whereby workers are required to obtain a particular qualification to practise their occupation, are relatively rare outside of the professions and occupations, such as gas fitter, where there is a direct threat to public safety. Marketization of education and training has become a key feature with the shift to the idea of parental/student choice, public providers competing against private providers, and private sector companies providing and certifying qualifications.

Apprenticeships were once a key part of the initial training system for young men (Vickerstaff 2003). Unions played a substantial role in their management and content, while state intervention was limited. This system declined from the 1970s, forcing the Conservative government in 1994 to develop a state-funded model that grew out of earlier youth training programmes designed to address unemployment and social unrest (Fuller and Unwin 2003). Currently, there are only around 5 to 7 per cent of 16- to 18-year-olds working as apprentices in what has become an all-age system where 'adult apprenticeships', for those aged over 24, constitute the major growth area (Wolf 2011: 166). Provision is of highly variable quality and often dependent upon sector. Many apprenticeships last less than a year, and there is limited employer involvement with the bulk of training delivered by private training providers, particularly in areas such as retail and hospitality (Keep and James 2011; Fuller and Unwin 2012).

The majority of initial VET takes place within further education (FE) colleges where students can take a wide variety of mainly 'competence-based' vocational qualifications. Many of these qualifications are low-level and have little or no value in the labour market (Wolf 2011). Competence-based National Vocational Qualifications (NVQs), which have dominated vocational provision, were originally designed for accrediting competencies acquired in the workplace. These qualifications have been seen to entrench a British view of skill as the ability to carry out narrowly defined tasks in a country where qualifications bear little relation to collective agreements and wage structures (Clarke and Winch 2006). Although widely criticized for their neglect of underpinning

---

[3] The situation contrasts with Scotland where residents receive free tuition and Wales where a more generous system of loans and grants is available.

[4] Tripartite Industrial Training Boards (ITBs) were introduced from 1964 with the power to operate levies. However, their impact was varied and withdrawal from the levy system began in the early 1970s. All but two ITBs were abolished in 1988, leaving only the construction industry and electrical construction industry with a compulsory levy and the film industry which subsequently introduced a voluntary levy (Gospel and Casey 2012).

knowledge and understanding (Hyland 1994), they were subsequently adapted for use in colleges with highly detailed competence-based curricula. In addition, unlike in Norway and France, there is little substantive general education within UK vocational programmes which hinders progression in learning, including to higher education (Green 1998; Brockmann et al. 2011).

In terms of governance, there is very little that resembles social partnership. Over the last thirty years, tripartite bodies have been replaced with ostensibly 'employer-led' agencies set up and funded by government. Sectoral bodies are weak, and there are no legal requirements for employers to negotiate or consult with trade unions over training. Under New Labour, as skills became the policy lever of choice for achieving national competitiveness and social inclusion (Keep 2009), the system became increasingly *centralized*, state-led, and state-financed (Keep 2006; Wolf 2011). Government funding and state subsidy were central mechanisms for boosting investment in training among employers and individuals and for directing providers in accordance with national skill targets, most of which went unmet.

Despite the increase in funding, survey evidence indicates that between 1997 and 2009 there was a 44 per cent decline in the volume of training undertaken by employees, a trend that predated the recession (Green et al. 2015). Austerity has meant a substantial tightening of state budgets and the removal of funding from a large area of adult learning (Keep 2015a). Against this backdrop, the Coalition government and its Conservative successor have emphasized the need for 'employer ownership' of skills, whilst signalling their intention to move towards a training market in England. A higher proportion of public funding will be routed through employers who will be given a greater say over the content of vocational provision and certification and will be expected to contribute more of their own money to skills development (Keep 2015b: 2). However, concern that employers will not 'step in' to fill the funding gap has led to the introduction of a compulsory apprenticeship levy system which will commence in 2017.

Norway

Norway's education policy has been founded on 'social democratic progressivism' (Telhaug and Volckmar 1999), with an emphasis on equalization, social solidarity, and personal freedom. The past thirty years have nevertheless seen an increasing emphasis by policy-makers and the social partners on education being used to meet the needs of the economy and to strengthen the country's ability to compete (Telhaug and Volckmar 1999). There is a high level of participation in post-compulsory schooling, with 92 per cent of 16- to 18-year-olds in upper secondary education, primarily attending public schools that offer general education and vocational programmes. The academic and vocational divide is far less pronounced than in the UK or France, with little stigma associated with undertaking vocational study (Kuczera et al. 2008: 11). The numbers in higher education have been steadily rising, with a system based on universities and colleges, funded primarily by the state. Around 80 per cent of institutions are state-owned, with free tuition and a generous grant and loan system covering maintenance costs. Students are generally older than in the UK and France, with 20 per cent aged over 30 and many taking time to complete their studies, with years-out being commonplace (Clark et al. 2009). Reflecting the flat wage structure in Norway, returns to higher education are relatively low compared with other OECD countries (OECD 2015a).

Over the last twenty years, initial VET provision has been based upon a 2+2 apprenticeship system which combines two years of training in school followed by two years of training in the workplace (Skule et al. 2002). Around half of all those completing lower secondary education enter the vocational route, substantially higher than in France and the UK. During the school phase, students study a vocational area along with an extensive curriculum of general education which supports progression in learning and enables students to move across pathways and access higher education. Those successfully completing vocational training obtain a craft or journeyman certificate which confers skilled worker status and which is recognized within collective agreements and pay awards.

Although there is said to be 'a high level of confidence' in the initial VET system among the state and social partners, there are well-documented problems with 'drop-outs', particularly in the vocational track, along with evidence that academically weak students struggle to obtain apprenticeship places (Kuczera et al. 2008: 11). The OECD's PISA tests of literacy and numeracy of 15-year-olds, where Norway emerged as an average performer, have also raised concerns over the quality of Norwegian schooling more generally (Ure 2007: 57–8). The system remains highly unified, and there is a strong tradition of 'democratic education' founded on principles of active citizenship, social solidarity, and egalitarianism that is deeply rooted in the teaching profession, including school leaders. However, some local authorities, notably Oslo from 1997, allow parents and students a choice over which school they attend (Brugård 2013).

VET has traditionally been an area where the social partners have exercised significant control and influence (Skule et al. 2002). Høst (2008) has argued that recent years have seen a move away from a VET system controlled and managed by the social partners to one where they are merely consulted. Nevertheless, as both Høst (2008) and Souto-Otero and Ure (2012) note, there remains substantive social partner mediation of VET policy, which continues to be based on a high level of trust and consensus.

Ongoing training is generally seen to be the responsibility of individual companies, with a relatively high level of adult participation in work-based training. Unions and employers' associations frequently operate a jointly negotiated levy of employers and workers in a sector, which provides funds for training and development (Skule et al. 2002). Adults who lack post-secondary education qualifications have the right to access free education, while recognition of prior learning is well developed, again offering access to skilled status and higher wages in collective agreements. Subsequent efforts by the main trade union confederation, LO, to advance a right to paid educational leave through the national bargaining rounds, as part of the so-called Competence Reform (1999–2006), were blocked by employers, with other initiatives yet to be forthcoming (Bowman 2005; Payne 2006; Ure 2007).

France

The education system in France is often described as academic and centralist. Although there has been some decentralization to region, district, and council levels since the early 1980s, the Ministry of Education continues to play a key role in terms of the employment of teachers, finance, curricula, and examinations. There have been few attempts to adopt aspects of marketization, performativity, and choice that have been seen in Norway and more prominently in the UK. The system is based upon ideals of equality and republican elitism (Géhin 2007), with social selection based on academic criteria. Initial VET is described variously as 'statist', 'public', and 'schools-based', with an emphasis placed upon providing general education to vocational students and limited employer coordination and involvement. For example, apprenticeships, never as extensive as in the heyday of the UK system, have been partially revived but still account for only 7–8 per cent of the 17–19 cohort (similar to the UK today). Continuous training is based around a mix of levies, individual legal rights, social partnership, and collective bargaining.

France has operated a model of mass higher education for many years, but with a relatively high failure and drop-out rate from universities. The main distinction is between the 'elite' selective institutions, in particular the *grandes écoles*, and the non-selective universities which are open to anyone with a baccalaureate. Both operate with nominal fees and provide grants for lower income students. However, the elite institutions are widely criticized for reinforcing existing class structures (Duru-Bellat and Kieffer 2008). Education and training became an increasing focus of policy attention in the late 1980s and 1990s with a further expansion of university education and an increasing focus upon vocational training (Culpepper 2003). While there is formal equality between vocational and academic routes, there remains a strong presumption that the more able students will follow the general route. Most initial VET is provided in public vocational colleges (*lycées professionelles*), with the number of places linked to the needs of the local economy rather than student demand as in the UK. Vocational programmes 'attempt to prepare students for life in the broadest sense; rather than preparing them for the immediate demands of the labour market at a given point' (Méhaut 2006: 3). Students, including those in private colleges and apprentices, are required to follow a range of general subjects alongside their vocational studies, and qualify with national diplomas which form part of a qualification progression ladder that can provide access to higher education.

As with Norway and the UK, a central aim has been to raise the qualification levels of young people. The introduction of a vocational baccalaureate, which allows access to higher education, together with improved pathways from lower level vocational qualifications, have helped to raise attainment levels to just below those of Norway. Staying-on rates up to 18 are high, although 18 per cent of those following the vocational path undertake lower level qualifications (RRS 2015: 102). There are strong socio-economic patterns of participation, amid concerns about polarization in educational attainment and increasing problems with basic numeracy and literacy (Mattei 2012).

Continuous education and training involves highly structured relationships between employers, trade unions, and the state, with a system based on social dialogue. There is not a legal requirement to train workers but all firms must contribute to training levies which are jointly managed by trade unions and employer associations through sectoral bodies. Fundamentally, the view is that training is financed by the employer and not by the individual (Méhaut 2006). Employers are required to negotiate over company training plans, although there has been some shift towards individual legal rights, including a right to 20 hours' training per year and access to paid training/educational leave of up to one year. The latest figures on workplace training show levels between that of Norway and the UK (see Table 4.1), with 58 per cent of workers aged 25–64 receiving training in 2011.

A Comparative View

Successive governments in all three countries have sought to raise participation in education and training and increase qualification levels (Figure 4.1).

Table 4.1. Education and training features

	UK	Norway	France
Public spending on education as percentage of GDP, 2011[1]	6.0	6.7	5.7
Percentage of 15–19-year-olds studying at institutions, 2013[2]	81	87	85
Percentage of employed receiving formal or non-formal education and training in 2011[3]	41	67	58

[1] Eurostat: tsdsc510.
[2] OECD (2015a: 316).
[3] Eurostat: trng_aes_103.

Industrial Relations, Skill Formation Systems, and Workplace Development

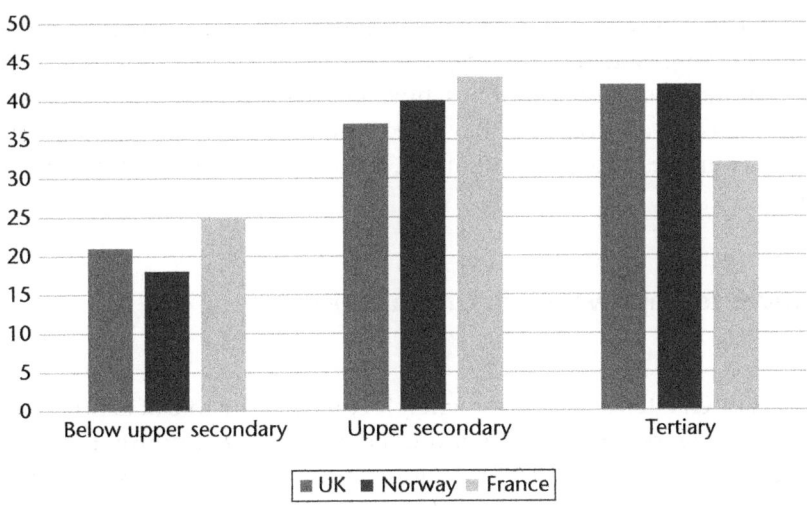

Figure 4.1. Educational levels aged 25–64, 2014
Note: 2013 France.
Source: OECD (2015a: 42–4).

Both Norway and France have been more successful in raising the participation of 16- to 19-year-olds (see Table 4.1). In contrast to the UK, they also provide a core of general education within vocational programmes, and there is greater coherence of pathways and progression between academic and vocational studies. Initial VET in the UK tends towards a training model, despite provision being increasingly situated within the full-time education system. There is little social partner coordination or state regulation, with employers freely able to determine training investment. Norway is characterized by the strong role afforded to the social partners, a distinctive 2+2 apprenticeship model, and sectoral collective agreements that cover training. France has a predominantly school-based model of initial VET, with little employer involvement, combined with considerable legal regulation of employers' training activities and a substantial role provided for the social partners.

The UK and Norway have both expanded higher education, with participation levels now above those in France, traditionally seen as the home of mass higher education. In England, higher education has become increasingly marketized with costs shifted onto individual students, again in contrast to the other two countries. At the same time, France and Norway both operate a social partnership model across education more broadly which does not exist in England and only in a much weaker form in Wales and Scotland (see Chapter 5). Unions and employers' associations are much stronger and more influential in Norway, while their role and position in France is enforced through a strong system of legal regulation.

The following section examines how far work organization has figured explicitly on the agenda of policy-makers, employers, and trade unions in the three countries and what initiatives, if any, have been brought forward in this area.

Initiatives to Improve Work Organization

UK

The UK is often cited as a pioneer when it comes to the role of action research in improving work organization and job design, most famously through the activities of the Tavistock Institute and its 'socio-technical' experiments with autonomous group working beginning in the British coal mines (Trist and Bamforth 1951). It is somewhat of an irony that their legacy and influence would prove to be far greater in Scandinavia, where they would spawn a substantive number of public programmes aimed at 'workplace development' (see the next section on Norway), than on British soil where there was little interest from either the state or trade unions (Payne and Keep 2003). There were some isolated experiments with 'job enrichment' in the 1960s and 1970s but nothing to compare with the efforts to develop autonomous work groups, most notably at Volvo in Sweden (Berggren 1992; Sandberg 1995). British unions tended to concentrate their energies on informal job controls and bargaining over wages and conditions. There was limited state support through the establishment in 1974 of the Work Research Unit (WRU), within the Department of Employment, whose remit included helping firms to develop joint solutions to organizational change (Purcell 2000). The election of the Conservative government in 1979 turned a tradition of limited state involvement into one of vehement opposition to any *perceived* threat to managerial prerogative. The WRU was duly wound up in 1993, having long ceased to be proactive (Purcell 2000: 174).

From 1997, successive New Labour governments continued with a non-interventionist approach. Insofar as New Labour concerned itself at all with the question of how employers designed jobs or managed their employees, it did so mainly by *exhorting* them to adopt 'high performance working' (see Chapter 2) and by supporting 'partnership at work', although the latter did not necessarily have to involve trade unions (Terry 2003). Both met with little success. There was no attempt to develop anything that might resemble the publicly funded workplace development programmes that one still finds in a number of other European countries, such as Finland and Norway (see Payne and Keep 2003; Ramstad 2009).

Industrial Relations, Skill Formation Systems, and Workplace Development

The only recent initiatives in this area have been some modest developments in Scotland and Wales, under the banner of 'skills utilization'. In both countries, there has been a recognition by devolved governments of the importance of not just the education and training system but 'the way in which jobs are designed, filled and subsequently executed' (Scottish Government 2007: 31; Welsh Government 2014). A number of pilot projects have been funded to explore ways to improve skills utilization in organizations and sectors but these are small scale, in what remains a fledgling and fragile area of policy (Payne 2012).

Despite having no legal right to bargain over skills, UK unions have in recent years taken a more active interest in the area of workplace learning, and have successfully achieved state funding for learning initiatives and the statutory recognition of workplace union learning representatives. However, there has been little attempt to tie this to a broader agenda around skills utilization and job design, in part reflecting broader difficulties unions face in negotiating or consulting with management on these issues (Lloyd and Payne 2007; Green 2010). The 2011 Workplace Employment Relations Survey indicates that unions appear to play little role in decisions pertaining to work organization and job design at workplace level. Only 8 per cent of managers reported that they negotiate with staff or representatives on important changes in technology, 12 per cent on changes in work techniques, and 14 per cent on changes in work organization, although this figure has increased from 5 per cent in 2004 (van Wanrooy et al. 2013: 20–1).

Norway

Industrial democracy and 'local workplace participation' arrived on the agenda of Norwegian unions in the 1960s and 1970s, when the main employers' association and LO launched their famous Industrial Democracy Programme. Inspired by the UK's Tavistock Institute, experiments were conducted in selected industrial enterprises often with the aim of developing autonomous work groups (Emery and Thorsrud 1976). For unions, the idea was that the democratization of work required not only formal institutions of collective bargaining and co-determination rights but efforts to increase worker participation and involvement at the level of the job. Dølvik and Stokland (1992: 154) note that the overall impact of this project was 'limited, partly because it was initiated from above without sufficient motivation at the workplace'. For the most part, union attention still remained focused on traditional collective bargaining over wages and conditions, with legislation seen as the preferred means of promoting industrial democracy.

Its legacy, however, was that it helped to cement the view that unions and management had a joint interest in working together to build profitable organizations which 'gradually emerged as an almost indisputable dogma in

Norwegian working life' (Heiret 2012: 53). This view also helped to bring forth the development of co-determination legislation in the 1970s, with new rights for employees to be involved in company decision-making, and had a major influence on the 1977 Work Environment Act which focused attention on the need for good working conditions and a participatory workplace. The labour market parties came to accept the view that the active participation of a skilled workforce with decent working conditions, autonomy within the job, and opportunities to contribute to product and process innovation, could support competitiveness and flexible adjustment under conditions of globalization and intensifying competitive pressures.

The Industrial Democracy Programme would also be the forerunner to a 40-year history of expert-driven workplace development programmes aimed at improving the innovation capacity and competitiveness of Norwegian firms through an approach centred on broad employee participation and labour–management cooperation (see Qvale 2002). These included Enterprise Development 2000 and Value Creation 2010, state-funded programmes with social partner involvement, which focused upon 'action research' as a developmental method. Those involved with these programmes insist that better ways of working can only be developed locally and must start from the needs of the individual organization, as there is no one best way (Gustavsen 2007). Considerable attention has also centred on the question of diffusion, or how to build 'critical mass', given that organizations are not usually persuaded by 'star cases' of what works in other sectors or organizations. The focus has shifted towards building 'development coalitions' and 'learning networks' (e.g. sector, region, supply chain) which bring organizations together to share experiences in ways which allow lessons to be adapted (Gustavsen 2007).

Action research approaches emphasize the importance of facilitating change through constructive 'democratic dialogue' between management, workers, and their representatives, with researchers helping to create a dialogic space where all voices are equal (Gustavsen 1985). A key question is whether such approaches can deal with hierarchical power structures within organizations or whether management will set the agenda and leave critical researchers compromised as a result (Johansson and Lindhult 2008; Huzzard and Björkman 2012). How far have such programmes contributed to the development of better forms of work organization? Evaluating their impact is difficult, given that typically 'soft' evaluation methods are used, comprising qualitative feedback from project participants who are also in receipt of public funding (Payne and Keep 2003). As noted in Chapter 3, some commentators argue that it is the wider macro-social and institutional environment constraining employers which holds the key to understanding why Scandinavian countries have managed to achieve higher aggregate levels of task autonomy (Gallie

2007). While these programmes may make a contribution to more autonomous forms of working, exactly how big a part they play remains unclear.

Co-determination may also be significant and has become increasingly focused on issues of productive efficiency (Hagen and Pape 1997: 34). Company groups (*Konsernfaglid Samerbeid*)—consultative works councils involving local union representatives and management—occupy an important position in Norwegian working life, and it is now said to be common practice in larger enterprises for unions to take part in strategic decisions relating to mergers, acquisitions, and company closures (Heiret 2012). In the public sector, similar arrangements have been developed, with union representatives emerging as central 'restructuring actors' although it has been suggested that the influence wielded by professionals has reduced (Heiret 2012: 60).

France

In response to the 1968 revolts and subsequent strikes in France, the early 1970s witnessed attempts by the state to improve conditions within the workplace. Key issues were seen to be 'authoritarian management, rigid occupational hierarchies and the dehumanising effects of Tayloristic work practices' (Grumbrell-McCormick and Hyman 2006: 482). According to Lane (1989), the state was driven by a desire to facilitate dialogue between unions and employers, improve conditions at work and help modernize the economy. Employers resisted attempts to expand bargaining at the workplace, while unions were politically reluctant to engage with work organization issues, viewing this as a process of incorporation rather than opposition to capitalism. Tchobanian (1995: 125) argues there was a 'tacit understanding that leaves company organization to the company itself and focuses union activity mainly on the distribution of income and other material benefits'.

As noted earlier, the Aurox laws in 1982 provided new legal rights and institutions designed to encourage workplace negotiations and reduce levels of overt conflict. This period saw the strengthening of the role of union and employee representatives and works councils, while workers were given the legal right to participate in the workplace by discussing in groups 'the content, organisation and conditions of work' every two months (Parsons 2005: 142). However, the results have generally been limited. Works councils have no co-determination powers, and their rights to consultation and information are often ignored. The 'right of expression', as it is called, is said to have been hijacked by managers or to have fallen into disuse (Moss 1988; Tchobanian 1995). Nevertheless, Milner and Mathers (2013: 130) have argued that legal rights do provide 'informational, relational and material resources' which can have a constraining effect on employers.

A national agency, Agence Nationale pour l'Amelioration des Conditions de Travail, aimed at improving working conditions and company efficiency, was established in 1973 and remains in place today. It has a budget of 11 million euros and can provide funding for small and medium-sized enterprises (SMEs) to undertake initiatives, although this appears to be predominantly around occupational health issues. Various governments (particularly on the left) have continued with legal interventions aimed at improvements in work organization, predominantly by encouraging the social partners to negotiate national agreements under the threat of legislation if they fail to agree. Since 2010 annual company bargaining must take place in relation to reducing 'harm' in the workplace, i.e. health and safety, stress, and the effects of routine work. A 'quality of working life' national agreement[5] was signed in 2013, which includes reference to the interest of the work, involvement, the degree of autonomy, and responsibility. Some unions have criticized the agreement for only providing broad principles, and there is little indication of substantive change at the workplace. Only 2 per cent of company level collective bargaining agreements signed in 2014 refer to conditions of work and only 1 per cent cover training (MTEFD 2015: 533).

A Comparative View

Norway has a long history of workplace development initiatives and programmes, with cooperative approaches between management, unions, and employees at workplace level sustained by strong legal rights to co-determination and participation, and established social norms and ways of working that have gradually been built up over time. In the UK and France, employers have effectively resisted engagement with what they consider to be an area of managerial prerogative. While French governments have attempted to encourage social partnership in this area, there has been little concerted pressure from unions. In UK workplaces, engagement with these issues has largely been informal and piecemeal, with unions over the last thirty years unable to push for effective legal regulation or national programmes in this area.

Outcomes

This section considers the performance of the UK, Norway, and France in relation to a range of employment and work-related outcomes. Issues of employment, equity, and social protection are discussed before outlining the

---

[5] 'Accord national interprofessionnel sur la qualité de vie au travail du 19 juin 2013'.

Industrial Relations, Skill Formation Systems, and Workplace Development

available evidence on patterns of skill and work organization in the three countries.

Employment, Unemployment, and Poverty

Norway has the highest out-of work benefits, high and relatively equal wages, and an employment rate that is significantly above that of France and the UK. Unemployment has also remained low since the 1990s. Participation is built around a full-time model of employment for women throughout the lifecycle, whereby over three-quarters of core age (25 to 54 years old) female employees work full-time, as in France, compared to only two-thirds in the UK (Table 4.5). Supported by high quality and subsidized childcare provision, parental leave, and a large public sector, it also has a smaller gender pay gap (Tables 4.6, 4.7). All three countries have experienced a gradual shift towards more full-time participation for women, although the UK maintains substantially higher levels of part-time work, reflecting the very high costs of childcare and limited maternity leave payments.

France has comparatively low levels of employment participation among the young and the over-55s, owing partly to low retirement ages and persistently high levels of unemployment since the mid-1990s. Both France and the UK experience particular problems with high levels of youth unemployment, with rates for the under-25s in 2014 of 24 per cent in France and 17 per cent in the UK (Table 4.5). As noted earlier, temporary work has also increased in France and is considerably higher than in both the UK and Norway. Notwithstanding differences in the use of part-time work, UK employees on average still work 12 per cent more hours annually than their French counterparts and 18 per cent more than workers in Norway (OECD 2015b).

The UK and France have fairly similar median wages, although the UK has substantially higher levels of wage inequality, which considerably worsens when part-time workers are included. Around 22 per cent of full-time workers in the UK are 'low paid' (i.e. earn less than two-thirds median earnings) compared to 6 per cent in France and 7 per cent in Norway (Table 4.2). The low figures for the latter two countries reflect France's relatively high minimum wage, and the tendency for most Norwegian employers to apply collectively agreed pay minima, even if they are not signatories to the agreement, alongside high levels of unemployment benefits. While in all countries women are more affected by low pay, there is a bigger gender gap in the UK. Low-wage workers in Norway are predominantly the young, with 86 per cent of low-wage jobs undertaken by those aged under 30. In the UK and France there is a much more even distribution across the age groups, although the young are still more likely to be low paid than other age groups.

Table 4.2. Pay and low-paid work (%)

	UK		Norway		France	
	2006	2010	2006	2010	2006	2010
Median hourly earnings (euros)	14.95	12.62	21.54	24.98	13.23	13.74
Median hourly earnings (euros purchasing power parity)	13.24	12.98	16.25	17.49	11.94	12.12
Low wage work (%)	21.8	22.1	6.5	7.3	7.1	6.1
Male	15.0	16.7	4.9	6.0	5.4	4.5
Female	28.5	27.6	8.8	8.6	9.3	7.9
Aged below 30	50.0	40.6	34.1	26.2	19.9	12.4
Aged 30–49	14.4	14.7	3.1	2.3	6.5	5.0
Aged 50+	18.5	18.3	1.6	1.3	5.6	4.7

Notes: Median hourly earnings: all employees excluding apprentices. Low wage work: employees excluding apprentices earning two-thirds or less of national median gross hourly earnings in that country.

Sources: Eurostat: earn_ses_pub2s; Eurostat: earn_ses_pub1a, earn_ses_pub1s.

Despite the higher cost of living in Norway, social protections outside of the labour market, coupled with higher wages at the bottom end, ensure that levels of poverty, and in particular child poverty, are lower (Table 4.8). France is similar to Norway in terms of in-work poverty, but is more affected by high and increasing levels of child poverty (nearly 19 per cent). In both countries in-work poverty is found predominantly among the young. In contrast, the UK, with its low wage floor and limited welfare provision, has a much higher level of poverty, including child poverty and in-work poverty, which affects similar proportions across the age range. Out-of-work benefits are based upon a low minimum safety net rather than the much higher income-related benefits received in Norway and France. 'Conditionality', or what a person is required to do in order to receive unemployment benefit, is also far more stringent in the UK and is increasingly so as recent governments have toughened up eligibility criteria (Wiggan 2012). Although sickness and disability benefits, pensions, and unemployment benefits are relatively high in France, they are predominantly income-related. For those without the required period in employment, however, support is quite low.

Evidence indicates that social mobility is relatively high in Norway in terms of earnings, occupational status, and educational outcomes, compared to both France and the UK, with the latter found to have one of the worst records of any developed economy (OECD 2010b: 187). While there is substantial evidence about lack of progression out of low wages along the life course in the UK (D'Arcy and Hurrell 2014), France appears to do better although is still some way behind Norway (Thompson and Hatfield 2015: 22). In Norway the numbers in low-paid jobs among the over-30s are extremely small, suggesting that all but a few are successful in moving out of low-wage work.

Skill, Discretion, and Over-Qualification

As noted in Chapter 2, there are major difficulties when it comes to estimating the skills required in jobs. The OECD (2013) Survey of Adult Skills (PIAAC) reveals some differences between the three countries (see Table 4.3). England[6] appears to have fewer jobs at graduate level and more jobs that require very minimal levels of education. Nearly 40 per cent of jobs in Norway and France ask for a tertiary qualification, compared to 33 per cent in England (OECD 2013: 168). While less than 12 per cent of Norwegian jobs require education levels at ISCED1 (primary school level), this rises to nearly 18 per cent in France and 23 per cent in England. Levels of over-qualification, however, are very similar between France and England but appear to be less of an issue in Norway, reflecting the higher qualification demands of jobs. Breaking down the data, over-qualification in Norway and France predominantly affects those with middle and lower level qualifications, while in the UK it is mainly found among those with tertiary education or lower level qualifications. Norway has particularly high levels of over-qualification among young people (aged 16–25). In France, rates are highest among foreign-born workers and those on fixed-term contracts.

In relation to work organization, there is evidence of different patterns across the three countries. As we saw in Chapter 3, survey data indicate that Norway is towards the top in terms of the percentage of jobs combining high levels of worker discretion and learning intensity, while the UK and France are in the mid-to-low position depending on the range of comparator countries. Table 4.4 shows patterns of work organization based on the European Working Conditions Survey (EWCS) in 2010. These figures, however, must be treated with some caution. In comparison with earlier surveys, there are strong fluctuations in the French results. The proportion of French workers experiencing jobs characterized by 'discretionary learning' went from 38 per cent in 2000 (Lorenz and Valeyre 2005: 435) to 47 per cent in 2005, before dropping

Table 4.3. Measures of qualification demand

	England	Norway	France
Percentage of jobs requiring education at ISCED1	22.8	11.8	17.6
Percentage of jobs requiring education at ISCED5+	33.1	39.4	38.7
Percentage of over-qualification	30.2	19.8	31.3
Percentage of under-qualification	12.4	15.2	12.9

Notes: Self-reported: over-qualified is where the qualification of worker is higher than that required in the job; under-qualification is where the qualification level of the worker is lower than that required in the job). ISCED1 = primary school; ISCED 5 = higher education.

Source: OECD (2013): Tables A4.24, 4.25a, 4.25b.

---

[6] The study only includes England and Northern Ireland. Here figures from England only are included.

Table 4.4. Patterns of work organization 2010 (percentage of employees)

	Discretionary learning	Lean production	Taylorist	Traditional/simple
UK	28.4	36.6	19.6	15.5
Norway	54.7	27.8	11.7	5.8
France	30.6	27.7	19.7	22.1

Source: Lorenz (2015).

16 percentage points to 31 per cent in 2010. It seems unlikely, even taking into account the effects of the recession, that patterns of work organization could have swung so markedly in such a short space of time.

For Norway and the UK, the survey data both from PIAAC and the EWCS are consistent with the findings from qualitative studies discussed in Chapter 2. They are also indicative of the recurrent debates in the UK that lack of employer demand for skill is the substantive issue rather than failures of the education and training system. Evidence from France is more mixed. Recent workplace studies that include France have tended to show workers with a broader range of tasks and more functional flexibility compared with similar workers in the UK (Caroli et al. 2010; Gautié and Schmitt 2010).

Nevertheless, a common feature of these studies is the high level of work intensity in France. This picture is confirmed by surveys of French workers which show that working conditions have deteriorated substantially, particularly between 1994 and 2003. Work intensification and associated job stress continue to be the major issues (EFILWC 2007), highlighted by increasing media publicity and union concern around work-related suicides. There is some limited survey evidence which suggests that, despite working fewer hours on average, levels of work intensity are relatively high in Scandinavia, including Norway, and are increasing (Oinas et al. 2012). The UK witnessed a substantial increase in work intensification in the 1990s (Felstead et al. 2007) and a renewed upward movement in work pressures against the backdrop of high unemployment and public sector austerity (Felstead et al. 2013b). Overall, the picture from the three countries is consistent with other data which show an intensification of work pressures across most European countries (Green 2006).

Conclusion

The chapter has outlined the key features of the UK, Norwegian, and French institutional setting, with a specific focus on the industrial relations institutions and the regulatory, welfare, and skill formation systems. It has also sought to consider how these different models are changing over time. In the UK, Conservative governments in the 1980s and 1990s played a critical role in driving forward a process of liberalization, dismantling weak corporatist institutions, and launching a frontal attack on trade unions. Notwithstanding some modest shifts in policy during the New Labour years, there has been the entrenchment of a neo-liberal growth model, centred on a lightly regulated labour market and an economy still heavily reliant upon finance and debt-fuelled consumption. Bank bail-outs and soaring public debt have provided governments since 2010 with a pretext for rolling back the state and a further weakening of welfare provision.

While commentators have long questioned the sustainability of the 'Nordic model' (Lindbeck et al. 1993), the Norwegian story is one of remarkable continuity and resilience. Norway has consistently defied the neo-liberal Cassandras of doom, emerging largely unscathed from the financial crash of 2008. Continuity is particularly marked in terms of the industrial relations system. Norway has always been considered rather 'unique' (Kasvio et al. 2012) even within the Scandinavian context, with lucrative oil wealth, a large concentration of small firms, and fewer transnational companies compared with Sweden. A powerful labour movement and a relatively weak domestic employer class mean that trade unions are 'still able to balance the class power of capital' (Bieler 2012: 235). It is of course tempting to dismiss the Norwegian case as simply an anomaly that bucks the dominant trends. However, it continues to stand as an example of a more progressive social model that appears to have weathered the processes of globalization and financialization that dominate contemporary debates.

France has experienced some trends towards liberalization, including privatizations and moves to decentralize collective bargaining to firm level. The latter raises the prospect of derogations from sector agreements and an increased ability on the part of employers to determine working arrangements, although how far and to what extent remains unclear. A central question is whether weaknesses in the French economy, including stubbornly high levels of unemployment, and the declining power of trade unions, will add to pressure on its social model and the divide between permanent workers and those subject to precarious employment.

On the evidence of these three countries, it is hard to make the case that we are witnessing a simple process of convergence and it is clear that their institutional environments remain very different. There is also considerable variation across a range of outcomes associated with these different national systems, although some of these indicators appear to be moving in the same direction, for example reports of work intensification. While, as noted in earlier chapters, available measures of work organization and skill are far from unproblematic, Norway emerges as some way ahead, with a number of features that may help to create conditions supportive of higher skilled jobs and more autonomous forms of work organization. These include a powerful labour movement and strong unions, higher wages and compressed pay differentials, established norms of cooperation through legally backed mechanisms of co-determination and participation, a well-regulated labour market, a supportive VET system and extensive tertiary education, and high unemployment benefits. Labour is relatively expensive, making it hard for organizations to compete through cost cutting and numerical flexibility.

In France, while the high cost of labour, employment security, and a regulated training system geared to social partnership might be considered conducive to skilled work, these features exist alongside other limiting factors, notably union weakness at workplace level, divided employers, and conflict-ridden employment relations. The UK is characterized by weak employment protection, relatively low labour costs (particularly at the middle and lower end), fragmented employers' organizations, and weakened unions that have limited legal rights to organize in the workplace. Consequently, there is little to prevent many employers competing through 'low road' strategies. On the other hand, unions have traditionally been stronger in the workplace than in France, which may enable them to have more influence over aspects of work organization.

The countries also differ in terms of the emphasis placed upon developing better jobs within the public policy arena. Norway has a long history of publicly funded workplace development programmes involving the labour market parties, with little to compare in either the UK or France. These programmes stress the importance of broad employee participation and constructive democratic dialogue. However, disentangling the contribution of workplace development programmes in delivering better forms of work organization from the wider institutional context is difficult. One conclusion might be that developing better forms of work organization is a long-term process, requiring both a supportive institutional context and specific, targeted workplace programmes.

This chapter has concentrated on the big picture of national models and how they may influence job quality and broader social outcomes. As noted in Chapter 3, however, comparative research needs to move beyond the macro-level if it is to examine the interplay of national institutions, sectors, and organizational approaches in shaping work outcomes, particularly in the service sector. In contributing to this research agenda, the following three chapters provide detailed studies of the work of vocational teachers, fitness instructors, and café workers in the UK, Norway, and France. The aim is to explore the possibilities for developing better jobs, the ways in which this might be achieved, and the prospects for progress.

Table 4.5. Labour market data, 2014

	UK	Norway	France
Employment rate (%)[1]			
aged 15–64	71.9	75.2	64.3
aged 15–24	48.1	50.1	28.4
aged 25–54	82.1	83.9	80.4
aged 55–64	61.0	72.2	47.0
female aged 15–64	67.1	73.4	60.9
female aged 25–54	76.2	81.4	76.1
male aged 25–54	88.0	86.2	84.9
Part-time (%)[2]			
aged 15+	24.1	18.8	14.2
female aged 15+	38.1	27.7	22.3
female aged 25–54	34.2	19.8	20.3
male aged 15+	11.7	10.8	6.6
Unemployment (%)[3]			
aged 15+	6.1	3.5	10.3
aged under 25	16.9	7.9	24.2
Temporary employees (%)[4]			
aged 15–64	6.3	7.9	16.0
aged 40–59	4.2	3.1	8.6

[1] Eurostat: lfsi_emp_a.
[2] Part-time employment as percentage of total employment (OECD 2014) less than 30 hours per week in main job; OECD (2015), 'Incidence and composition of part-time employment', in *OECD Employment Outlook 2015* (Paris: OECD Publishing). <http://dx.doi.org/10.1787/empl_outlook-2015-table86-en>.
[3] une_rt_a.
[4] Percentage of total employees: lfsa_etpga.

Table 4.6. Support for childcare

	UK	Norway	France
Statutory maternity/paternity leave	6 weeks 90% pay 33 weeks maximum £140[1]/week 13 weeks unpaid	49 weeks full pay	16 weeks full pay
Childcare costs as percentage of earnings[2]	34	11	10
Childcare provision	Part-time free from 3 years old	Available from 1 year old	Free from 2 years old

Notes: [1] 2015 equivalent to approximately 50% of weekly wage of full-time worker on national minimum wage.
[2] Net childcare costs for dual earner couple with gross earnings of 150% of average wage for two children in full-time care; 2012 OECD Family Data Base Chart PF3.4B.

Table 4.7. Measures of income inequality

	UK	Norway	France
Gender pay gap[1]	19.7	16.0	15.1
P50:P10[2]	2.0	1.9	1.9
P90:P10	4.2	3.0	3.6
P90:P50	2.1	1.6	1.9
S80/S20	5.9	3.8	4.6
Gini index[3] income inequality	0.35	0.25	0.31

Notes: [1] Percentage difference between average gross hourly earnings of male and female paid employees in enterprise with 10 employees or more, 2014, Eurostat: tsdsc340.
[2] Income ratios 2010, S80/S20 ratio of average income of top 20% to bottom 20%. P90/P10 ratio of the upper bound value of the ninth decile to that of the first.
[3] 2012 0 = complete equality; 1 = complete inequality. After transfers.

Source: OECD (2015) Income inequality (indicator). doi: 10.1787/459aa7f1-en (accessed 9 December 2015).

Table 4.8. Measures of poverty (%)

	UK		Norway		France	
	2005	2014	2005	2014	2005	2014
At risk of poverty	19.0	16.8	11.4	10.9	13.0	13.3
At risk of poverty (under-18s)	22.9	19.9	9.4	10.2	14.4	17.7
In-work poverty	8.2	8.6	4.5	5.0	6.1	8.0

Note: At risk of poverty after social transfers (below 60% national median income).
Source: Eurostat: tessi120; tesov110.

5

Professional Work, Autonomy, and Innovation

Vocational Teachers

Introduction

The chapter uses a comparative study of vocational teachers to explore the factors shaping the work of public sector professionals,[1] focusing upon issues of discretion and autonomy. As noted in previous chapters, although professional work is characterized by relatively high knowledge requirements, there is some evidence of cross-country variation in the way that professionals are managed. For those working in the public sector, state policy is a key domain shaping service provision and the work of professionals. Alongside this, there are often long-standing industrial relations and labour market institutions which potentially provide opportunities for professionals and their representatives to exert power and influence.

In recent years, most Western governments have introduced reforms to public services with the aim of improving effectiveness and efficiency. Considerable attention has focused on 'new public management' (NPM), involving marketization and the use of private sector management approaches such as quality auditing and accountability for results (Hood 1991; Pollitt 1993). The UK was the first country in Europe to embrace NPM in the 1980s and is regarded as an NPM 'enthusiast' (Bach and Bordogna 2011). While the impact has been variable across the devolved nations of the UK, as well as different parts of the public sector, studies have shown that many professionals have

---

[1] There is a substantial literature on the nature of professional work. Here we use the term 'professional' in the sense of an occupational category rather than to indicate particular levels of qualification requirements, status, or autonomy.

been subject to new 'performativity' demands and heightened managerial controls that have eroded autonomy (Felstead et al. 2004; Bach 2010).

Today, NPM is considered a 'powerful orthodoxy' whose influence has spread far beyond the USA and UK, although early assumptions that there would be a process of global convergence have proven misplaced (Bach and Bordogna 2011: 2283; see also Pollitt 2007; Goldfinch and Wallis 2010). While certain aspects have been observed in other European countries, there is considerable variation in form, depth, and effects. In Scandinavia, for example, Demark and Sweden are said to have been relatively receptive, introducing elements of marketization, while Norway is regarded as a more 'reluctant NPM reformer' (Ibsen et al. 2011). France is described as 'not an NPM laggard but a model apart', reflecting a 'neo-Weberian' state tradition very different to both the UK and the Nordic countries (Kickert 2007; Bordogna and Neri 2011: 2329). The picture, therefore, is one of 'different reform trajectories which are embedded in, and mediated by, country-specific legal, institutional and cultural conditions' (Bach and Bordogna 2011: 2283).

Cross-national comparative research has been mainly concerned with understanding convergence and divergence at the level of policy reforms. As noted in Chapter 3, few studies have sought to drill down and compare directly the *work* of public sector professionals across countries. This chapter extends existing research through a comparative study of vocational teachers in England, Wales,[2] Norway, and France undertaken at sector and workplace level between 2009 and 2010. As a key part of the education and training system, this group has been increasingly subject to reforms as skills policy has acquired greater political salience. Notwithstanding a burgeoning literature on teachers in Further Education (FE) colleges in the UK, there is little in the way of international comparative studies. Reflecting the knowledge and learning demands of professional jobs, the chapter focuses upon vocational teacher education and training, and the scope teachers have to deploy their knowledge and expertise within the job.

The chapter begins by locating the discussion in the context of the initial vocational education and training (IVET) sector and provides a background to public provision in each country at the time of the research, before comparing approaches to vocational teacher education. The main part of the chapter explores teachers' work in depth by probing their levels of discretion and autonomy in relation to 'what they teach' (curriculum), 'how they teach' (pedagogy), and the extent to which they are subject to managerial monitoring and control. The chapter then reflects on alternative approaches to managing public service sector professionals, focusing upon

---

[2] Education and training in the UK is a devolved responsibility; however, England and Wales shared a common framework prior to 1999 and retain many similar features.

the quality of teaching and learning and the scope that teachers have to innovate within the job.

The Changing Context of Initial Vocational Education and Training

As noted in previous chapters, many governments have looked to restructure their IVET systems in pursuit of economic competitiveness, higher productivity, and social inclusion. Attention has focused on raising participation and attainment, controlling public expenditure, and ensuring that the system *performs* effectively. Teachers are seen as pivotal in terms of their ability to deliver 'quality' in teaching and learning (OECD 2005). Education reforms have taken place against the background of a globalizing discourse of NPM applied to the public sector (Pollitt and Bouckaert 2004). In the UK, NPM involved a new framework of performance controls, borrowed from the private sector, with a particular emphasis upon market mechanisms and the decentralization of responsibility for results to local managers. This was combined with a strengthening of central government control through the use of targets, auditing, and other measures aimed at driving improvement, which intensified during the New Labour era (Hood 2006). For many public sector workers, the result has been an erosion of professional autonomy, heightened managerialism, and an intensification of labour (Ferlie and Geraghty 2005). In education, the emphasis has been on competing for students and national inspections of schools and colleges, with tough action towards those deemed to be 'failing'.

The rhetoric of NPM emphasizes 'competition', 'choice', 'consumers', 'clients', 'quality', and 'accountability'. As Newman (2000) argues in a critical discussion of NPM in the UK, the question of what constitutes performance or quality is controversial, however, not least in education where goals and purposes are contested and much of what is valuable in student learning cannot easily be quantified or measured (see also Hodkinson 2008). At the same time, the use of targets and audit controls is not unproblematic, in part due to their potential for negative, unintended consequences, such as 'teaching to the test' and high levels of bureaucracy. An alternative view, favoured by teacher unions, emphasizes the importance of professional expertise, autonomy, and teacher-driven innovation as the most effective means of improving teaching and learning. Teachers, it is argued, need sufficient scope to exercise their professional judgement and to work collaboratively within learning communities (Coffield 2008) that allow them to 'develop their creativity and ability to innovate, while becoming more actively engaged and thus more motivated' (Eurydice 2008: 9). Such an approach, however, requires a high degree of trust, autonomy, and engagement, along with effective supports to enable teachers to work together to improve teaching and learning (Cribb and Gerwitz 2007).

This chapter discusses these issues in the context of country-specific IVET systems where the impact of NPM is said to have been either quite different to that of the UK (Norway) or where it remains rather alien (France). Does this mean that vocational teachers have more opportunities to use their professional expertise and judgement in these countries? Is it reflected in their training, job design, and management at the organizational level? How much discretion and autonomy do teachers have within their work and how much influence do they wield in relation to decisions both at workplace level and within national policy-making through their collective organizations? How does this context shape the scope and opportunities that are available for teachers to work together with their colleagues to improve the quality of teaching and learning?

These questions are addressed through in-depth research involving interviews at sector level and in four FE colleges in England and Wales, three Norwegian upper secondary schools, and three vocational colleges in France. To aid comparability, the focus is on one group of vocational teachers, namely those teaching hairdressing. A more detailed discussion of the method adopted is provided in Appendix 1. In most cases, semi-structured interviews were held with the head of the institution, departmental heads or leaders, and between three and five teachers at each site. In total, 54 interviews were undertaken at workplace level. The next section outlines the central features of each country's IVET system and the institutional structures shaping teachers' employment.

England and Wales

In England and Wales, FE colleges are the main providers of IVET. FE colleges are large institutions, providing a wide range of academic and vocational programmes for young people and adults, from basic skills courses to higher education. Traditionally associated with working-class education, FE has tended to be regarded as low status and is said to increasingly work on a 'deficit model of provision', offering a 'second chance' to those who have struggled in mainstream schooling (Jephcote et al. 2008: 164). The sector has undergone major upheaval over the last twenty years as governments have implemented forms of NPM that are even more extreme than those seen in other areas of the education system (Gleeson et al. 2005). Colleges, removed from local authority control in 1992, were granted corporate status (referred to as 'incorporation') and required to operate in a 'quasi-market' with other providers as levels of funding were cut back. State control intensified after

New Labour took office in 1997, although with increased resourcing designed to help meet government skills targets.

Since 1992 funding has been linked to student recruitment, retention, and certification. College managers are accountable for results, with quality measured through high stakes inspections of management and teaching conducted by Ofsted in England and Estyn in Wales. Over time, the curriculum has become 'increasingly centrally controlled, prescribed and codified' (Simmons and Thompson 2008: 611), following the introduction of competence-based qualifications, most notably NVQs. Efforts to increase participation and support social inclusion have seen increasing numbers of young people entering FE with complex social lives and learning and behavioural difficulties.

The period following incorporation in 1992 was one of bitter industrial conflict as unions fought unsuccessfully to retain national bargaining and highly regulated employment conditions. College managers, operating within shrinking budgets, were largely able to reduce costs through suppressing pay, compulsory redundancies, increased workloads, and widespread casualization (Williams 2003). Despite subsequent increases in funding under New Labour, between 40 and 50 per cent of FE teachers continue to be on some form of casual contract. Although union membership remains high compared to the national average, the two main unions, the Universities and Colleges Union (UCU) and the Association of Teachers and Lecturers (ATL), have limited power and influence.

Employer organization has also become increasingly fragmented, although intervention by the Welsh government, following political devolution in 1999, supported a move towards more cooperative and collective relations in Wales. By 2010, only around 40 per cent of colleges in England were estimated to comply each year with national collective bargaining (UCU official), while in Wales (with separate negotiations) this is a government requirement. In England, local disputes, particularly over issues such as compulsory redundancies or the imposition of new contracts, are not uncommon as terms and conditions have become increasingly varied.

There is no formalized social partnership for the FE sector in England at national level, with policy decisions increasingly centralized in the hands of senior ministers and civil servants (Coffield 2007). A defining feature is the bewildering institutional complexity and the frenetic pace of policy change, with a seemingly endless succession of 'top-down' reforms to institutional arrangements, qualifications, funding, and programmes (Keep 2006; Coffield et al. 2008). In terms of union influence, a UCU official claimed in 2009: 'You can have input around the margins but you can't deflect them [policy-makers] from the central tenets.' A representative of the employers' organization, the Association of Colleges (AoC), observed that the pace of reform had become 'so relentless' under New Labour that the FE teacher 'managed change as part of their natural state'. In Wales, differences in the political settlement and policy process, which predate devolution in 1999, are said to have allowed a more prominent voice for teacher professionals (Rees 2007).

Research has highlighted how the 'world of FE' in England became 'one of diktat and discipline, performativity and managerialism' (Simmons 2008: 360). Teachers were said to have become 'delivery agents' of government priorities, weighed down with heavy workloads, onerous administrative demands, and constant changes to institutional arrangements, funding, and programmes (Avis 2003; Coffield et al. 2008). Despite a weak and fragmented professionalism, particularly for vocational teachers with diverse occupational backgrounds (Robson et al. 2004), most teachers retained a strong commitment to students, with many seeking to work in, and around, performativity demands to meet student needs (Gleeson et al. 2005). Despite political devolution and a more inclusive policy process in Wales, similar workplace issues have been identified in a sector where 'incorporation' has cast a 'long shadow' (Jephcote et al. 2009).

Norway

In Norway, vocational teachers work in upper secondary schools that are under the control of the nineteen counties and which receive block grants from central government. The majority of schools provide both general and vocational education and, with an average of 425 pupils, are much smaller and less diverse in terms of provision than colleges in England and Wales. After 1994, all students were given a *right* to three years of upper secondary education and to receive teaching adapted to their individual needs. Participation at age 16 is near universal and around half study for vocational programmes. The main model is the 2+2 apprenticeship, combining two years in school and two years of work-based training, as noted in Chapter 4. The Ministry of Education and Research has overall responsibility for national policy development and the administration of education and vocational training. The counties, or 'school owners' as they are referred to, have considerable autonomy, however, and are responsible for the employment of teachers, the number of programmes offered, and student admissions. Schools recruit and manage teachers, and are responsible for local examinations. Unlike in England and Wales, there is no system of school inspections.

Norway's lacklustre performance in the OECD's PISA tests over recent years has resulted in pressures to introduce certain elements of NPM into schools, in particular a greater focus upon quality measures, outcomes, and auditing (see Helgøy and Homme 2007; Møller and Skedsmo 2013). This shift has introduced new tensions in the system as school leadership has traditionally been based on non-hierarchical relations, trust in teachers' professionalism, and close working relationships with teachers and their unions (see Møller et al. 2005; Tjeldvoll 2008). Successive education reforms since the 1980s are said to have led to 'reform weariness' among the teaching profession, with teachers increasingly required to perform the roles of 'counsellor', 'social worker', and 'paper administrator' (Lyng and Blichfeldt 2003: 69–70).

Vocational teachers in schools are employed under the same national terms and conditions as those teaching general subjects, which are an outcome of national bargaining between the teachers' union and local government. There is near universal union membership through the Union of Education, Norway's third largest union. Teaching is a highly secure form of employment, with temporary positions rarely used. The Union of Education is represented on the tripartite National Council for VET, alongside the main labour market parties, NHO and LO, and the Ministry. Norwegian school teachers are said to experience 'more professional autonomy than many of their European colleagues' (Czerniawski 2013: 386). Although there is no specific research on vocational teachers, Helgøy and Homme (2007) argue that teachers in Norway have a high level of autonomy at the 'collective' level, which they call 'old professionalism', compared with their counterparts in Sweden, but less autonomy within the classroom.

As noted in Chapter 4, the policy formation process around VET has changed in Norway in recent years, with the Ministry taking a more directive approach, albeit in consultation with the social partners. A national officer with the Union of Education interviewed in 2010 insisted that the union retained a major input into national policy deliberations: 'we had a huge hearing on the latest curriculum and the government changed it...You can't change everything but they really consider it and I think we have a lot of say.' There is some suggestion, however, of an erosion of influence over the last few years, as unions failed to stop the introduction of national testing in compulsory schooling (Johnsen 2012). Nevertheless, teacher unions represent a powerful constituency that remains opposed to an extension of controls over teachers' work, and centre-left governments have modified the testing regime in light of their concerns. A departmental head at one school visited remarked that if it had not been for the unions, Norway would have adopted 'the English model' of inspections and targets 'a long time ago' (head of arts and crafts, Norway2).

France

In France, most initial vocational education takes place within state vocational colleges (*lycées professionnelles*), which students enter at age 15, although there is also a substantial private sector (covering around 20 per cent of students). Colleges are similar in size to upper secondary schools in Norway, with most specializing in specific subject areas (RRS 2015). Vocational courses have lower status than academic programmes and are disproportionately comprised of students with poorer school results and from lower socio-economic backgrounds, many of whom struggle with learning, find themselves on courses they have not themselves chosen, and have limited options in the labour market. Research by Jellab (2008) indicates that certain vocational colleges struggle to maintain discipline, with student violence directed towards teachers a major concern (see also Troger and Hörner 2007).

Vocational colleges are controlled by the Ministry of Education which is responsible for education policy, national curricula, exams, and the employment of teachers. The Ministry operates through thirty regional *academies*, with colleges run by locally elected Regional Councils which manage investment and operations, non-teaching staff, the matching of courses to local economic needs, and the allocation of students. The college principal is appointed directly by the Ministry, and the *academies* deal with the employment, training, inspection, and allocation of teachers. Colleges themselves are not subject to inspections and there are no output-oriented targets. Recent years have witnessed a major squeeze in the education budget as governments have sought to tackle the public deficit, with the result that teacher numbers have been shrunk through natural wastage.

The most defining characteristic of teachers in France is that they are civil servants (*fonctionaires*) with *titulaire* status and are subject to a legal and regulatory framework that covers all of the different Ministries. Excluding casual workers (where there is a lack of data), only around 10 per cent of vocational teachers in public colleges do not have civil servant status, and less than 6 per cent of *titulaires* work part-time (RRS 2015: 287). Civil servants have lifetime employment and their pay and conditions are negotiated between trade unions and the Civil Service Minister. All teachers are employed on a common grid or pay spine, with their position related to tenure and performance, and there are additional pay supplements available for taking on extra responsibilities. There is a system of individual teacher inspections, undertaken by *academie* inspectors, which are used primarily to assess training and development needs and determine promotion and acceleration up the pay spine.

Characteristic of French industrial relations, there are a number of trade unions operating within the education field, together with a history of rivalry, mergers, and splits. Teachers, however, are relatively unionized compared with other sectors. Union density is estimated to be around 25 per cent (Amossé and Pignoni 2006), although influence at workplace level remains uneven. Unions have been able to unite around issues such as opposition to pension reforms in 2010 and reductions in the number of new teachers recruited from 2011. There is also evidence of activism at local level, with regular reports of strikes at individual institutions, related to issues such as discipline, arrest of undocumented students, bullying management, and the loss of specific courses.

At national policy level, there is formal social dialogue through various public committees. Change is slow, both in terms of administrative procedures and political processes, with requirements for extensive consultation with unions, employers, and other interest groups (Cros and Obin 2003). The general technical committee, which covers the whole education system, negotiates over the management of staff, training, work organization, equality, and rules on promotion. Each specific area of education, for example vocational colleges, has an administrative committee, and there are a variety of other committees at regional and local level. Despite their legally-backed role in these forums, however, unions have not been able to prevent some changes which they regard as detrimental, including the reforms to initial teacher education, discussed in the following section.

The main differences in terms of the context within which vocational teachers work in the four countries are summarized in Table 5.1.

Table 5.1. Public sector initial vocational education and vocational teachers

	England	Wales	Norway	France
Institutions	FE college	FE college	Upper secondary school	Vocational college
Number (2014/15)	216	12	345	901
Average size (students)	12,000	12,000	460 (2013)	409 (2014)
Employer of teachers	College	College	County	Ministry of Education
Collective bargaining coverage	50% approx	100%	100%	100%
Union membership (education)	50% (UK)	50% (UK)	Over 90%	10–20%
Average wage level, compared to median in each country[3]	£34,159 full-time (UK) (2014) 126%	£35,739 full-time (2014) 147%	494,500 NOK (2014) 97%	€41,610 (2011) 120%
Vocational teachers (public sector)	68,000 FTE (all college) 59% women	5,390 FTE (all college) 59% women (2015)	25,000 (all upper secondary) 49% women	58,279 49.5% women (2014/15)
Employment contracts	62% of contracts part-time; 40% fixed-term, casual[2]	70% of contracts part-time; 50% temporary/casual[1]	Typically full-time, permanent	Typically full-time, permanent; 7% part-time; 10% non-civil servants
Union role in policy	Minimal	Minor role	Extensive formal role	Extensive formal role
Effective influence	Limited	Limited	Extensive	Moderate

[1] Staff contract numbers for teaching staff (staff may have more than one contract) 2008/9 Statistics for Wales.
[2] Lingfield (2012); Frontier Economics (2014).
[3] ASHE ONS, OECD, Insee, Statistics Norway.
Sources: Education Mirror (2014): RRS (2015); The Education Workforce Council (Wales), DBIS (2015).

Vocational Teacher Education

As VET has achieved increased political salience, policy-makers have turned their attention to the competence, qualifications, and professional development of teachers. Often neglected in the past, IVET teachers were often seen as practitioners and specialists in their vocational field rather than qualified *teachers*. In many countries, attempts have been made to develop a more professionalized workforce, with measures aimed at initial teacher education and continuing professional development (Parsons et al. 2008). Commenting on approaches to vocational teacher education, Grollmann and Rauner (2007: 20) note that, 'Huge differences exist with regard to...how teachers and trainers are recruited...and how they are prepared in order to cope with their daily work.' They distinguish between a 'professionalised model', based on high wages, strong professional status and a sound knowledge base, and a more 'ad hoc model', which emphasizes work experience and more flexible recruitment and employment patterns. How does the situation compare across the four countries in this study?

Prior to 2001 in England and 2002 in Wales, there was no statutory requirement to hold a teaching qualification, and in 2005, around half of FE teachers in England and one-third in Wales still did not possess such a qualification (Estyn 2006; Jephcote and Salisbury 2009: 967). The qualification requirements in both countries were later revised in 2007, and teachers in England only were required to register with a new professional body, the Institute for Learning, and undergo a process of 'professional formation' (LLUK 2007). There were a number of qualifications available at different levels, ranging from a minimum 'threshold' award at level two to a level five diploma which conferred 'fully qualified' status. Qualifications could be taken prior to entry or post-entry within certain time limits. 'Associate teacher' status was also introduced for those undertaking a more limited teaching role and with a lower level qualification. A minimum core of literacy and numeracy at level two (equivalent to lower secondary school qualifications) was also stipulated. In 2013, the UK Coalition government rescinded the statutory requirement in England to obtain a teaching qualification, insisting this was a matter for colleges and their staff in what was widely condemned by many commentators as a retrograde step (Simmons 2013).

In Norway, all forms of teacher education have been regulated by the same law and subject to the same criteria since 1995. Those wishing to teach vocational programmes in upper secondary schools must obtain either a three-year vocational teaching degree (which is increasingly the norm) or a one-year teaching certificate. In 2007, around 10 per cent did not hold a teaching qualification, having entered the profession prior to these requirements (Utdanningsdirektoratet 2007: 87). The Union of Education argues that teaching should become an all Master's-level profession, a requirement which currently applies only to those teaching *general subjects* at upper secondary level.

In France, the status and education of vocational teachers was unified with other teachers in 1989 (Cros and Obin 2003). Until recently, teacher education consisted primarily of two years at a public teacher training institute (IUFM). The first year involved preparation for a highly competitive national examination (*concours*), which selects candidates for a fixed number of places, where the focus is on developing subject knowledge of the vocational specialism. Those who passed entered a second year as paid trainees, alternating between undertaking vocational teacher education at an IUFM and teaching placements in a college. Successful completion automatically provides teachers with full *titulaire* status, that is, a permanent, full-time job as a civil servant. Changes were introduced in 2010, despite an extended period of strikes and unrest at IUFMs, with the aim of teaching becoming an all Master's-level occupation, and with IUFMs incorporated into universities. Having been somewhat overlooked, it has since been accepted that vocational teachers in craft areas would not need a Master's qualification. The process of entering the profession is still through the *concours*; however, the second year for the trainee involves increased teaching hours in the college and a less structured provision of pedagogic training.

As summarized in Table 5.2, vocational teachers in France and Norway are required to have a higher level of vocational qualification and longer professional experience before they can enter teaching training. In England and Wales, these prerequisites (apart from level two numeracy and literacy) are at the discretion of individual colleges. Initial teacher qualifications are also substantially higher in France and Norway. High standards in written and oral French are crucial to success in the *concours* and in fields such as hairdressing, where the *concours* is often closed over a number of years, competition is intense. Teachers in both these countries will normally have continued with first language studies and maths until 18. Vocational students in England and Wales will typically drop these subjects at 16, with some evidence of remaining difficulties for future teachers. One university tutor in England commented in 2010 that many students on the FE postgraduate diplomas struggled with the level two literacy and numeracy tests.

As well as level of qualifications, it is important to consider the 'knowledge' developed within these different teacher education programmes, and how they may affect teacher status and approach. Grollmann and Rauner (2007) note that teaching profiles which require in-depth subject knowledge tend to raise the status of VET teachers but may also lead to entrenched subject-based identities which can prevent effective cross-disciplinary working. Teachers in

Table 5.2. Teacher education requirements in England, Wales, Norway, and France

	England/Wales	Norway	France
Teacher qualifications	Threshold licence; Certificate (associate teacher); Diploma ('full' teacher); Cert Ed; PGCE From 2013: *voluntary* in England	(a) 3 year vocational teaching degree or (b) 1 year vocational teacher education	CAPLP (obtained through competitive exam)
Entry requirements	None, but normally Level 3 qualification (craft) in specialist teaching area	(a) Craft certificate + 2 years professional practice (b) Craft certificate + 4 years professional practice + 2 years further study	For craft-based subjects: BAC or equivalent + 7 years professional practice
Course content	Threshold licence (30 hours + one hour of observed practice) Certificate (120 hours + 30 hours teaching practice) Diploma (150 hours + 100 hours teaching practice) Cert Ed/PGCE 1 year full-time or 2 years part-time. Education theory and practice. Minimum core of literacy and numeracy (level 2)	(a) 3 year degree: In-depth study of vocational area (1.5 years), vocational specialism (1 year), educational science (1 year) + 12–14 weeks teaching practice (b) 1 year pedagogic theory and vocational didactics + 12–14 weeks teaching practice	1 year preparation for *concours* (exam) based on subject knowledge (1 year) [not compulsory] Trainee: 1 year part-time educational science and vocational pedagogy + 6 hours a week teaching practice (10 hours + from 2010)
Delivery	Universities or FE colleges	University colleges	Public teacher training institutes (IUFMs) Universities (from 2010)
Status of learner	Student/college employee	Student	1st year student 2nd year paid trainee

France and Norway require greater vocational knowledge and experience but they are also subject to very different approaches to learning to teach.

In England and Wales, the concept of 'vocational pedagogy'—how teaching is tailored to subject specific traditions and learning methods—is weakly developed. Those wishing to teach vocational specialisms attend the same generic course as those teaching academic subjects in FE, the *assumption* being that whether one is teaching bricklaying or biology the principles are the same (Huddlestone and Unwin 2007). Adaptation to subject area is made during teaching practice, usually with the support of a mentor from the same area. In contrast, in Norway and France, there is a strong focus upon 'vocational pedagogy' (*yrkesdidaktik* in Norwegian or *didatiques* in French). Students learn to teach in relation to their subject and are taught by vocational specialists.

In Norway, teachers are expected to develop competence in a *broad* vocational area (e.g. arts and crafts) to accommodate a wide range of student choices during the first year, along with their particular specialism (e.g. hairdressing). Social competence, including team working, is afforded more emphasis, with the teacher expected to be a guide or facilitator of students' learning. In contrast, the French model is strongly focused on the teacher as a subject expert and specialist, alongside a more traditional conception of the organization of learning and instruction (see Grollmann and Rauner 2007; Troger and Hørner 2007).

What about the place of educational theory? The occupational standards model used in England and Wales assumes that professional knowledge can be prescribed and codified into written statements, and makes only a few vague references to theory. This model has been criticized for its 'technicist' view, where teachers learn generic teaching skills or techniques to deliver a prescribed curriculum. It is argued that a narrow, skills-based teacher training limits the scope available for teachers to interrogate the purpose of vocational education, accountability pressures, and the way education can function to reproduce or counter social inequalities (Avis et al. 2013). In Norway and France, educational theory is a major component, with pedagogical competence tailored to the characteristics of the particular trade or vocational area. As well as allowing more opportunities for trainees to deepen their knowledge of their vocational area and its place in society, this approach allows more scope to reflexively explore the purpose of education.

In summary, France and Norway embody a more 'professionalized' model of vocational teacher education, compared with England and Wales. In France, the professional status of vocational teachers is further reinforced by civil servant status, lifetime employment, and a seniority-based promotion ladder. In England and Wales, attempts by the state to move to professionalize the workforce have been limited, with regulations recently abandoned in England, while the widespread use of temporary and part-time staff (with restricted teaching roles) has produced a 'balkanized' workforce which further compounds the problem.

Vocational Teachers at Work

The formal requirements and teaching approaches, alongside the sectoral context, would lead to an expectation of a more autonomous and professional workforce in Norway and France. To what extent does the evidence from the

Skills in the Age of Over-Qualification

Table 5.3. Characteristics of the case study workplaces

College/ School	Background	Student numbers		Numbers of hairdressing teachers		
		College/ school (FTEs)[2]	Hairdressing	Full-time	Part-time	Temporary, hourly paid, agency
England1	Low prosperity town Grade 1 (Ofsted)[1]	5,000	200	7	6	7
England2	Average prosperity town Grade 3 (Ofsted)	5,000	350	3	2	10
Wales1	Average prosperity, inner-city Grade 2 (Estyn)[1]	5,000	200	1	5	7
Wales2	Low prosperity town Grade 3 (Estyn)	15,000	100	3	3	2
Norway1	High prosperity city, ethnically diverse and lower income students	1,000	60	4	0	1
Norway2	High prosperity town	1,000	30	3	0	0
Norway3	High prosperity town	700	45	3	2	0
France1	Average prosperity town	600	75	4	0	0
France2	High prosperity inner-city, mainly female students	600	125	5	0	0
France3	Low prosperity town, includes residential students	600	110	6	0	0

[1] Ofsted/Estyn are inspections bodies. Grade 1 is the top score (outstanding), Grade 4 is the lowest (inadequate). FTE = full-time equivalent.
[2] Approximate numbers to ensure college/school cannot be identified.

workplace support this view and are there consequences for the quality of teaching that is being delivered?

Table 5.3 summarizes key data on the case studies in each country.[3] Departments in England and Wales were normally much larger than in the other two countries, with more staff and a greater variety of programmes and student profiles. While, at national level, the gender balance of vocational teachers overall is fairly even, all of the teachers in the hairdressing departments in this study were women. Most were aged 35 plus, having worked for a number of years as hairdressers prior to entry. Reflecting the higher levels of education demanded in Norway and France, teachers from these countries typically had

---

[3] Pseudonyms are used for the schools and colleges, and for teachers; further details can be found in Appendix 1.

Table 5.4. Teacher contracts and programmes taught in the case study hairdressing departments

	England/Wales	Norway	France
Typical class size	18–20	15	15 (practical) 30 (theory)
Full-time teacher contracted hours	37	35	35
Class contact hours	22–24	22	18 + 1 compulsory overtime
Additional required hours on site	8+	7–9	0
Programmes	Level 1, 2, 3; full-time, part-time, apprenticeship	2 + 2	CAP, MC BP (by apprenticeship)
Typical qualification of teachers interviewed	Level 3 Hairdressing Cert Ed teaching	Apprenticeship Vocational degree or 1 year teaching certificate	Brevet de Maîtrise CAPLP

both higher vocational and teaching qualifications than in England and Wales. In the four countries, teachers held practical sessions with between fifteen and eighteen students, and taught theory elements in classrooms, with numbers in France doubling to a maximum of thirty students (Table 5.4). Hours of work and teaching contact time were similar in England, Wales, and Norway. In France, contracts specify shorter teaching hours, although all teachers undertook additional compulsory paid overtime.

The most striking difference in terms of employment contracts is that in England and Wales, full-time permanent teachers were in the minority, with a heavy reliance on fractional contracts and part-time, hourly-paid staff (Table 5.4). By contrast, in Norway and France, full-time, permanent teachers were the norm. Unfortunately access was not available to casualized workers in England and Wales, thereby potentially presenting a more positive picture of the work environment. The other main cross-country difference was the expectation of time spent in the workplace. In France teachers were only obliged to be on site when they had classes, whereas in Norway, England, and Wales there were specified additional hours when teachers were required to be present.

The next section examines the extent to which teachers felt they had discretion, autonomy, and control over their work. The focus is, first, on what teachers teach and their choice over teaching methods, and, second, managerial monitoring and control and the influence teachers felt that they and/or their representatives had over decision-making within the school or college.

Discretion and Autonomy in Teaching

Curriculum and Assessment

All four countries operated with a centralized curriculum that teachers were required to follow, but the key issue was the level of prescription and the specifications in relation to assessment. In England and Wales, the NVQ curriculum for hairdressing, as developed by the relevant awarding body, ran to over 100 pages and prescribed in considerable detail the specific competencies and theory elements on which students had to be assessed. Although some teachers were able to add additional elements outside the formal curriculum, most spoke of having little opportunity due to lack of time:

> You can't go ahead and teach them something that isn't in the unit because you've got the time constraints. (Liz, Wales2)

Another commented on the lack of time to introduce 'competition work' and 'cutting workshops':

> it doesn't happen, it's very basic and it is like you are teaching what you've got to teach... it is just stand there and do this. (Debbie, Wales2)

The heavy assessment requirements, associated with NVQs, meant that teachers spent considerable time 'tracking' and marking students' portfolios of work. The content, frequency, and method of assessment, as specified by the awarding body, provided little space for teacher discretion. A teacher described how she was constantly bombarded with 'big files' of student work to assess:

> From an assessors' point of view, it's quite a job during a practical session to actually track the work they have completed in that time. And if you have got eighteen learners in a class then it is quite a lot of time... just filling in folders... we are constantly signing and marking those. (Janet, England1)

For the theory element, one college had adopted the awarding body's online multiple choice method of assessment, thereby removing teachers completely from the examination process.

In France, the hairdressing curriculum was a highly prescriptive 60-page reference manual (referential) which set out the knowledge areas that teachers had to cover and the assessment processes. Teachers felt that there was some scope to introduce additional material or, as one teacher explained, 'a margin to manoeuvre'. 'There is a referential and over two years, we have to do it all... [but] they have some things which are a bit I find old fashioned... but you are able to give it a little less time' (Brigitte, France2). Another teacher reflected the widely-held view that teaching needed to be up to date with the latest trends in hairdressing and to develop more in-depth skills and techniques which were not in the referential: 'we want to give the impression to our pupils that the job is not just about basics... we also want to show them a global image of the profession' (Agnes, France3). Unlike in England and Wales, assessment was not particularly burdensome, outside of the final exam period, and was more under teacher control. Recent reforms had replaced national tests with local assessments that were set and marked by teachers within the school. Teachers continually evaluated students throughout the course but there was no guidance or any requirements.

In Norway, a country with a tradition of centralized curricula, the 2006 Knowledge Promotion Reform had afforded teachers greater scope for autonomy and local decision-making. Teachers welcomed the new curricula which were focused on broader 'learning outcomes' and summarized in just 'a couple of pages'. As one teacher put it, 'we have got the freedom, nobody is telling us this, this, this. We have got the goals... how we get the students there is up to us' (Kristine, Norway3). Another referred to the role of the teachers' hairdressing association—there was no equivalent body in the other countries—where all hairdressing teachers met annually to collectively discuss new plans for teaching.

> We meet once a year for three, four days and we go through what we are going to do, how we are going to do the teaching, what has changed since last year and all the new plans that come for teaching. (Eva, Norway2)

Assessment was also the responsibility of the hairdressing team and was regarded as manageable. Formal examinations set by the college took place at the end of the year and teachers, as in France, determined the number of assessments carried out throughout the year.

Pedagogy

The teachers in England and Wales were highly constrained by the curriculum and assessment process, but felt they had more autonomy in relation to how they taught. A teacher explained:

> There's nothing telling us how to teach students... so yes there is flexibility there in teaching... we are encouraged to use a little bit of Powerpoint... [and] varied teaching methods, to stimulate students, but nobody says you have to do it this way, you have to use these lessons. (Tina, Wales2)

Despite this apparent freedom, however, there was strict monitoring and intervention by management in relation to the teaching process. Across the colleges, quality assurance schemes and ongoing monitoring were seen as an essential element in improving the learning experience. Students regularly evaluated teachers with responses collated by senior managers before being fed back to the relevant teaching group.

Observation of teaching was also common, whether from other teachers (particularly internal verifiers of NVQs), heads of departments, and designated internal inspectors, or from awarding bodies and, most significantly, the national inspectorates which, together with funding, drive managerial behaviour. Interestingly, many teachers commented on the positive role of national inspections, which they felt helped to improve their performance: 'it keeps us on our toes' (Rachael, Wales1); 'it is good to give you a little shake up' (Tina, Wales2); '[it shows] anybody who isn't up to scratch' (Lisa, England2). At England2, managerial intervention in the teaching process had intensified after the department received two successive '3' ratings (satisfactory) in their Ofsted inspections. Each teacher was required to meet with the vice-principal four times a year during which they had to show their schemes of work and lesson plans:

> He [the vice-principal] wants to see me reflecting on my scheme of work...I have got to reflect on my scheme of work and I've got to reflect on my lesson plans. They also advise you to reflect on your day. (Sarah, teacher, England2)

Teachers spoke of having five formal teaching observations in the previous year. Therefore, while teachers insisted that they had freedom in how they taught, the prescribed nature of assessments, the use of student evaluations, formal observations of teaching, and ongoing course reviews ensured that in practice the teaching process was extensively monitored and controlled.

On the surface, vocational teachers in Norway appear to have less autonomy in relation to their actual teaching methods. The teaching profession has been characterized by an 'anti-authoritarian' or democratic approach, which values relatively egalitarian teacher–pupil relations and learner-centred pedagogy, where teachers are trained to act as a 'guide' or 'facilitator' of student learning (Czerniawski 2013). In line with students' right to receive 'adapted' learning, teachers are expected to agree with each student the approach which works best for them. At one of the schools, teachers felt this approach considerably reduced their discretion.

> The opportunities to choose how to teach are not that good because it is supposed to be the student's choice...they have to come up with the ideas themselves and then we advise them. (Anna, Norway1)

At the other two schools, the teachers interviewed considered the adaptive approach to be largely impractical, arguing that many students lacked both the knowledge and capacity to make informed choices and that it was often necessary for teachers to plan and direct their learning. As one put it:

> they [students] have never been in the hairdressing trade before, how do they know what [content] to choose? We ignore it. (Eva, Norway2)

Their ability to 'ignore' national policies derived from belief in their own professional knowledge, alongside a lack of monitoring and consequences.

As in England and Wales, Norwegian students also evaluated their teachers via student feedback forms submitted to school heads. The information was then fed back to the relevant teacher. Unlike in England and Wales, however, there was no compulsory observation of lessons (although teachers did observe each other), and teachers generally rejected the idea that they were being 'watched' or 'monitored' by 'management'. Issues related to the quality of teaching were largely considered to be the preserve of individual teachers and their teaching teams, with intervention only undertaken when a 'problem' was identified.

In France, teachers have far more freedom in relation to how they teach than what they teach. A teacher explained: 'I am going to conduct the lesson as I want, with the support I want and in the manner I want' (Brigitte, France2). There was no monitoring of teachers by the principal, with individual departments run by a coordinator who had no responsibility for managing staff. 'He [the principal] doesn't intervene in our pedagogy, he trusts us, and . . . as far as I'm concerned it would be fairly badly received' (Nadine, France2). However, a number of teachers pointed to the role of the *academie* inspectorate which was seen to be increasingly prescribing particular teaching methods in line with requirements set out by the Ministry of Education. The introduction of project work which required interdisciplinary working, alongside the requirement to integrate theory and practical work, were felt to be part of a more centralized, directive approach.

The inspectorate was able to influence teaching pedagogy through provision of training and individual teacher inspections. The inspector is likely to visit a teacher every four years, spends around an hour observing a teacher's class, and will follow this up with a lengthy discussion with the teacher, and the allocation of a mark. While some teachers claimed the inspector had no influence on how they taught, others explained how the link to individual evaluations (and their mark) could have an effect. 'She [the inspector] told us clearly that if we didn't work with this new pedagogy, our pedagogy mark would not rise' (Martine, France2). For others, it was more subtle: 'Increasingly we now feel that through inspections there is a way of thinking how to conduct the course; we are more and more directed' (Marie, France1).

Unlike in the other countries, there is no student evaluation of teachers in France. Teachers interviewed simply did not regard this as appropriate given their status as professional experts. Such views reflect French educational philosophy which 'emphasises the authority of the teacher' (Misra 2014). As one teacher remarked, 'I would never ask a pupil what they thought of my course, *on principle*' (Nadine, France2, emphasis added). Another stated that she was 'not against student evaluations' and that she regularly asked pupils what they expected from her, but was also sceptical as they could favour 'cool teachers who don't give too much work' rather than the profession's notion of a 'good teacher' (Brigitte, France2).

To summarize, teachers in England, Wales, and France confront a far more prescriptive curriculum than in Norway. However, in England and Wales, competence-based qualifications and the dominant role of awarding bodies also bring a particularly heavy burden of assessment. In Norway, the requirement to develop local course structures and assessments with few guidelines demands a higher level of skill and knowledge from teachers. Although teachers in England and Wales felt they had freedom over their teaching methods, they are subject to high stakes national inspections of their teaching which, together with the effects of the funding regimes, results in a high level of managerial monitoring of their work. There was, however, little in the way of resistance to these restrictions, and many teachers felt that these types of measures were required to ensure performance. In contrast, French teachers experienced a relatively high level of classroom autonomy and little monitoring of pedagogic practice. There was widespread discussion about, and defence of, teachers' autonomy and the mechanisms through which they felt it was being both extended and eroded. Teachers in Norway have experienced a considerable loosening of curriculum constraints, are not subject to national inspections, and face little managerial interference in their work. One of the central differences across the countries is the pressures on college managers in England and Wales that have resulted from marketization and audit, an area that is considered in the next section.

Governance and Management Systems

In England and Wales, all interviewees referred to the relentless pressure upon colleges to deliver in accordance with the key performance metrics of student recruitment, retention, and certification. As a human resource manager at Wales1 commented, 'It's literally getting the students in, retaining them, and then getting results... the 3Rs—recruitment, retention, results.' National performance benchmarks were said to be constantly increasing with severe penalties for failure. Under-performance could mean the closure of particular courses or departments, or even culminate in the removal of the senior management team. The impact of such pressures varied across the colleges but in all cases resulted in increased levels of bureaucracy and paperwork. England2 had undergone two full Ofsted inspections and two monitoring visits in the space of just two years. On both occasions, the college and department had been graded only 'satisfactory', a process described by the head of hairdressing as 'horrendous'. Teachers were required to provide their head of department with student retention data and undertake extensive follow-ups:

> You're getting it from the college for retention and early warning reports, and from the awarding body itself and having to get in paperwork for the whole of the curriculum. (Cheryl, teacher, England2)

Even at a college judged to be 'outstanding' by Ofsted, teachers felt under pressure:

> If we are not performing and we lose learners then courses will cease and I believe more and more that management... only want success, so the courses where you have got a poor or below benchmark success rate and retention rate, they will remove from the curriculum. (Sharon, England1)

The only department that did not feel this constant pressure was at Wales1 which had just been given a top score in their first inspection for eight years. The college had the advantage of a good location and buoyant applications, while a strict recruitment process and an initial probationary period for students helped to keep retention rates high. Departmental managers enjoyed the process of inspection, seeing it as an 'opportunity to show off'. Feedback was provided to the faculty management on a yearly basis in respect of recruitment and retention targets, and teachers did not feel unduly burdened with paperwork: 'we don't have that much really' (Rachel, Wales1). Teachers' views on the manageability of administrative demands were not shared by departmental managers, however, who complained of endless 'bureaucracy' and the 'constant changes' driven by the Welsh government.

Researchers have drawn attention to the fear and resentment felt by FE teachers in some colleges towards 'punitive performance management' and, in some cases, outright bullying (Mather et al. 2009). While there is no denying that such practices exist, the picture is variable. As noted earlier, there was little evidence of overt opposition to the efforts of managers to monitor teachers' work or, for that matter, the process of external inspection. These findings may reflect the particular colleges selected or the specific occupational group, most of whom had entered the profession relatively recently and had no prior experience of a world without audit and who struggled therefore to envisage any alternative (see also Hodkinson 2008). Nevertheless, concerns were raised that inspections placed too much emphasis on crude performance metrics (retention and results in particular) rather than on the quality of the learning experience. As one department head recounted, this led to intense pressure to pass students who were not always up to the grade:

> It's stressful because the college wants retention to be good and it's all really about 'bums on seats'... I often have difficulty weighing up my standards on whether I pass somebody or not... I try to keep my principles... but it worries me sometimes. (Jan, England2)

Most of the problems experienced were considered to be externally driven by government and awarding bodies, although complaints were also directed at senior college management. A teacher from one college reflected a widely-held view that managers were a 'long time out of teaching' and operated at some distance, such that 'they don't always consider what the teacher does on the ground' (Julie, Wales1). It was clear from the interviews that teachers felt they had little opportunity to influence decisions made by college management. Very few of those interviewed were members of a trade union, and most saw unions as dealing mainly with individual grievances, rather than exerting influence within college decision-making processes.

In Norway, most students attend their local upper secondary school, with funding allocated by the county according to the number of classes at the start of each academic year. School choice and competition for students is relatively limited. The exception is the densely populated capital of Oslo, where several schools offer vocational programmes within commutable distance of each other and schools are able to select students on the basis of their grades from lower secondary education. The research uncovered examples of funding practices in Norway which bore the imprint of NPM. One Norwegian local authority had recently introduced a system, whereby funding was withdrawn according to the number of students who dropped out during each academic year. Norway1 had a high concentration of students with low grades, poor motivation, and behavioural issues, which resulted in a 'drop-out' rate of around 35 per cent. As a result, the school lost the equivalent resources of between ten and twelve teachers that year. Although the local authority also set targets to reduce drop-out, failure to meet the target did not carry any repercussions for college management. As the principal noted, 'We have a sort of New Public Management but there are no consequences'; heads and teachers would not lose their jobs.

The research confirmed that Norwegian teachers have experienced increased demands in terms of paperwork. Teachers referred to the need to monitor student attendance and absenteeism, and to document meetings with students and parents. The Head of Arts and Crafts at Norway2 commented, 'If you go back ten years in Norway... it is very clear that the bureaucracy is much more and time consuming and the reporting is taking the time from their direct contact with each individual student.' When asked about paperwork, the response was mixed. One teacher replied: 'Oh God yes... A lot of feedback that students have got to have' (Eva, Norway2), while another stated that it was 'not that much' (Helga, Norway1). It is particularly striking that at Norway1, despite a challenging student intake, teachers considered levels of paperwork to be reasonable and felt there was little managerial interference with their teaching. Rather their primary concerns revolved around the day-to-day challenges of dealing with students who had complex learning needs and behavioural problems.

There are long-established norms of non-interference in teachers' classroom practice in Norway, with many school principals and teachers sharing a common commitment to the values of 'democratic education' and 'democratic leadership' (Møller et al. 2005). Within the schools, unions played a prominent role. All but one of the teachers interviewed belonged to a trade union and considered that their representatives were actively involved in decisions relating to the organization and management of the school. Regular meetings, fortnightly in the case of Norway1 and Norway2, were held between union representatives and school management. As the Head of Department at Norway1 commented, 'they [the union] have a lot of power and...take part in decisions that affect the school, especially when it comes to salaries'. Referring to an unpopular new system of performance bonuses that had been introduced at the school in the previous year, the unions and the principal had jointly evaluated applications. All those who applied received them leading to an abandonment of the policy the following year.

Head teachers and other senior staff generally regarded discussions with unions as vital for securing consent and effective management, the principal of Norway1 insisting that she wanted 'a strong union rep so that I know what the problems are'. In addition, the less hierarchical relations meant there was more opportunity for debate and discussion. As one teacher commented, 'We have the vice principal, the door is always open to listen to whatever we have to say and it's quite a good relationship, it's not like a hierarchy, where we are here and they are there' (Heidi, Norway3).

In France, student recruitment is undertaken at regional level, with programmes linked to the needs of the local economy. Funding is allocated according to criteria related to course needs and the number of students, with colleges free to bid for additional money to support particular projects. Colleges have a contract of objectives with the *academie* which are very general, for example becoming an 'eco-college' or gaining status as a higher level vocational college (*lycée des metiers*). Failure to meet these carried no penalties for college heads who are appointed by the Ministry. Asked what happens if objectives were not met, the *chef de travaux* (head of works) at France1 replied that it was a matter of 'conscience'. In contrast to the UK and Norway, there are no external targets in relation to pass rates, absenteeism, or drop-out rates. Colleges set their own objectives but these tend to be in terms of where they would like to be for the following year rather than hard targets. As one teacher observed, although there was a general aim to improve pass rates, she had 'never been pressurized' in relation to results:

> I am not a failure if only 80 per cent pass. Because I estimate that only 80 per cent deserve it... for us it is all the more important in the vocational area as the pupils

are going to find themselves on the labour market... it is the reputation of the establishment. (Nadine, France2)

Issues of drop-outs and absenteeism were viewed to be a wider social problem 'that is outside of the establishment [college]' (*chef de travaux*, France1). The *chef de travaux* at France2 argued that exam results reflected the types of students recruited: 'the pupils who quit, it isn't the good students at the top of the class, it is those who are absent and those who cause problems... lack motivation'. Nathalie, a teacher at France3, when asked about targets, commented: 'We don't do the recruitment, so they can't ask us for pass rate targets. We aren't a private company.' Colleges are subject to occasional audits but they are not graded and the process would seem to have little effect on teachers' work. There were some concerns around increased levels of bureaucracy and paperwork, related primarily to the move towards work placements in the initial hairdressing qualification (the CAP) and new requirements for project work, alongside the increased use of consent forms and the ordering of stock and equipment. However, these were not considered to be major issues.

When asked who supervised their work, teachers replied either 'no one' or the *academie* inspectors rather than the college principal or deputies. A *chef de travaux* (France1) stressed that it 'isn't in the culture' to measure teachers' performance. The inspector's mark is important for individual teachers and their pay progression but, as one inspector explained, 'before it was more on the sanction-evaluation, while today we try to be on the advice-evaluation... It is very rare to lower a mark.' Even for teachers with major problems, lowering marks had to follow a strict procedure, and ultimately for those who were civil servants, 'nothing' could be done as they had lifetime employment. A plan of training could be put forward but ultimately the teacher does not have to follow it.

Although principals did not interfere directly in teachers' work, they could still affect their working lives through the distribution of resources, including funding for training and time off, the allocation of administrative duties, the financing of projects, and the general organization of student life. Colleges are hierarchical, with principals having considerable power in these areas. In the colleges visited, principals at France1 and France2 were said to be 'open' to staff involvement in decision-making or at least 'listened' to them, but at France3 teachers were frustrated that their requests were ignored. As one explained, 'if we ask for something, we have to wait ten years to have it!' (Agnes). Another spoke of wasting time and energy having to 'fight for things that other colleges naturally have' (Jocelyne). Teachers complained of having only one functional salon, not being released for any training, and not having the correct equipment and products.

There was far more awareness among the teachers of union activities in schools than in England and Wales, and the teachers generally saw unions as important. Unions were active in France2 and France3, where their role related primarily to individual grievances and organizing strike action against national policies. However, at France3, there had been a one-day strike protesting at student violence and demanding action from the college principal. While such action was not uncommon, there was, nevertheless, a feeling among teachers that unions had lost power and influence.

To summarize, French teachers experienced the lowest levels of managerial monitoring and surveillance, with minimal interference in teachers' classroom practice. In Norway, teachers felt they were still largely trusted to get on with their job, with relatively little intervention from heads or other senior staff, although concerns over drop-out rates were increasing levels of student monitoring and paperwork. By contrast, teachers in England and Wales face considerable pressure to reach targets, with the threat of job losses if they are not successful which can extend to the removal of the senior management team if the college is deemed to be failing. The result of introducing the market into these colleges, together with extensive centralized controls and auditing, has been a proliferation in paperwork, monitoring, and evaluation that far exceeds that in Norway and France.

Scope for Teacher-Led Innovation and Improvement

How do these different systems impact upon teachers' experience of work and their ability to contribute to the performance of the IVET system? Writing in relation to FE in England, Coffield (2008) argues that improving the quality of teaching and learning is more likely to come about through gradual experimentation and the fostering of vibrant 'teacher learning communities' than through 'top-down' performance management systems which may have negative, unintended consequences. He emphasizes the importance of trust, collaboration, research-informed practice, and 'bottom-up' innovation. Lipowski et al. (2011: 689) also observe that 'teacher cooperation in professional learning communities helps establish a positive environment and to enhance understanding of professional teaching'. To do this effectively, teachers need meaningful continuing professional development (CPD) as well as sufficient time and space to explore the research base, share ideas, and try out new innovative approaches to pedagogy and assessment.[4]

In England and Wales, there was only one college where teachers were generally positive about their environment and the opportunities they had

---

[4] A comparison of the opportunities available to vocational teachers to access CPD in the case study countries has been published elsewhere and will not be repeated here (see Lloyd and Payne 2012; Larré et al. 2013).

to share ideas with each other. The department was highly successful and was located in a high performing Welsh college (Wales1), with fairly limited concerns over discipline or drop-out numbers. Teachers spoke of a departmental culture that encouraged the exchange of ideas and where there was time available to reflect on, and improve, teaching provision. The other three colleges painted a much bleaker picture due to the pressures of audit and mounting paperwork. At Wales2 and England2 in particular, many felt that if they had more time it would not only improve their work–life balance but also enable better preparation of teaching and more space to share ideas, which many saw as important for quality. Indeed, there were notable tensions between a belief that inspections and monitoring were inevitable and necessary to improve performance and a feeling that these same processes took time away from vital parts of the job.

> I still think if you take half the paperwork away there is obviously going to be improvement for the quality of teaching because you can have more impact, more input in the student. (Donna, teacher, Wales2)

> What everybody lacks is the time...You sit down and talk to some of them [teachers] for a little while and you get these amazing ideas coming out and that's what they need, the time together to be able to thrash ideas out, inspire each other. (Head of department, England1)

In the three colleges, there was no scheduled time provided to reflect on teaching. As a result, teachers worked extra hours and adopted a more individualized or informal approach to development:

> It's down to the individuals...most of the people that work here are very professional and do put themselves forward to do things, but I wouldn't say it comes from the top, there's nobody sort of encouraging us to do that. (Sharon, teacher, England1)

Many of these teachers struggled to manage the job within their contracted working time, engaging in 'underground working' (James and Diment 2003), that is, working beyond their official contracts in order to provide students with a positive learning experience. As one put it, 'my home life gets squeezed because I won't let things slip' (Tina, Wales2). Working beyond contracted hours was a particular problem for casual, hourly-paid lecturers who are only paid for the hours they teach and are often not 'around' to participate in team discussions. When preparation and marking time were taken into consideration, one part-time teacher estimated she was putting in around double her contracted hours (Debbie, Wales2). The consequences of a casualized workforce were also experienced by full-timers who were required to take on more administrative responsibilities.

In Norway, the majority of teachers interviewed felt that the job could, for the most part, be managed within their contracted hours. At all schools, time was made available each week for the staff to meet and discuss pedagogic issues. The response of teachers to these meetings was rather mixed. At Norway1 and Norway2, teachers found that either they focused on the problems of individual students or the meetings were disrupted by other demands.

> We do have some time in between that is just for us but then usually either she has got to go to a meeting with a parent or something or she has got something going somewhere... we are never together as there is always something else going on. So you see that is a bit difficult. (Eva, Norway2)

At Norway1, teachers stated that there was little encouragement from the school management to consider pedagogic issues as a group and that they tended to focus on the immediate problems presented by poor student motivation and behaviour. At Norway2, teachers were more active when it came to sharing ideas with each other.

> I think that we are looking at new ways of doing things quite a lot and then we just talk together and say 'I have got an idea, let's try that' and we do it. (Anya, Norway2)

Norway3 provided an example of a particularly vibrant department. Weekly meetings were held with the team setting their own agenda and using the opportunity to 'share experiences and ideas and developments' (Kristine, Norway3). In addition, once a week one person from each team across the school, a specially trained coach, and the vice-principal met to explore ways of providing a better education. The staff felt there was enough time to discuss ideas with each other and that they were 'always in each other's classrooms'. There were also opportunities for the two teachers who were undertaking part-time Master's degrees to share their experiences with colleagues:

> Yes, the university gives me ideas and when Linda is at her course at the university she gets ideas, and when Kristine is she gets her ideas and together we put some of them out, and we give each other ideas. (Heidi, Norway 3)

These views echo the work of Czerniawski (2013: 394–5) who found that 'collaborative learning... was particularly prevalent' among Norwegian school teachers, in part because of formalized time assigned to meetings for such activities but also due to teachers generating such opportunities themselves as they were not constrained by a prescriptive curriculum.

In France, hairdressing departments held regular team meetings, but again these were concerned predominantly with coordination issues, the organization of teaching and projects rather than pedagogic issues. Whilst informal discussions existed, there was no regular dedicated time for these activities.

> When we are on a course, we have discussions among ourselves, or with colleagues you see from time to time... it's informal. (Corinne, France1)
>
> When you ask colleagues to discuss this or that issue, it is yes, yes, yes we will see, then we don't see. I have ended by working with my colleague X, we work well together and the pupils feel that but not with all my colleagues. (Martine, France2)

There was the suggestion of a more individualist teaching culture in France, with some teachers said to be quite protective of their own classroom. Referring to peer observation, one teacher commented: 'the French take it very badly, they can have a horror of being judged... and many don't want it' (Brigitte, France2). Some, however, spoke of how they had benefited from going into the classes of colleagues teaching related subjects, such as chemistry, biology, and English, even if the opportunities to do so were fewer than they would have liked. As with many of the schools and colleges in other countries, teachers complained of the lack of time available for these kinds of activities.

Although teachers in France had the shortest teaching hours of the countries in this study, many stated that that they worked well beyond their contracted hours, in some instances more than 45 or 50 hours a week. Teachers felt that this was necessary to complete preparation and marking as well as develop project work:

> I wait for my children to go to bed and then work. Sometimes I start at 9.30 p.m. and finish at 1 or 2 in the morning... By the end of the week I am exhausted. (Martine, France2)
>
> I have to be in front of the class... I attend 99 per cent of meetings. I must have some projects. What do I sacrifice? Preparation? Evaluation of students' work? This weekend I will be marking assignments. My husband says 'stop'. What can I do? (Corinne, France1)

There were many common elements in the experience of teachers across the four countries. Teaching is a complex and challenging job that can be stressful as well as hugely rewarding. Many spoke at length of the personal fulfilment they derived from helping individuals to grow in confidence and develop as people and learners, and in contributing to the future of their craft. Dealing with challenging students with motivational and behavioural problems is something that teachers in all of these countries have to deal with but which varies significantly between schools according to their intake. In England, Wales, and Norway, these pressures were particularly pronounced in schools or colleges that tended to draw more students from lower socio-economic groups (Wales2, England1&2, and Norway1). The worst affected by poor student behaviour and violence were France1 and France3. It was reported that a quarter of teachers were absent due to occupational ill-health at France1, placing additional strain on other staff. The effects across the countries were generally considered to be less pronounced for those teaching popular vocational programmes, such as hairdressing, compared to the more challenging task of delivering 'general subjects' to vocational learners.

Discussion and Conclusions

There are several common strands running through the experiences of vocational teachers in this study—the increasingly challenging nature of many young people, mounting paperwork, the satisfaction derived from helping learners to progress, and weariness with policy change. Notwithstanding such apparent similarities, as well as some variation between individual schools, colleges, and departments, the research highlights significant differences in vocational teachers' work across countries.

Vocational teachers in France and Norway are required to have longer professional experience as well as higher level of vocational and teacher qualifications than their counterparts in England and Wales. FE colleges in England and Wales pursue a flexible approach to recruitment in the context of widespread casualization, while France and Norway adopt a more 'professionalized model', based on stricter regulation (Grollmann and Rauner 2007). Consequently, vocational teachers in France and Norway have a stronger knowledge base on which to ground their professional status. The study also indicates that vocational teachers in Norway and France have managed to retain higher levels of autonomy and control over their work.

In England and Wales, a system subject to marketization and increasing state control, together with a highly prescriptive curriculum, has served to reduce teachers' autonomy and subject them to increasing 'performativity' demands. The result has been an intensification of work pressures and high levels of bureaucracy and paperwork which impinge upon the process of teaching and learning. In both countries, incorporation in 1992 has left an enduring legacy which has shaped similar outcomes at local level, despite differences in the political and policy process. While NPM has also been applied in the compulsory schooling sectors, the fragmented nature of the occupational group and relatively weak unions may partly explain why these types of reforms went further in FE.

In England, teacher unions have no role in national policy-making in a country where notions of social partnership are very weak and the state has been reluctant to cede control over skills policy. Similarly, unions' ability to influence managerial decisions is limited, depending on the financial position of the college, management orientations, and the capacity to mobilize members. Since 2010 UK governments have favoured a training market with more funding flowing through employers in the context of austerity and deep cuts to the FE sector which adds to the pressure on colleges to deliver 'more with less' (Simmons 2013). While the political and policy process in Wales is somewhat more inclusive of teacher professionals and unions, funding formulas determined by the UK government mean that FE teachers are coming under similar pressures.

In Norway, while recent decades have seen education increasingly expected to serve the goal of economic competitiveness, it nevertheless remains heavily imprinted by the country's social democratic welfare state tradition, with its commitment to equality, comprehensiveness, and strong citizenship rights. Marketization remains limited, and while there are moves towards greater accountability and quality auditing, they are modest in comparison with England and Wales. Undoubtedly, head teachers experience growing tensions between these new demands and a tradition of democratic management, but these are hardly comparable to the pressures and tensions experienced by college managers in England and Wales.

Values, cultures, and traditions clearly play an important role, but so too does power. Norwegian teachers are strongly unionized, and possess a developed 'collective professional identity' (Helgøy and Homme 2007). Reflecting the country's social partnership tradition, teacher professionals in Norway are actively involved in national policy-making, and there are strong cooperative and participatory cultures at school level. It is questionable whether political and social actors could easily break with such a model, even if deemed desirable (Bach and Bordogna 2011). Pressure from coalitions of public sector unions was a major factor in why centre-left governments were forced to backtrack on NPM-type reforms in education and health (Bieler 2012). While union influence is stronger when left governments are in power, a multi-party, consensus-oriented political system, geared towards coalition-building, militates against radical policy shifts (Helgøy and Homme 2006). This does not mean that pressures to adopt NPM measures have disappeared, and future outcomes will depend upon the ability of all public sector unions to resist changes in this direction.

In France, vocational education is similarly lodged within a national competitiveness and social inclusion agenda, although, as with Norway, there is an enduring focus on education for citizenship which includes providing a strong core of general education to those on vocational programmes. Marketization of public services has been rejected by successive governments, which remains reliant on 'the traditional strength of the French administrative tradition' (Bordogna and Neri 2011: 2328). Hierarchy and rules are central to this process, which includes the position of teachers as civil servants and professional experts with lifetime employment. Reforms to teaching are ongoing but unlike the position in England and Wales, unions have involvement in various committees set up for social dialogue. While some changes are forced through, even in the face of sustained mobilization by unions, there is a more deliberative process because of these formalized systems and the ability of unions to organize strike action.

The centralized structure of French education, particularly in relation to the curriculum, ensures that teachers are constrained to a greater extent than in Norwegian schools, but their professional status and rules regarding their management ensure that they retain considerably more autonomy than in England and Wales. Nevertheless, the lack of union engagement with issues such as work intensity can potentially be seen as a factor in long working hours. The national approach has been to win additional (compulsory) paid overtime hours rather than to increase the number of teachers. Weaknesses in workplace organization can also leave teachers powerless in the face of college principals' unilateral decision-making over issues such as resources, training, and student behavioural policies. Pressure on the sector continues through a combination of increased student participation and a tightening of resources.

What then of performance? While there is a broad consensus that teachers have a key role to play, the question is whether improvements in teaching quality are best achieved through marketization and audit, or by providing teachers with the time, scope, and resources to collaboratively improve their own practice. The study found examples of teachers in all of these countries who sought to be creative in their approach to teaching and who looked to share ideas with like-minded colleagues, on a largely informal basis. In England and Wales, this space was all too often hemmed in, however, by pressures of audit, heavy workloads, and time constraints. An exploratory study by Ertl and Kremer (2010) also found that discussions around innovative teaching were more frequent in Germany where the policy process and qualification structures are relatively stable. Opportunities for systematic and structured reflection are not common in any of the four countries, suggesting that the development of vibrant teacher learning communities remains challenging in all contexts. In terms of the potential for teacher-led innovation, the Norwegian system has the advantage of providing teachers with more time, a teaching culture that is less individualistic and more collegiate than in France, and a curriculum that affords teachers greater flexibility. Time, of course, is a necessary but not sufficient condition for innovation, which still requires commitment on the part of teachers and their teams as well as resources, meaningful and targeted CPD, knowledge of the research base, and effective support and leadership (Coffield 2008).

None of these systems are static and all face pressures of various kinds. Both Norway and France highlight the possibility of a way of managing public service professionals that, unlike in England and Wales, does not rely on marketization and extensive monitoring and control. The explanation for these differences would seem to reside in different state traditions, the political process, and the relative power wielded by teacher professionals and their unions, issues which are taken up in the concluding chapter of this book.

6

Regulating the Middle

Fitness Instructors

Introduction

In comparing service sector jobs across countries, this chapter focuses on what might be classified as an 'intermediate' job, namely that of fitness instructor. In the UK and USA, the idea of the 'hourglass' economy, or the hollowing out of the 'middle', has gained currency following the widespread loss of skilled manufacturing jobs and the subsequent growth in occupations at the top and bottom of the labour market (Nolan 2001; Goos and Manning 2007; Kalleberg 2011). However, as Anderson (2009) notes in relation to the UK, associate professional and technical jobs have emerged or expanded to fill much of this middle. The difficulty is that this occupational category is very broad, including lab technicians, artists, youth workers, police officers, and estate agents (to name only a few), with contrasting levels of qualification as well as widely varying skill demands.

Drawing on the analytical framework developed in Chapter 3, we might expect middle-level jobs in Norway to have broader job design and higher task discretion and skill content than their equivalents in the UK and France. However, comparative research on middle-level *service* sector jobs is limited, with earlier studies concentrated on intermediate jobs in manufacturing. Service sector jobs, particularly in the private sector, are likely to vary much more in terms of trade union organization than those in manufacturing, while in new sectors, such as the fitness industry, there is the question of how far they are integrated into existing institutional structures. Are these jobs better in Norway? Moreover, what can a comparative study of fitness instructors tell us about the role played by national institutions and sector dynamics in shaping work organization? What light can it shed on the role of trade unions at national, sector, and workplace level?

As noted in Chapter 3, there is the possibility that well-organized groups of workers with a strong skills base may, under certain conditions, be able to exert influence over work organization and push for more broadly designed jobs. However, in contrast to many skilled jobs in manufacturing, which have typically been obtained through apprenticeships or other forms of extended vocational training, middle jobs in the service sector are not necessarily associated with particular qualification levels or length of training. There are nevertheless examples of intermediate jobs, such as nurse in the UK and kindergarten worker in Norway, that have shifted to 'professional' or 'graduate status' with associated increases in pay through concerted effort on the part of their trade unions and help from the state. An important research question is what role qualifications and their regulation *might* play in raising workers' skills and status, and the impact that this might have on work organization, the opportunities to use skills within the job, and wider aspects of job quality.

The job of fitness instructor offers a good opportunity to consider these issues. The fitness industry is relatively new, having emerged over the last thirty years at a time when institutional structures of collective organization and education and training have been in considerable flux. Classified by the ISCO[1] as an associate professional occupation, instructors are responsible for providing advice and guidance to customers within a gym environment. However, there are a range of possibilities in terms of how the job might be designed, from a relatively skilled job providing ongoing advice and individual training programmes to those with major health problems or elite athletes to a fairly routine service function passing on basic health and safety rules, and meeting and greeting customers. Qualification regulations of fitness instructors also vary substantially across the UK, Norway, and France. France is a country well-known for its detailed labour market regulations, including those governing qualifications requirements for entry to particular jobs, and fitness instructor is no exception.

The chapter begins with a discussion of the factors shaping intermediate jobs and asks what role 'occupational licensing' might play in raising skill levels and service quality. Having outlined the research methods, a brief background is provided to the fitness industry in each country along with their key industrial relations institutions. The chapter then compares national approaches to fitness instructor education and training, before examining the organization of work itself. Two key aspects of work organization are considered: first, the scope and design of the fitness instructor role and, second, how instructors are monitored and controlled. Finally, consideration is given to broader aspects of job quality and the relationship between skills and performance.

---

[1] International Standard Classification of Occupations.

Intermediate Jobs

While there is no generally agreed definition of an intermediate occupation (Elias and Bynner 1997), it is typically referred to as the '"layer" between semi and unskilled employees and the managerial and professional layer' (Rolfe et al. 1994: 11). Much of the research in relation to this group has been on craft and trade apprenticeships, with a number of international studies comparing issues such as the breadth and depth of the qualifications undertaken and, to a lesser extent, the job role (see Clarke 2011 for one of the few recent studies). Job quality in these areas has often been linked to labour market power, reflecting either labour shortages or trade union organization, and the collective influence of workers on the scope and nature of the job tasks.

The strength of the German apprenticeship system in creating intermediate skills, allied to forms of work organization and product market strategies which rely on these skills, has attracted considerable commentary (Streeck 1992; Culpepper and Finegold 1999). The record of French and UK organizations is far less impressive. Indeed, intermediate vocational skills have long been regarded as a major weakness of both these systems. There was evidence of a greater segmentation of skills in the UK even prior to the mass expansion of higher education in the 1990s. Research has uncovered a preference for graduates, alongside semi-skilled workers, in parts of manufacturing (e.g. Mason and Wagner 1994) as well as in other areas such as banking (Quack et al. 1995). The spread of jobs makes it difficult to generalize, but evidence from both France and the UK indicates further moves towards the 'graduatization' of many intermediate level jobs, particularly in the service sector, despite seemingly little change in their knowledge and skill requirements (Mason 2002; Nauze-Fichet and Tomasini 2002; James et al. 2013).

Countries with a strong apprenticeship system that covers much of the service sector, as well as manufacturing, for example Norway and Germany, usually find it easier to delineate middle jobs from high- and low-skilled jobs. These middle jobs normally require an apprenticeship and are typically linked to 'skilled worker' status and higher pay through recognition within collective bargaining agreements. In the UK, the regulation of qualifications, particularly for this middle layer, remains rare compared with Germany, the Nordics, France, and even the USA. The effect of 'occupational licensing' or 'licence-to-practise', where qualifications are used to regulate entry to a trade or profession, has rarely been studied outside the USA. The research findings, which are limited in number and overwhelmingly based on US professional workers, suggest that licensing is generally associated with higher wages, lower employment, increased prices, and little difference in service quality (Forth et al. 2011). UK studies of jobs with relatively low qualification requirements—care work, childcare, security guards—find limited impact on pay, skills, or employment

Skills in the Age of Over-Qualification

(Fernie 2011; Gospel and Lewis 2011). However, the research base is at present limited in relation to intermediate jobs and has little to say about the impact on skill use and the organization of work.

Researching the Fitness Industry

The evidence in this chapter is based on research conducted at sector level and in workplaces in the UK, France, and Norway (see Appendix 1).[2] Interviews were held with providers of fitness instructor qualifications in the three countries, and in the UK with senior officials of the sector skills council and the qualification regulator, in Norway with representatives of the main employers' associations, and in France with a key civil servant in the Sports Ministry and a previous head of the employers' association. The work practices and management of instructors were examined through case studies of individual gyms (see Table 6.1). Day visits were made to four gyms in the UK, two in the private sector (UKgym1, UKgym2) and two in the public sector (UK-LA1, UK-LA2). In Norway, research was conducted in three gyms comprising a large chain (Ngym1), two sites from a smaller chain (Ngym2), and a not-for-profit gym, based in a university (Ngym3). In France, six gyms were included reflecting the smaller size of the organizations. These included two sites from a larger chain (Fgym1), two regional chains (Fgym2 and Fgym3), two independents (Fgym4 and Fgym5), and a US-based franchise (Fgym6). In each case,

Table 6.1. Characteristics of case study gyms

	Ownership	Market position	Typical membership fee	Location of gym(s)
UKgym1	Large chain	Mid/high	£65	Medium city
UKgym2	Large chain	Low/mid	£40	Large city
UK-LA1	Local authority	Low	£37	Small town
UK-LA2	Local authority run by charitable trust	Low	£36	Small city
Ngym1	Large chain	Mid/high	550 NOK (£54)	Oslo
Ngym2	Small chain	Low/mid	320 NOK (£31)	Oslo
Ngym3	Quasi-public	Mid	410 NOK (£40)	Oslo
Fgym1	Large chain	Mid/high	€82/104 (£66/£100)	Paris
Fgym2	Regional chain	Mid	€50 (£40)	Large city
Fgym3	Regional chain	Low/mid	€42 (£34)	Large city
Fgym4	Independent	Low	€44 (£35)	Large city
Fgym5	Independent	High	per session	Large city
Fgym6	US-franchise	Low/mid	€39 (£31)	Large city

Note: FGym1 included two gyms, one targeted at the mid-market, one at the higher end.

[2] Pseudonyms are used for the gyms and those interviewed, where relevant.

semi-structured interviews were undertaken with the gym manager, fitness instructors, and, where they existed, gym supervisor and personal trainers. The fieldwork took place between 2009 and 2011. In total, sixty-four people were interviewed, including twenty-nine instructors and personal trainers.

Developments in the Fitness Industry

The fitness industry took off in the USA in the 1970s as a scattering of small gyms catering for weight-lifting and body builders was rapidly transformed into a major industry with broad consumer appeal. The UK industry followed closely behind, with substantial development from the early 1980s, while in Norway and France it would be another decade before the industry developed in earnest. Expansion of the industry in most countries involved the large-scale building of new gyms, alongside a process of consolidation as larger companies swallowed up many of the independents and smaller chains. The subsequent slowdown in the industry from the early 2000s, particularly in the UK, led to a number of these large companies failing and a further wave of mergers and acquisitions. The sector, however, remains predominantly a domestic one, with a limited role played by multinational companies, typified by the extension of branded chains across borders to close neighbours, for example from the UK to Ireland, and Sweden to Norway.

Table 6.2 outlines some of the key features of the industry in the three countries. The UK and Norway have similar levels of membership, although the structure is quite different. The UK is dominated by a number of large fitness chains, such as David Lloyds and Fitness First, which have over fifty clubs each and have largely squeezed out the independent sector. Alongside these companies there exists substantial public sector provision through local

Table 6.2. Key features of the fitness industry

	UK	Norway	France
Turnover	£3,800m	£320m	£700–1,000m
Percentage membership	12	12	5.6
Employment	51,500	7,000	15–18,000
Fitness instructors	28, 000	NA	NA
Number of gyms	5,660	475	3,295
Structure	Private (60%): 7 large chains (50+ clubs) Public sector (40%)	Private: 2 medium-sized chains (40%), small chains and independents Voluntary gyms (10%)	Private: 1 medium-sized chain, small chains, independents

Note: NA = not available.
Source: Mintel (2011a); IHRSA (2011); Kvarud Analyse (2011); Sports.gouv.fr (2012).

authority-run leisure centres that account for around 40 per cent of total gym membership (SkillsActive 2010: 14). By contrast, Norway and France have no similar types of publicly-run gyms. Over the years, public provision in the UK has been increasingly managed through a process of contracting out to a range of profit and not-for-profit organizations.

In Norway, the sector has two large private chains, SATS and Elixia, which dominate a market otherwise comprised of small chains, independents, and voluntary-run gyms (Steen Johnsen and Kirkegaard 2010). In France, gym membership rates are considerably lower and the sector highly fragmented. There is only one medium-sized company—Club Med Gym—alongside a range of small local chains, independents, and a growing number of franchise operations (some French, others foreign owned). It is estimated that 90 per cent of clubs are very small firms (Viallon et al. 2003). The industry view is that it is very difficult for larger chains to be successful outside of Paris. There is also a high rate of company closure as many individuals attempt to set up gyms with inadequate levels of capital (Perez 2009).

As well as differences in organizational structure, there is a context of national-based attitudes towards health and fitness. The UK is described as having 'Anglo-Saxon' private clubs with a focus on physical fitness. However, public sector provision is different, being more aligned to the 'public health agenda' concerned with combating obesity and sedentary lifestyles. Norwegians, on the whole, are more physically active but are said to be reluctant to engage in indoor gym activity, partly due to the popularity of outdoor sports and a suspicion towards private companies. Many sporting activities are provided by voluntary organizations funded by the state. Gyms focus predominantly on those who are already active and membership prices are relatively low compared to the high cost of living (see Table 6.1). In contrast, there is the suggestion that the 'French' are really not that interested in physical fitness, particularly outside of Paris (Laurent 2010), with group exercise classes said to be far more popular than individual work outs.

The last decade has witnessed, particularly in Norway and the UK, an intensification of competition in the sector due to over-expansion and an influx of low-cost providers. UK industry reports indicate that since the financial crisis of 2008, few new sites have opened, with organizations increasingly focused on maximizing revenue from existing clubs and members (Mintel 2009). Private sector growth is also sluggish in Norway, resulting in 'aggressive competition and excess capacity' in the sector (SATS 2010: 29). While France never experienced the rapid expansion of the other two countries, low-cost entrants, such as franchises, along with 'instructor-free' and even 'staff-free' gyms, are placing downward pressure on prices.

The fitness market, however, is highly differentiated in terms of price and services provided. The premium sector, with the highest membership fees, focuses on 'exclusivity', offering the latest equipment, swimming pools, racquets, saunas, etc., a high staff-to-member ratio and the comfort of towels, toiletries, and high-quality fixtures and fittings. The low-cost end consists of a range of providers, including the UK public leisure centre, where the equipment may be of variable quality, the gym small, and the amenities and décor fairly basic but access to gym instructors is contained in the price. These exist alongside the 'mass discounters' with the latest equipment but few 'frills' and virtually no guidance from instructors. There are also a number of small independents with limited equipment, shabby premises, and basic changing facilities. In between, on different points of this quality–cost continuum, are a range of other providers that include franchises, hotel gyms, and workplace gyms. Competition is also localized as distance to a gym is a major factor in membership decisions.

Collective Organization

Collective organization across the three countries is generally weak in relation to both employers' associations and trade unions. Rather unusually for the UK, employers were relatively quick to organize. The Fitness Industry Association (FIA) was established in 1991 and represents around a third of operators in both the public and private sector. As is typical in the UK, it acts mainly as a lobby group and has no role in collective bargaining or in advising over industrial relations issues (see Chapter 4). It does, however, have a major focus on the training and qualifications of instructors, where it has worked closely with the sector skills council, SkillsActive. For instructors, there is a lack of collective voice within the industry and very few appear to be union members. There is no longer a union representative on the board of SkillsActive, nor is there any input (union or otherwise) on the various committees that oversee the qualifications and regulation of instructors.

For those working in the private sector, there is no evidence of any collective bargaining. In the public sector, however, instructors are normally covered by national collective bargaining for local authority workers (Perkins and White 2010), although many of those working for contracted-out operators are outside these agreements. Since 2007, there has been a national pay spine, with the allocation of jobs to the spine decided locally. Instructor pay can, therefore, vary quite substantially depending on how the job has been evaluated, as can entitlement to unsocial hours payments. In the private sector, pay rates are very low; instructors are paid at or slightly above the minimum wage and receive no supplements for weekend working or unsocial hours. Pay is generally higher in the public sector, where instructors also receive other benefits derived from collective bargaining, such as enhanced rates of holidays, sick leave, maternity pay, and pensions.

In Norway, the core features of the national model, notably strong employer and trade union organization, are not reflected in the fitness industry. Norges Treningssenterforbund was established in the early 1980s to promote the interests of commercial fitness clubs. It covered only about a quarter of the market and appeared to have little influence and no role in collective bargaining. It was not until 2010 that the 'big two', SATS and Elixia, joined with this organization to form Treningsforbundet to act as a lobby group and raise professional standards in the industry. The following year it affiliated to HSH (now called VIRKE), the second biggest employer federation in Norway.

Data on trade union membership are not available, but interviews with industry stakeholders suggest it is very low. A sectoral collective agreement, however, was negotiated between NHO and LO in 2010 which provides a minimum pay rate of NOK 114.15 per hour for a new entrant, rising to NOK 126.47 for someone with four years in the same company. These rates are low by Norwegian standards; for example, the legal minimum in cleaning, agreed in 2011, was NOK 151.67. Indeed, fitness instructor pay is similar to that of a café worker (see Chapter 7). Some clubs, notably Elixia, have signed workplace collective agreements with LO, although coverage remains limited, and there is some indication of resistance from management (Ringerikes Blad 2009). One of the reasons for the difficulty in organizing employees is that many instructors work part-time, and a high proportion are students who see the job as temporary. In common with the UK, but rather uncharacteristically for Norway, there are no institutionalized channels for employee voice within the sector or within training organizations.

In France, the fitness industry conforms to the national picture of weak workplace unions and fragmented employers. In 1994, an employers' organization, the National Union of Facility Operators and Sports Services (Syndicat National des Exploitants d'installations des Service Sportifs [SNEISS]) was created to represent commercial fitness operators and was instrumental in the development of new training programmes specifically for fitness instructors (Viallon et al. 2003). This organization has since collapsed and been replaced by Union Patronale Fitness Bien être et Santé (UPFB), which claims 300 members and is seeking to take the industry out of the sports collective agreement and into a more specific active leisure sector agreement which they hope will be more favourable to employers.

Unions are active in the sector but workplace organization appears confined to the largest fitness group, Club Med Gym, where there is a company collective agreement. There is some evidence of company-level works councils in the sector but generally union membership is extremely low, even by French standards. Since 2010, all gyms have been covered by the sports industry collective agreement, which sets down detailed employment conditions and minimum pay rates according to job categories based on skills and responsibilities. There is

Table 6.3. Industrial relations institutions and fitness instructor pay

	UK	Norway	France
Employer organizations	Active (not collective bargaining)	Recently formed	Weak, collapsed
Workplace unions	Weak	Weak	Weak
Collective agreements	Public sector only	Some companies	Industry-wide Some companies
Pay levels (typical pay in the wage distribution)	Bottom 10–30%	Bottom 25%	Bottom 20–40%

no specific level for an instructor, although the job could be argued to be at least at the level of 'Technician A', affording a pay rate of the minimum wage (SMIC) + 18.23 per cent, equivalent to 11.11 euros in 2012. Despite the requirement to have a national qualification to undertake the job, the position is generally seen as being low paid. Unions have representation on a large number of bodies related to the broader sector, such as the commission on qualifications and training. These bodies are dominated by professional sports organizations and individual sports federations, with the fitness industry a marginal player.

As summarized in Table 6.3, collective bargaining covers all instructors in France, and nearly all of those working in the public sector in the UK. These institutions, however, are not specifically designed for the industry, but are long-standing arrangements that cover a broader sector, i.e. sports and local authority employees. The fitness employers' associations have little or no input into these bodies, while instructors lack representation of their specific occupational interests. In Norway, although there has been a move to develop new institutions for the fitness industry, there has been little progress. Across the countries, there are a number of common industry features: low levels of unionization, the weakness of employees' collective voice, and pay levels which are typically in the bottom third of the pay distribution.

Fitness Instructor Education and Training

This section outlines approaches to skill formation used in each country, examines their appropriateness for the job, and considers the structure of labour supply. Table 6.4 identifies the typical minimum qualifications in the three countries.

In the UK, although there is no statutory qualification requirement to be a fitness instructor, minimum standards developed by the industry have been in place for more than a decade and are widely followed. Concerns about

Table 6.4. Qualification and training provision for fitness instructors

	France		UK	Norway
Qualification type	BPJEPS	DEUST	Level 2 REPS	University module/ private course
Internal equivalence	BAC Prof	BAC+2	5 A–C GCSEs	–
Contact hours	600	1,200	60–120	90–130
Work placement hours	374	400	0	0
EQF level	4	5	3	University: 10 ECTS (degree level)
Typical recruits	Early 20s		Young	Part-time students
	Older career change		Older career change	Gap year young
				Ex-elite athletes

Note: EQF is the European Qualifications Framework; ECTS is the European Credit Transfer and Accumulation System.

'cowboy' operators and media coverage of poorly trained instructors risking consumers' lives, combined with a confusing plethora of entry routes and qualifications, led the FIA and the industry training organization to develop a Register of Exercise Professionals (REPs). The aim was to raise the professional status of fitness instructors by verifying that qualifications met approved industry standards. The Register is organized into skill levels: 'level two fitness instructor', 'level three personal trainer', and 'level four exercise referral', each of which aligns with various qualifications. There are multiple entry routes into each of these levels alongside many different types of qualifications and awarding bodies, typical of the UK's broader approach to VET (see Chapter 4). A level two qualification, for example, could be obtained through a ten-day intensive private training programme, an in-work NVQ with associated self-study, or a one-year full-time diploma undertaken in an FE college. Many instructors have level three qualifications, which can be completed in as little as nine weeks of full-time study. Other entrants include those with university degrees in areas such as sports science or health club management, who often follow this up with a level two fitness qualification that is recognized by the REP.

Despite the introduction of the REP, there remains considerable debate around the level of qualification required to be an instructor. Concerns have been raised that entry standards are insufficient for the demands of the role and are at odds with efforts to raise the professional status of instructors. The overwhelming view from managers and instructors interviewed in this study was that level two is 'entry level'. If the job had been designed to include only tasks at this level, then there was not felt to be a problem. As one manager explained, 'I just want someone who is going to have a smile on their face, who can talk to people' (manager, UKgym1). In practice, however, job roles were typically more complex. A survey undertaken by SkillsActive/REPS/FIA (2008: 16), for example, found that 'most fitness instructors are expected to deal with most clients who enter the gym, including special populations'.

These include those with a variety of health issues, such as back pain or cardiovascular problems, and others seeking nutritional advice, for which instructors may not be sufficiently qualified or trained. The higher level three qualifications, which cover nutrition but not 'special groups', were viewed positively in the main by both managers and instructors. However, some concerns were raised about the limited theoretical content and low standards, such that 'nobody ever fails it' (Jamie, fitness instructor, UK-LA1). One general manager (UK-LA2) felt that ideally all instructors should be at level four, as one in four members of local authority gyms have 'high risk issues'.

Fitness and sports-related courses are extremely popular and are provided across most colleges and universities, as well as by a range of private providers. The result is that there are a large number of would-be entrants hoping to find jobs in what is still a relatively small field. Recruitment of qualified applicants is not a problem in the industry, but 'job readiness' is a common concern among both employers and instructors. High levels of turnover are characteristic of a sector which draws predominantly on young people leaving education, although it also attracts older workers seeking a career change. One survey indicated that just under a quarter of fitness instructors had been in the industry for less than a year (SkillsActive 2008: 21).

In Norway, there is no apprenticeship available for fitness instructors nor is there any regulation of their qualification requirements. Since 2005, the Academy for Personal Training (AFPT) has provided short courses for fitness instructors and personal trainers, effectively setting its own qualifications, curriculum, and standards. Courses for fitness instructors are taken over six weekends, while the course for personal trainers comprises twelve weekends. The Norwegian School of Sports Science (NIH), a university, offers similar short courses (both part-time and full-time) for fitness instructors and personal trainers. Both sets of qualifications are recognized by the big chains, SATS and Elixia, which are said to increasingly require instructors and personal trainers to be qualified.

The basic fitness qualification was seen by managers and instructors as a real minimum. Even a private training provider admitted that 'you don't go that deep'. Consequently those completing the course still required workplace supervision, along with in-house training. As the sports manager at Ngym3 explained, the qualification is 'OK for healthy people' or for simply showing clients around the gym. The numbers taking this qualification were not substantial, and managers of clubs were generally content to recruit part-time university students studying medicine, physiotherapy, or sports science, or those who had been elite athletes. However, views from the training providers and the employers' association stressed a need for the industry to professionalize the workforce and to raise the level of qualifications. As a lecturer from a university provider argued, 'you are not serious if you are just having people from the street working for you'. However, for most of those on the ground, there appeared to be few concerns about qualification standards.

In contrast to both the UK and Norway, fitness instructors in France, as with all paid teachers of sports activities, must legally possess a recognized qualification. There are two qualifications designed to cover gym instructing and teaching exercise classes (in the UK and Norway these are separated). The DEUST-MF is a level III qualification (i.e. BAC+2) which is delivered by a group of five universities and takes two years. The idea is to provide instructors with 'a wide portfolio of skills, who also understand how to run a company and are capable of assuming managerial responsibilities' (Viallon et al. 2003: 90). Around 150 places are available each year. The BPJEPS-AGFF is a lower level (BAC equivalent) qualification which takes one year and is provided through CREPS (regional centres of sports training and organization under the Ministry of Sport) and certified private providers. Students can also be on a paid apprenticeship or 'professionalization contract'.[3] Both qualifications must deliver a minimum number of teaching hours and include extensive work placements. Entry is highly competitive, with selection based on detailed application forms and interviews, and all candidates are required by law to pass physical fitness tests.

Overall, the most positive response to qualifications came from French employers and instructors. Both qualifications were considered to be of a good quality, with the lower level qualification seen as being more practical and the higher more academic. They were clearly understood and recognized by employers and managers, and were also seen to provide instructors with the necessary skills to undertake personal training. The courses were invariably described as 'difficult'. Discussions about whether the DEUST was 'too theoretical' and the BPJEPS 'too short' were ongoing, but remain relatively marginal issues. For most instructors, work placements, which covered a third of their time when studying, were viewed positively and ensured that they already had contacts within the industry and were 'job ready'. The general restrictions on the numbers taking these qualifications meant that it was reasonably easy to obtain a first job. Instructors in France tend to be older than in Norway and the UK as normally they are unable to start the qualification until they are 19. Many also enter as older adults, seeking a career change. Although there are no figures available, the general view was that

---

[3] The professionalization contract is aimed at all young people between the ages of 16 and 25 inclusive, and job seekers aged 26 years and over. It is a training contract which can be part of a fixed-term or open-ended employment contract and involves a mix of employment and formal training. Its objective is to allow employees to acquire a professional qualification and to promote integration or reintegration into employment (Insee 2014).

five years working as an instructor was fairly typical before moving on to other positions.

The job in France has, arguably, a higher status than in Norway and the UK, being widely referred to as *professeur de fitness*, implying a teacher rather than a deliverer or instructor. Underpinning this difference in title and status is the requirement to possess a rigorous state diploma. In the UK, attempts at 'professionalizing' the role through a voluntary Register have been partially undermined by low entry level qualifications which can be obtained over just a few days. Perhaps surprisingly, there are no regulations governing the qualifications required of fitness instructors in Norway which may explain its status as a predominantly part-time job for students. The next section considers the relationship between these different approaches to the education and training of instructors and the organization of work.

Work Organization

At a general level, it is possible to identify certain differences in the fitness instructor role across the three countries. In the UK and Norway, fitness instructors work mainly in the gym, offering advice and guidance to members. They may also teach some group classes, such as aerobics, spinning, or circuit training, but this is normally voluntary, worked outside of their shift, paid at a higher hourly rate, and limited to a few hours a week. Outside these core tasks, the job may include reception work, selling membership, and cleaning the equipment, gym, and even the changing rooms. In France, most fitness instructors are required to be 'polyvalent' which means providing both tailored programmes and advice in the gym as well as undertaking at least two to three hours of group exercise classes each day. There is also a tendency to do less non-core tasks, at least in the larger gyms.

Examining the work undertaken by fitness instructors in the gym (rather than in relation to exercise classes) reveals a complex pattern both between and within countries (see Table 6.5). In all but one French gym, in two of the three Norwegian gyms, and in the two public sector gyms in the UK, the instructors' role was relatively broad. They induct new members, offer general help and advice, and write individual exercise programmes. One-to-one sessions are provided for members and are either included within the membership fee or involve a small additional charge (e.g. Ngym3). In some cases (UK public sector gyms, gyms in France, Ngym2), programmes can be reviewed and rewritten allowing instructors to follow individuals over time, making the job more rewarding.

At UK-LA2, fitness instructors were expected to carry out ongoing reviews taking into account changes in the customer's life and adapting programmes

Skills in the Age of Over-Qualification

Table 6.5. Qualifications, job design, and pay in the case study gyms

Gym	Qualifications in recruitment	Job design	Personal trainers[1]	Cleaning	Typical pay per hour	Coverage by collective bargaining
UKgym1	Level 3 REPS	Middle	Yes	Equipment	£6.00	No
UKgym2	Level 2 REPS	Narrow	Yes	Equipment	£5.73	No
UK-LA1	Level 2 REPS	Broad	No	All gym	£7.00	Yes
UK-LA2	Level 2 REPS	Broad	No	All gym	£8.20	Yes
Ngym1	No minimum	Narrow	Yes	No	120 NOK	No
Ngym2	No minimum	Middle	No	All gym	150 NOK	No
Ngym3	1 year relevant university	Middle	No	Equipment	145 NOK	Yes
Fgym1	BPJEPS/DEUST	Broad	No	No	€12.0	Yes
Fgym2	BPJEPS/DEUST	Broad	No	Equipment	€12.0	Yes
Fgym3	BPJEPS/DEUST	Broad	No	Equipment	€12.0	Yes
Fgym4	BPJEPS/DEUST	Broad	No	All gym	€11.5	Yes
Fgym5	BPJEPS/DEUST	Broad	No	No	€14.0	Yes
Fgym6	BPJEPS/DEUST	Narrow	No	Equipment	€10.0	Yes

[1] Refers to separate job.

accordingly (e.g. pregnancy, injury, or any other health issues). Instructors at the other gyms also identified a broad role which required extensive technical skills and knowledge:

> Inductions, personal programmes... if anybody needs help with anything, there is always people asking for different exercises to do or if they are doing something wrong, you have to put their technique right. (Jamie, UK-LA1)

> we interview them [the customers] about their motivations, any possible goals... to try and devise a programme that will be a motivation for that specific individual. (Artur, Ngym3)

In a number of cases, particularly where there were no ongoing programme reviews taking place, instructors felt the job lacked challenge and became fairly routine. One manager (Henri, Fgym1) argued: 'here you have to do little programmes for people who want to do some little work out and their knowledge is somebody who knows everything for doing very specific programmes for high athletes... they are bored'.

For instructors in UK local authority gyms, there is added variety in that the membership base is often broader in terms of age, income, and level of physical fitness than in private sector gyms. The two gyms contributed to the National Health Service's Exercise Referral scheme, where doctors can refer patients with various health conditions to gyms for guided physical activity. One local authority had trained a group of fitness instructor specialists[4] to deal with

---

[4] At the time, instructors undertook a number of specialist modules at level four, although not a full qualification.

referred clients across all gyms in their area. At UK-LA2, only one person in the gym was trained and designated to work on referrals. She explained the benefits:

> I find it far more rewarding and challenging to work with clients that have cardiac conditions... and see the results for them and the gains. (Jessica)

While this scheme represents a higher skilled job, the numbers account for only an estimated 6 per cent of fitness instructors in the UK (SkillsActive/REPS/FIA 2008).

In France, in all but one gym, instructors were also undertaking a range of group exercise classes each day, with pre-choreographed routines supplied by the Les Mills Company in widespread use. As Felstead et al. (2007) show, these programmes involve a standardization of exercise-to-music teaching, with instructors required to be trained by the Les Mills company, in what can be seen as a process of routinization and deskilling. Instructors had a mixed view of pre-choreographed classes but all felt they reduced levels of creativity. Many instructors complained about the requirement to take several high impact classes a day, which could take its toll in terms of physical injury and exhaustion. As the chief executive of Fgym1 explained:

> Fitness is a very hard job. On average they stay three or four years. Because if you do four or five courses of Body Attack or Step [Les Mills high impact classes] a day, at the end of four or five years you will have problems with articulations... with backs, knees, ankles.

Reduced staffing levels, designed to cut costs, compounded the problem, with instructors expected to cover the classes of colleagues who were on holiday or off sick. One instructor who had suffered a physical injury explained, 'employers forget that if they give us too many classes, we get injured'. Instructors in the UK and Norway did not report these kinds of complaints and often mentioned their ability to pursue their sporting interests in their own time.

A Narrower Job: The Future?

An important factor impacting on the design and scope of the *instructor* role was the extent to which some organizations sought to extend the use of personal trainers. In the UK and Norway, intensifying competitive pressures had led a number of private companies to increase revenue by growing personal training and capturing a greater proportion of client fees. The approach identified in the two large private gyms in the UK and Ngym1 was to encourage members to pay for advice and guidance from a personal trainer, partly by reducing the scope of the instructor role to that of a generalized helper, with narrow tasks and limited knowledge requirements.

At UKgym2, for example, fitness instructors undertook basic inductions, demonstrated the use of equipment, and offered a generalized service to customers, ensuring that they were happy, answering basic questions or queries, telephoning low-use members, and keeping the gym clean and tidy. The gym manager claimed that they were 'basically just hosts pretty much' in a 'simple job' that was 'not very challenging', and which was mainly a 'stepping stone' to becoming a personal trainer. A similar role was found at Ngym1, where fitness instructors were given the title of 'motivators' and required to constantly 'walk the floor' and interact with as many customers as possible. The gym manager described the role as 'very demanding and draining...[as] you have to be very flexible and able to interact with all types of people from all walks of life'. Because of the high energy levels required, only part-timers working a maximum four-hour shift were employed. The understanding in both organizations was that these instructors would not give detailed advice or write tailored programmes.

> It's kind of a line...I am allowed to do it [write exercise programmes], but it is a kind of grey area...you don't want to be going into personal trainer territory... because then why should they pay a personal trainer? (Dan, instructor, UKgym2)
>
> The motivators are not supposed to be out there to give people instruction, they are supposed to be out there for people who have got questions, so they are normally brief questions. (Fitness manager, Ngym1)

The expansion of personal training led to a narrowing of the instructor role and a stripping out of knowledge requirements as well as a reduction in the number of instructors employed. The manager of Ngym1 explained that recruiting well-qualified instructors would require a substantial increase in pay: 'you can't afford to employ the best staff because they are not pulling in any revenue for us'. The emphasis upon generalized customer service in place of, rather than complementary to, an expansive knowledge base, can be seen as consistent with the deskilling of the instructor function.

In the UK, personal training, once the preserve of the independent self-employed individuals who paid a fee to a club and dealt directly with clients, has increasingly become 'owned' by the club. Today job advertisements across the private sector chains rarely refer to fitness instructors, with entry instead via the role of an 'employed' or 'self-employed' personal trainer. In some clubs, like UKgym2, personal trainers are recruited as self-employed, with the requirement to pay the club either a set fee or provide unpaid hours working as a fitness instructor. Another approach, found at UKgym1, is to start the employee as a paid fitness instructor while they grow a client base for personal training, with the aim of becoming a full-time (self-employed) personal trainer within a year or so. In Norway, one of the main gym chains (Ngym1) offered a similar model but with personal trainers being employees, as required by law, and thereby provided with relevant benefits, such as sick pay and holidays. Pay was solely dependent on the number of training sessions sold, with trainers receiving a fixed percentage of the client fee.

At the other clubs in the study, personal training was either not permitted or was extremely limited. The view was that the instructors should be providing a broad service for all customers as part of the general membership fee, reflecting the public sector ethos in the two UK local authority gyms and the responsibility of the not-for-profit Norwegian gym to serve the needs of its student population. The other gym in Norway pursued an approach that integrated personal training with the instructors' role, thereby offering an alternative package to the two main chains. In France, personal training is not well developed and much of it takes place in the home.

In Norway, the impact on instructors of this narrow role was considered less of an issue because these are mainly part-time and temporary jobs. In the UK, it is more problematic as many instructors are relatively new entrants into the labour market seeking a career in the industry. They may have limited qualifications or experience, yet are expected to rapidly move into a personal trainer role and compete for clients with a growing number of other recruits and more established trainers. The result has been very high levels of labour turnover. In France, the only case of narrow job roles was in a US-franchised outlet (Fygm6), which operated a standardized 30-minute workout, where resistance machines are set up in a circle and the individual changes place every 30 seconds. All the exercises and music were predetermined by the franchise, leaving the qualified instructor (required by law in France) to simply act as a motivator and help any new members to use a machine.

> Labour turnover is high. The concept isn't ideal for an instructor. It is repetitive, you don't evolve... There is a lack of freedom, creativity. Always doing the same thing, it is hard. (Manager and instructor)

A new development in France has been the opening up of low-cost gyms without classes and with no instructors. Companies have sought to exploit a regulatory loophole which arises from having regulations on those teaching and instructing but not whether gyms have to provide instructors in the first place. These low-priced centres have proved popular, but many within the industry are concerned about the 'race to the bottom' as well as the potential health and safety issues that could arise with members of the public who have been provided with no assessment or guidance. There have already been moves by the Ministry of Sport to introduce norms and recommendations for 'instructor-less' gyms.

Job Roles Downwards

Instructor roles also differ in terms of the extent to which the job is stretched downwards to such tasks as working on reception and cleaning. Overall, French instructors were less likely to be performing these types of 'non-core' activities. The example of cleaning illustrates the differences across countries and organization. In all but three gyms (Ngym1, Fgym1, Fgym5), the job included some cleaning activities, although the type of cleaning varied. In a number of cases, instructors only cleaned the gym equipment (UKgym1, UKgym2, Fgym2, Fgym3). Overall, French instructors were less likely to be undertaking non-equipment cleaning; the only case of regular cleaning was at a small owner-run gym (Fgym4) where all staff (including the owner) did everything. The most onerous cleaning demands were found in the two local authority gyms in the UK and in one of the gyms in Norway (Ngym2). The instructors in these gyms were required to wash floors and windows, and in Ngym2 clean the changing rooms and toilets. They viewed their cleaning role far more negatively, seeing it as a purely cost-cutting exercise. As two instructors explained:

> I have no education in washing, I want to work with people and health and exercise. (Maria, Ngym2)

> If there is something in the changing room and it's on the floor, there's litter, then pick it up, fair enough; mopping and cleaning the changing rooms when you are meant to be working in the gym, I just think that is an absolute disgrace, I think it is just not acceptable when there are customers who constantly need help. (Joe, UK-LA1)

While using instructors to clean saves on the cost of employing dedicated cleaners, it could be argued, as did many of those interviewed, that this does not make the most effective use of their skills and knowledge nor does it do much for their professional image! Indeed, some managers in the UK argued that there were better things that instructors could be doing with their time, for example undertaking research, planning events, and developing new programmes. However, with pay rates of instructors similar to those of a cleaner, there was little cost incentive to employ specialist cleaners.

Monitoring and Control

Were there any differences in the way instructors were managed, in respect of levels of autonomy and discretion, the use of targets, and other forms of control? Direct managerial supervision is somewhat problematic due to the

Regulating the Middle

nature of the job and hours worked. Instructors work on a one-to-one basis with clients, when they cannot be easily monitored, and the clubs are open from early in the morning to late at night making it costly to have managers always on site.

Gyms in all three countries, although less so in France, used some standardized forms in relation to inductions and exercise programmes, but the detail was left to the discretion of the staff. There was a general recognition that instructors would have their own approaches, which would depend on individual experience, education, and outlook:

> We are sports technicians, it is us who decides in relation to the person. (Nicolas, Fgym2)
>
> Training again is all individual, everyone has got their own methods and techniques as to how they train someone, how I train someone is completely different to [my colleague]. (Jack, UKgym1)

Only Ngym2 used a 'set method' for training which instructors were required to follow when designing their own programmes, while the franchise gym in France (Fgym6) followed a standard programme from the parent company.

The gym or club manager normally establishes the framework within which instructors work; for example allocating shifts, specifying process and length of time to be taken on each induction, and 'one-to-ones' for programme writing. The extent to which an instructor's day was structured by managers varied. At some gyms (UKgym2, UK-LA2, Ngym1, Ngym2), the fitness manager specified the daily schedule, for example times for appointments, cleaning, and floor walking.

> The first thing they have to do in the morning is look in the book—then maybe from 11 to 12 you go to meet with a new person and make a programme for them... it's different things, you will see—some days it's many things, some days it's quiet. If it's quiet then yes I would say you should do this, or this. (Manager, Ngym2)

Others reported that outside of set times for classes and booked-in appointments, they decided on their own organization of time. At UKgym1, instructors spoke of being 'very much encouraged to go off and do our own thing', with minimum levels of direct supervision. As the manager reported:

> The way the club works is that you get on with it, you don't wait for someone to say jump and then you jump.

It was also quite common for instructors to be left on their own to run the gym without supervision when the gym manager was away or on holiday. As one put it, 'It's cool to get responsibility. I know that they trust me' (Maria, Ngym2).

In nearly all of the gyms in France and Norway there was a very 'light touch' performance management system. If targets were set with instructors, they were infrequent and very general, such as 'engage more with customers', 'improve the customer experience', and so on. Although gym managers of chains had financial and numerical targets, these were not cascaded down in the form of individual targets for instructors. At the Norwegian not-for-profit gym (Ngym3), the gym manager stated that if he felt an instructor was not cleaning properly or he heard that they were spending too much time on reception, he would simply 'have a talk' with them: 'I won't accuse them of anything because I have to trust them you know and I do.' Interviews with instructors confirmed that the management style was relaxed and 'built on confidence and trust' (Artur, Ngym3). In France, instructors' performance was generally assessed in an ad hoc process through any negative feedback from customers, with declining numbers in classes or lack of repeat appointments prompting intervention. The only manager who took a more direct approach spoke of ensuring that instructors turned up on time, wore the correct uniform, and were 'at their post'. In contrast, in the two UK private sector gyms, gym managers complained about the 'unrealistic' targets on personal training income and membership that they had been set by head office. During regular one-to-ones with instructors, the managers would then set individual targets for instructors on personal training income. Other elements of performance (apart from customer interaction) were generally monitored through day-to-day supervision.

One of the common challenges identified by managers across the three countries was ensuring that instructors interacted sufficiently with members, as this was seen as central to improving customer satisfaction and retention. Instructors and some managers often commented on the difficultly that instructors faced in approaching and engaging members, particularly in the larger, more anonymous, gyms. As one French manager (Fygm1) put it, many instructors 'don't go to the people... they discuss with the people they know or they talk amongst themselves'. Her response had been to ensure only one instructor was in the gym at a time and to encourage participation activities with the members. By contrast, the manager at UKgym1 set instructors a target of speaking to five members a day including a minimum number of new members, although there was no requirement to record these interactions. At Ngym2, instructors were required to record how many clients they had helped in the course of the day but were not set any actual targets.

The exception to the more 'light touch' management typical in France and Norway was at Ngym1. Here the role of the instructor was narrow, being designated a 'motivator' whose job was to provide basic advice and keep customers happy. 'Mystery trainers' were used to assess performance, with poor scores potentially leading to dismissal.

> I think especially through the mystery trainer is an example of how you are monitored and observed quite often. I was surprised at how many times I'd actually been evaluated... I was told it would be every once in a while but almost more than half my shifts I was getting reports. (Anders, instructor)

These assessments related to qualitative behavioural aspects of dealing with customers, rather than their technical competence or knowledge.

The UK gyms, however, stood out as having the most intense forms of target setting in relation to customer interaction. Three of the gyms (Ugym2, UK-LA1, and UK-LA2) sought to apply more quantitative measures to ensure instructors were making sufficient efforts to interact with and retain customers through the application of new computer technology. Using electronic cards or keys, the systems are able to track customers' use of the gym. The data produced enable 'low use' members (those considered most at risk of leaving) to be identified on a computer screen as soon as they enter the gym. At all three clubs, management set targets for instructors, from 85 to 100 per cent contact with customers deemed 'at risk' of relinquishing their membership. Instructors were required to record any interaction on the computer, enabling management to monitor how they were using their time. As one manager put it:

> This is the perception, instructors are sitting down doing nothing, reading a book right, whereas now this is a more qualitative and quantitative position to actually drill down and see what they are actually doing. (Group manager, UK-LA1)

He added that 'purely from a management side of it, what we are getting out of them [is] definitely more work'.

While some instructors were positive about the potential to see the progress that customers were making, many felt it symbolized a lack of trust. It was also considered to be self-defeating as recording each interaction took time away from proactively engaging with customers.

> What it's trying to do is get us to liaise with customers more, but all it's doing is keeping us on here [the computer] more. It's kind of a bit of a cheek really just to assume that we are not liaising with customers. (Jamie, UK-LA1)

An instructor at UKgym2 argued that it tended to turn what should be a natural and spontaneous process into something 'artificial'.

> It was OK at first and then they got league tables and they want you to be at 100 per cent all the time which isn't really realistic... your high risk members have to be spoken to and it is like you have got to kind of search people out... and just talking to them for the sake of so you can log it. (Dan)

One instructor (Scott, UK-LA2) suggested that once management had sunk money into the system and was committed to its success, there was a tendency to overlook other factors affecting customer retention, such as the poor state of the facilities and inadequate cleaning, which were repeatedly highlighted in customer feedback.

The evidence suggests a rather mixed picture in relation to managerial monitoring and controls. In the UK, instructors were more likely to be subject to tighter managerial controls than the instructors in France and Norway. This was related primarily to the use of targets in relation to interactions with members. While French instructors experienced the greatest levels of autonomy, the experience in Norway was more varied, with one gym subjecting instructors to tight levels of managerial controls, although not targets.

Better Jobs?

Instructors in France have more regulated qualifications, higher status, and, typically, more autonomy in the job than those in the UK and Norway. What does the role in France look like when broader aspects of job quality are taken into consideration? One issue that has already been highlighted is the physical strain associated with teaching high impact exercise classes. Furthermore, despite higher entry level qualifications, low pay is just as endemic in the French fitness industry as it is in Norway and the UK. However, instructors' pay in France places them higher up the wage distribution (see Table 6.3), and they are generally above the low pay threshold. This can be seen to reflect the relatively high level of the SMIC (national minimum wage), the collective agreement, and instructors possessing qualified status. Nevertheless, these rates are still not considered to reflect the demands of the job or the qualifications required. Without effective collective organization, instructors in France have been unable to link their qualifications and skill levels to higher pay. There is little in the way of workplace organization and, as one instructor (Nicolas, Fgym2) commented:

> In City X, I think it is the same in other towns, as there is not too much competition between gyms, all the bosses agree between themselves to define a [pay] band which they are not going to go above.

In the UK, the surplus of qualified individuals entering the industry and the absence of collective bargaining in the private sector has served to dampen pay pressures. As one private sector manager put it, pay is:

> rubbish, it's peanuts. It's terrible and it is across the board everywhere... [they] don't pay more because they don't have to. (Gym manager, UKgym2)

In Norway, pay is towards the bottom end of the labour market but the level is generally set in line with minimum collective bargaining rates and associated social norms, which are relatively high compared to France and the UK. Perhaps surprisingly, for instructors, as opposed to stakeholders, low pay was not considered a major issue in Norway as the job was mainly a part-time position for students. Although pay in France and Norway was felt to be low, in real terms the levels were generally well above the rates paid in the UK.

At the same time, many French instructors interviewed lacked access to continuous professional development (CPD) due to the limited availability of relevant courses and small employers who were not organized effectively to provide training. Fgym1, operating towards the upper end of the market, was the exception in terms of organizing substantial initial and continuous training at a variety of levels for its employees. As the training director commented, 'The salaries are not very high; we compensate with a coherent training plan where we develop other skills.' In the UK, there was a buoyant market in CPD courses, partly due to the requirement to undertake ongoing training to maintain membership of the Register. Instructors, however, were increasingly expected to fund their own training, despite often being in minimum wage jobs. In Norway, training access was limited, remaining dependent upon the individual club and the ability of the employee to negotiate opportunities. The larger chains in the three countries were able to provide progression opportunities, with some individuals able to move up to lower level management positions fairly quickly. However, in many cases, these posts are not very well paid and usually demand long and unsocial hours.

Despite the considerable investment in time or money in gaining qualifications in France and the UK, turnover in the sector is high. Low pay is one element, but working time is another. Clubs tend to open early in the morning and close late at night, are open at weekends, and experience peaks typically during unsocial hours (i.e. the evenings). These hours become increasingly problematic the longer individuals stay in the job, affecting work–life balance particularly for those with children. Social norms, however, impact on work scheduling, as more clubs in France close at the weekends or on Sunday afternoon and tend to start later in the morning, thereby reducing, although not eliminating, the amount of unsocial hours that need to be worked. Norwegian clubs generally overcame these problems by employing students on part-time contracts who prefer to work in the evenings and at weekends. In most cases, hours were negotiated on an individual basis with the manager and tended to remain fairly stable and predictable. Instructors received additional unsocial hours payments in only one workplace in this study, a unionized gym in Norway (Ngym3).

In the UK, instructors often faced the additional problem of having little say in work schedules, with rotas typically changing from week to week. Work scheduling in the French clubs was generally fixed once a year and those with longer tenure were able to negotiate more favourable hours with managers. In three clubs (Fgym2, Fgym3, Fgym4), however, instructors were required to work 'split shifts'; for example, a full-time instructor's day could include two shifts from 9.30 a.m. to 1.30 p.m. and 5 p.m. to 9 p.m. Split shifts were widely disliked, as one instructor commentated:

> Me, I have 20 to 30 minutes of journey to come to the gym ... it is a little bit rushed during the day, it is quick, I finish my work, I have to do something at home, hop there ... quick I have to go back to work, it is a little bit stressful ... there is also my family life, finishing late at night, not seeing the children, that is what poses me the most worries. (Antoine, Fgym4)

Despite negative aspects to the job in all three countries, nearly all of the instructors interviewed enjoyed their work. Considerable satisfaction was derived from helping individuals to transform their lives and bodies through physical activity, although some felt the pressure of the 'emotional labour' involved in having to constantly display 'enthusiasm' and 'be nice all of the time' (Hochschild 1983).

The evidence from this sector is that occupational licensing which provides for a high level of qualification, as in the French case, can impact on status and have some influence on the way a job is designed. However, licensing may be more successful when combined with other factors, such as labour market regulations, that limit the ability of organizations to generate substantial revenues from personal training. While these may provide a disincentive to creating the kinds of deskilled instructors' jobs found in a number of gyms in Norway and the UK, it is difficult to make the case that they have led to a major upskilling of the role in France. The French example also suggests that occupational licensing has, in this case, not been sufficient to raise pay substantially or bring about improvements in other elements of job quality.

Skills, Knowledge, and Performance

What can be said about the relationship between work organization, skills, and performance? Attempting to establish whether a more qualified workforce in France delivers higher levels of industry or organizational performance would be virtually impossible due to lack of accurate data, other intervening factors, and the distinctive national features of the fitness market. In terms of organizational strategy, might there be scope for more quality-focused service through higher skilled, more autonomous instructors who are paid above market rates? Certainly, there is evidence across Norway and the UK that some industry experts and managers consider that a higher level of instructor skills could improve performance. As a UK manager in one low-cost private gym commented:

> If we boosted the qualifications needed then not only would you have better staff and...a better product to offer and...stability is key because...[it is] hard to get any sort of consistency and performance. (General manager, UKgym2)

A manager of a private training provider also stressed the importance of ensuring robust qualification levels in Norway:

> I think that it's, they see that more and more people are educated in like their own health and if they come to like a club and meet people who don't know what they are doing then it is bad for the industry and nobody will win.

However, a direct link between product market position (e.g. membership cost) and the utilization of higher level skills was not borne out. The premium gym in Norway and the low-cost private gym in the UK both had narrow instructor roles oriented towards a 'meet and greet' service function. While the larger (and more upmarket) club in France provided more in-house training than other gyms, this was primarily justified in relation to employee retention and progression, rather than direct customer experience. Of relevance, and in common across the three countries, is the way in which quality tends to be defined by the organization and understood by the consumer. The qualification and skill level of the instructor is only one element whereas better equipment, facilities, and 'little extras' are the key selling points for many gyms seeking to position themselves at the upper end of the market.

The evidence, however, does indicate major industry concern in the UK and Norway about the competence of instructors that is not prevalent in France. For individual employers in the UK and Norway, there are added costs in recruiting, training, and mentoring new staff, as well as higher labour turnover. It is reasonable to assume that more robust qualifications standards also help ensure client safety. If the data were available, one might consider injury rates or liability claims across the three countries to ascertain whether customers in France accordingly experience fewer accidents and injuries. Yet these comparisons are unable to take into account national differences in the legal process and willingness of individuals to pursue litigation, while clients with more health problems, e.g. in the UK, may also be more likely to suffer from exercise-related problems.

As noted earlier, there are many in the UK who believe that the industry-led Register has resulted in a lowest common denominator approach and that higher minimum qualifications standards are necessary to guarantee customer safety and raise the professional image of the industry. However, these arguments have not been sufficient to persuade either the industry or government to act. In Norway, the qualification level of instructors can also vary enormously, with little guarantee that those providing instruction have the necessary knowledge or competence. Despite a growing recognition of this issue among the larger chains, which increasingly emphasize the need for qualified instructors, there are as yet no moves towards regulation. While there are tensions in the sector over issues of quality, these are not impinging upon organizational success sufficiently to bring forth industry solutions or to compensate for what would be substantially higher costs.

In terms of the balance between quality-focused and price-centred competitive strategies within the industry, it is hard to discern any clear national differences. One can see differences in the way the industry is structured which are particular to the countries studied. In the provincial regions of France, for example, the tendency is for relatively small middle range gyms, which is rather different from the UK where luxury gyms and mass discounters often operate in close proximity to one another. In Norway, rather surprisingly given its high cost of living, membership prices are quite low and there are examples of providers seeking to compete through a strategy of cost minimization. Indeed, in all three countries there is a quality–cost spectrum, with premium providers vying for market share alongside others more oriented towards price competition. The pattern of product market positioning that we might have expected, for example proportionally more high-cost/high-quality gyms in Norway and fewer low-cost/low-quality provision in the UK, is not apparent.

The other issue relates to the costs more generally to society of the education and training of instructors, their employment and future career prospects. In Norway, training provision generally matches the structure of the jobs, in that it is of short duration and provides the basics. The role of the instructor has not developed into a more technical/associate professional position as seen in France and is viewed more as an 'amateur'. Those undertaking the role largely see it as a better job than working in a bar or café when a student or as a short-term cross-over to being a personal trainer. The result may be considered satisfactory in that it is relatively low cost, and suits a certain group within the labour market, although there are concerns about the quality and safety of the gym instruction that is being provided.

The situation is different in the UK given the considerable investment that has been made by individuals and the state in training and education for this sector. There are vast numbers studying for qualifications which are often costly and are either paid for by the individual or else fully paid for, or subsidized, by the state. Many enter the industry hoping to build a career but low pay, limited progression opportunities, and unsocial hours lead to very high levels of labour turnover. Many of the qualifications, however, have no recognition outside of the industry or within the education system. A level three personal training certificate does not provide access to university. In France, the numbers taking qualifications are restricted which ensures there is not the vast oversupply of labour that characterizes the UK industry. Instructors in France tend to be older and have a higher status, with qualifications covering aspects such as gym management. While the latter supports progression in theory, the small size of many clubs places limits on available opportunities which, together with the intensive class-based teaching and hours not suited to family life, forces many to quit the industry. Nevertheless, the qualifications obtained in France are at least integrated into the national education system which allows entry to higher levels of study.

Conclusions

The chapter has compared the job of fitness instructor in the UK, France, and Norway, revealing a complex and variegated picture. Perhaps the most striking difference is that instructors in France are required by law to obtain a higher level of qualification. This helps to ensure greater consistency in instructor knowledge at a relatively high level, compared with the more variable (and frequently lower level) qualifications held by instructors in the UK and Norway. Overall, instructors in France appear to experience a higher level of discretion in relation to their gym work and are subject to little in the way of managerial supervision or the use of targets. Nevertheless, standardization is widespread in group instruction. However, it is in the UK public sector where some instructors probably had the greatest *demands* placed upon their skills and knowledge, by having to deal with a more diverse group of gym users, irrespective of whether they are sufficiently equipped through their education and training to deal with such challenges. In Norway, qualification demands are extremely limited, and less than in the UK, and there is little evidence to suggest that the job demands a higher level of skill or discretion. Compared to the UK only, there is less use of targets and performance monitoring.

The job of a fitness instructor does not seem to fit with the picture of Norway as a country that is relatively advanced in terms of work organization. Why might this be the case? Many of the key institutional features that are said to have supported the diffusion of more autonomous job roles in the Nordic countries, such as strong trade unions and well-developed systems of social partnerships around collective bargaining, are not found in the Norwegian fitness industry. In addition, the job has not been incorporated within the apprenticeship system as a recognized skilled occupation, resulting in rather ad hoc training practices and low status. This finding does not mean, however, that there is no evidence of any 'employment logics'. The recent introduction of individual targets for UK instructors, linked to computer-based technologies, is consistent with the 'rule-based' management systems that Dobbin and Boychuk (1999) suggest are typical of neo-liberal economies, and were not apparent in Norwegian or French gyms.

The UK employment regime provides employers with considerable flexibility when it comes to employment contracts, which has enabled a new and distinctive approach to managing personal training in the fitness industry. The growing use of self-employment status in private sector gyms, which is far more difficult in Norway and France, shifts the risks of uncertain revenues onto the worker, and has the longer-term effect of reducing the numbers of fitness instructors and of deskilling their jobs. Income insecurity is, therefore, a more prominent feature of the sector in the UK, alongside less stability in working hours and working time patterns. The shift towards a different model of personal trainers in the UK suggests a growing polarization of skills, particularly when compared to instructors in France. While French workers undertake a range of instructing tasks at different skills levels (including those similar to a personal trainer), the UK approach increasingly involves using more insecure personal trainers undertaking higher end tasks and directly controlled by the gym, alongside a smaller group of fitness instructors within a more restricted, lower skilled job role. Similar features appeared in a large fitness chain in Norway, although personal trainers have more secure employment. However, it is unclear whether this is a new development in the Norwegian context.

There are also some country-based differences in relation to other aspects of job quality that can be linked to the institutional and regulatory framework. Although lack of formalized entry qualifications in Norway, coupled with weak union organization, has left wages at levels towards the bottom of the pay distribution, they cannot fall to levels found in the UK or France. Wages remain underpinned by generous welfare provision, a relatively tight labour market, and a concern by employers that very low wages risk reputational damage. In France, national collective bargaining institutions, supported by a relatively high national minimum wage and strong regulation of qualifications, ensure that pay levels are somewhat higher than in the UK. However, institutions and regulations in France have not removed the high levels of work intensity or the physical strain associated with teaching substantial numbers of exercise classes. In the UK, voluntary regulation of entry standards on the part of the industry has done little to alter the oversupply of labour, allowing private sector employers to suppress wages and dictate local workplace conditions, in the context of union absence, a deregulated labour market, and low national minimum wage.

Trade union activism and mobilization are clearly important. Where trade unions are active, they can and do make a difference to the quality of work, notably in the UK public sector where pay and benefits are better than in the private sector, and in Norwegian gyms where pay is also higher and unions have ensured that unsocial hours payments are built into collective agreements. Nevertheless across the countries, high labour turnover and small workplaces make it difficult for unions to organize at workplace level. Even in France and the UK public sector, where unions have some influence at sectoral level, they have been unable to mobilize effectively in the workplace. This lack of workplace organization makes it difficult for instructors to apply pressure on management to improve working conditions and to advance their interests at the broader sectoral level.

The research draws attention to the need for comparative studies of work organization to be attuned to specific features of the national sector which shape differences in approach. The role played by UK local authorities in providing gym facilities contrasts with Norway and France where public sector provision is largely absent. The state-led public health agenda in the UK has increased the demands on instructors to deal with a more diverse client group with complex needs. Its impact can also be observed in the progress that has been made towards a more developed instructor role (including higher qualification requirements) for those dealing with medical referrals, even if the numbers involved remain relatively small.

What can be said about organizational strategy? While differences in approach can be found in all countries at the organizational level, it is hard to establish any clear link between product market position and the qualifications and knowledge base of instructors in those countries (i.e. Norway and the UK) where the regulatory framework allows gyms some degree of choice over the latter. In part, this reflects the different ways in which quality is defined, a question returned to in the concluding chapter. Looking beyond qualifications required to issues of work design and job quality, a clear link with product market position is equally difficult to discern (see Lloyd 2005).

Returning to the other questions, raised in the introduction, what does the evidence from the fitness industry have to tell us? Strong trade unions, more trust-based relations, and supportive national institutions may help explain Norway's relatively advanced position in terms of work organization viewed from the aggregate level of the national economy. However, the picture changes substantially when attention turns to a relatively new sector like fitness where these mechanisms are either absent or very weak. It is in France and UK public sector gyms where fitness instructor roles are, if anything, most demanding, despite differences in qualification levels. In the former case, the effect of strong qualification regulations in raising the status of instructors, coupled with the absence of personal trainers, has provided for a somewhat broader role. In the latter, the combination of the public health agenda and again the absence of personal training are significant.

The research questions, however, the extent to which regulating entry qualifications, even at a relatively high level as in the French case, impacts upon the organization of work and the skill content of the job. Job roles in France are typically at a higher skill level than in the other two countries. That said, there has been little push to make more of the skills that have been developed, such as enabling instructors to deal with more specialist client groups, to provide extensive nutritional advice, or to offer workshops or classes on the very latest fitness trends. Where trade unions are relatively weak and job design remains within the prerogative of employers, the potential provided by higher level qualifications and associated status may remain limited. It is certainly possible that with stronger, proactive unions more progress might be made but in many ways this remains a hypothetical question given their weakness in this sector.

7

Raising the Bottom

Café Workers

Introduction

A feature of many advanced capitalist countries has been the expansion of low-skilled jobs in the service sector leading to widespread concerns around poor job quality and the prospect of rising levels of 'over-qualification' and 'skills wastage' (see Chapter 2). These problems are no longer confined to neo-liberal economies, where large numbers of these jobs are low paid, but are increasingly felt in countries like Germany and Sweden (Bosch and Weinkopf 2008; Woolfson et al. 2014). Such developments return us to the core overarching question motivating this book around the scope for upgrading the skill content of jobs, including those at the lower end. This chapter examines this issue through an exploration of the work of café assistants in the UK, Norway, and France.

What role do national institutions play in shaping work organization at the bottom of the labour market? Is there a Nordic employment 'logic' or 'regime' that leads to higher levels of task discretion and skill across a wide spectrum of jobs, irrespective of their position in the occupational hierarchy (Dobbin and Boychuk 1999; Gallie 2007)? Alternatively, might there be specific sector dynamics which mean that some jobs are quite similar across countries with different national institutional regimes, especially when the focus moves beyond more unionized manufacturing (Crouch 2005; Arrowsmith 2010; Grimshaw and Lehndorff 2010)? If there is an 'employment logic' effect in the Nordic countries that plays out across sectors and jobs, then low-end service sector work would seem to present a good test case.

Even if there are powerful sector dynamics, this would not discount variation across organizations within a sector. In consumer services, there exists a range of product market positions available to firms, which may have implications for work organization and skills (Porter 1980; Schuler and Jackson 1987; Batt 2000). National institutional environments and levels of income inequality—through their effects, for example, on pay, labour market flexibility, and consumer purchasing patterns—may play a role in shaping the way firms tend to compete and the types of product and services they offer. We might expect that those countries operating with higher levels of 'beneficial constraints' (Streeck 1997b; Keep 2000), such as more regulation and lower levels of income inequality, to have more firms competing on quality and differentiation than in those countries where there are few limits to price competition. Nevertheless, even within countries such as the UK and USA with deregulated labour markets and relatively high income inequality, it has been argued that some service sector organizations can still choose a 'high road' quality-based approach (Carré and Tilly 2012). The assumption is that these firms will require a workforce with more training and task discretion which will need to be managed in ways that encourage higher levels of commitment and motivation. The suggestion, however, of a straightforward link between product strategy and skill in services is controversial, as discussed in Chapter 2, and requires further exploration.

How do national institutions, sector dynamics, and organizational approaches interact to shape work organization and skill requirements at the lower end of the labour market? Some commentators have argued that some low-end jobs may be very difficult or even impossible to redesign and that job improvement should, therefore, focus on wider elements of job quality (Keep 2000). Nevertheless, research suggests that, contrary to initial expectations, jobs in areas such as call centres and retailing differ across countries when it comes to work organization and often quite substantially (Doellgast 2009; Gautié and Schmitt 2010). However, other jobs, such as hotel room attendants, appear to show little cross-country variation.

This chapter examines whether there are differences in the work of café assistants and asks what can be done to develop better jobs. Café assistant is included within the European socio-economic classification under catering assistant and is defined as a 'routine, semi-skilled or non-skilled occupation'. The café subsector is a major new growth area within hospitality, which has generally attracted little research, despite being a significant source of employment. As such, it offers a further opportunity to explore whether, or to what extent, work organization and skills in a new industry, emerging after national institutional structures were laid down, match expectations derived from macro-level regime analysis.

The chapter begins by briefly revisiting the comparative studies of work organization at the lower end of the labour market, discussed in Chapter 3, and identifies the main factors which appear to make a difference. The next sections outline the research method, along with the main characteristics of the café industry in each country and the extent of collective institutional structures. The chapter then draws upon detailed workplace case studies to explore any national differences in the organization of work, skill requirements, and the degree of autonomy and discretion afforded to café workers. The final section assesses the extent of national differences in broader aspects of job quality, before offering some conclusions.

Work Organization and Skill at the Lower End

Surveys indicate that Scandinavian countries provide workers with higher levels of discretion and autonomy than in the USA and UK even for those in lower occupational categories (see Chapter 3). While these surveys provide useful indicators, case study research, although limited, has also suggested that in some cases national differences in work organization exist even for lower end jobs. The evidence from a small number of service sector jobs, including retail assistant, cleaners, nursing assistants, and call centre agents, indicate that there are a number of factors that appear to be significant for developing better designed jobs (Gautié and Schmitt 2010; Doellgast 2010). These include employment protection legislation, the role of works councils, employment law affecting employers' ability to monitor workers, trade union activism, and labour shortages, among others. Where few differences in work organization were found, as in the case of hotel room attendants, the lack of union organization, small workplaces, and an abundant supply of labour would seem to be part of the explanation (Vanselow et al. 2010).

One issue that has been raised is that there may be little scope in certain jobs or particular types of workplaces to reorganize work and raise skill levels (Keep 2000). Andersson et al.'s (2011: 272) study of Swedish supermarkets, for example, found that strong trade unions, extensive collective bargaining, and cooperative employment relations helped to 'institutionalize a high-road strategy in a low-skill sector with strong market pressures'. However, although there were positive job quality outcomes for workers and some improvements in responsibilities, they argue that there are 'limits to how varied and high-skilled it can be' when the 'majority of work consists of routine tasks like exchanging money, answering customer requests, cleaning and moving goods' (2011: 270–1). Similarly, Bailey and Bernhardt (1997) conclude that there may be limited possibilities for skill upgrading in many areas of service provision.

However, retailing is one of the areas where significant cross-country differences in work organization have been found, although it is Germany that offers an example rather than Scandinavia (Carré et al. 2010). Typically, retail workers in the UK and USA are undertaking simple tasks, such as working on a checkout, shelf-filling, and bagging, while in Germany they have broad responsibility for a specific area, including stocking, merchandising, and advising customers. Explanations for these differences have emphasized the high labour turnover and the low levels of skills and qualifications of the workforce in the USA and UK, compared to the widespread use of apprenticeship and more stable employment in Germany (Carré et al. 2010). Using the same data, Voss-Dahm (2008) takes a different view, arguing that Germany was different due to the twin pillars of the skill formation system and collective bargaining structure that lay down minimum standards of pay and conditions. These brought a stability to retail work and employer buy-in to a more professional form of retail working. Nevertheless, this model has been under threat as retailers have driven down costs by disengaging from collective agreements and apprenticeship training, while also taking advantage of tax incentives to create 'mini-jobs'. These changes have seen a dramatic expansion of low-paid, part-time jobs, frequently filled by married women who have an apprenticeship, constructed around narrow tasks hardly distinguishable from those in the UK and USA (Carré et al. 2010: 251). This change to the nature of retail work in Germany questions the view that skills alone are enough to ensure the sustainability of more broadly designed forms of work organization, and highlights the critical role of encompassing labour market institutions and supportive regulatory structures.

Office cleaning in Norway offers a further example of what can be achieved in terms of job redesign, given supportive conditions (Torvatn 2011). Strong tripartite organization in a sector where unions and large employers are able and willing to regulate the market, and the resulting high wage costs, have led firms to invest in new technology, develop training, and, in some cases, provide more autonomous forms of team-based working. Although these studies caution against jumping to conclusions that a particular job cannot be upskilled, it does not mean there are no limits as to how far particular jobs can be improved in terms of their skill content, nor does it discount the possibility that some may be difficult to redesign.

Our analytical framework, outlined in Chapter 3, draws attention to the role of organized labour at multiple levels, including the ability of labour movements to shape the national institutional framework, and union influence at the sector and workplace as central to explaining differences in work organization. Some sectors, however, particularly in private services, are likely to pose particular challenges for union organization, irrespective of national institutional and regulatory supports. Nevertheless, even without a union presence, there still exists the potential that firms pursuing approaches based on higher quality and differentiated products and services will design jobs that use more skills in the workplace. In addition, even though some jobs might be hard to upskill, there may be scope to improve other dimensions of job quality. The extent to which such an agenda can be advanced via employers opting to pursue a 'high commitment' approach as part of a 'high road' strategy, or whether regulatory constraints are required to 'block off' the 'low road', is a key question (see Chapter 2). Research suggests that workers in low-end jobs are more dependent than those in higher paid jobs upon labour market institutions and employment regulations for their wages and conditions (Carré and Tilly 2012). With comparative research in this area remaining limited, the rest of this chapter explores the case of café worker and begins by outlining the research method and the national industry context.

Researching Café Work

For the purpose of this research, a café is an establishment selling mainly coffee, tea, sandwiches, cakes, or light meals, with a counter service and normally a seated area. Interviews were conducted with outlet managers and workers in cafés in the UK (specifically, the Midlands region of England), Norway (Oslo), and France (a southern city and Paris) (see Appendix 1 for further details). The sample includes sixteen outlets from eleven companies in the UK, twelve outlets from nine companies in Norway, and sixteen outlets from twelve companies in France.[1] They ranged from branded coffee shop and sandwich chains, café/bakery outlets, department store cafés, independents, and a multinational company operating branded outlets at airports and railway stations in all three countries. Table 7.5 at the end of this chapter summarizes some key features of the organizations. Interviews were also undertaken with sector bodies including employer associations, training organizations, and trade unions. Over 100 interviews were conducted across the three countries in 2010 and 2011.

Obtaining precise data on the café industry is not straightforward as it is typically treated as a subsector of hospitality, which includes hotels and catering. The hospitality industry across Europe has been characterized as low value-added, with low levels of productivity and slender profit margins. It is, however, expanding and remains highly labour intensive, generating significant numbers of jobs, although often of poor quality and requiring low levels of formal education. Limited training, poor job design, insecurity, and low pay are said to be endemic (see OECD 2001; Holman and McClelland 2011). The sector across Europe is a major employer of young people and foreign-born workers, and is characterized by high rates

---

[1] Pseudonyms are used for the cafés and, where relevant, for those interviewed.

Table 7.1. Food and beverage services industry

	UK	Norway	France
Number of enterprises	115, 965	8,098	215,810
Turnover (EUR millions)	67,121	5,451	65,500
Employment	1,556,409	63,515	782,506
Employees full-time equivalent	1,051,090	36,077	588,923
Turnover per person employed (EUR '000s)	43.1	85.8	83.7
Gross value added per employee (EUR '000s)	19.4	37.6	33.7
Share of personnel costs in production (%)	31.9	36.9	36.0
Persons employed per enterprise	13.4	7.8	3.6
Gross operating rate (%)	16.7	7.1	5.9
Female employment (%)	51	65	43
Part-time employment (%)[1]	47	49	23

[1] Accommodation and food.
Source: Eurostat sbs_na_1a_se_r2 2013; Female lfsq_egan22d, Part-time lfsq_epgan2. Figures in euros.

of part-time work, unsocial hours, and temporary and undeclared working (Gerogiannis et al. 2012).

Comparing the narrower food and beverage sector in the three countries, the UK is the biggest in terms of share of employment with 1.5 million workers (5 per cent of the workforce); France has nearly 800,000 (2.9 per cent); and Norway just over 60,000 (2.2 per cent). Table 7.1 indicates that despite the larger size of UK businesses and their considerably higher profit margins, productivity and value-added are low compared to France and Norway. Across the three countries, there is a substantial over-representation of part-time workers in the broader hospitality sector compared to the national average, accounting for close to half of all workers in the UK and Norway and a quarter in France. While the general perception is of a female-dominated sector, this is not borne out by the data in the UK and France, where there is a fairly even gender balance. However, in Norway two-thirds of workers in this sector are female.

The café industry subsector in the three countries has experienced significant change, alongside substantial growth in recent years, including the rise of multinational players. Nevertheless, there are distinctive national consumption patterns and industry structures, which tend to reflect broader trends within the hospitality and retail sector in each country (Table 7.2). Since the arrival of the US conglomerate, Starbucks, in the mid-1990s, the UK has seen a proliferation in branded chains, whereby each high street and retail centre is dominated by the same range of coffee shops and sandwich bars. The three market leaders in specialist coffee outlets—Costa Coffee, Starbucks, and Caffè Nero—account for 30 per cent of the market, and employ around 15,000 workers. Greggs and the US-based franchise operation, Subway, control 60 per cent of the sandwich market (Mintel 2011b) and, together with Pret a Manger, have over 35,000 employees. Despite the recession and a general

Table 7.2. Structure of the café market

	UK	Norway	France
Coffee chains	Dominated by large chains	Small chains and independents	Medium-sized chains/franchise and independents
Bakery/sandwich	Dominated by large chains/franchise	Small chains and independents	Medium-sized chains/franchise and small independents
Contractors	Medium and large companies	Large companies	Large companies
Market leaders[1] 2013–14, number of outlets	Costa Coffee (coffee chain) 1,656 Greggs (bakery/sandwich chain) 1,690 Subway (US sandwich franchise) 1,650 Starbucks (US coffee chain) 730 Caffè Nero (coffee chain) 540	Baker Hansen (bakery chain) 28 WB Samsen (bakery chain) 21 Kaffebrennereit (coffee chain) 20 Subway (US sandwich franchise) 24 Wayne's Coffee (Swedish coffee chain) 16	Subway (US sandwich franchise) 510 Paul (bakery chain/franchise) 324 La Brioche Dorée (sandwich chain/franchise) 300 La Croissanterie (sandwich chain/franchise) 180 Pomme de Pain (sandwich chain/franchise) 100

[1] All predominantly national chains except where mentioned.
Source: Company websites; press reports.

flattening of the market, the major coffee chains in particular have relatively high profit margins, and continue to expand through opening new outlets and taking over independents and small chains.

Coffee is a traditional drink in Norway, which has amongst the highest per capita consumption in the world. In recent years, there has been the development of a strong 'café culture' in the main cities, driven by the younger generation, which is spreading to smaller villages and towns (Euromonitor International 2013). The specialist coffee shop, as in the UK, has been a major area of growth, although the industry structure remains distinctive. Highly fragmented, there are a large number of independents and only a few small national chains, the largest being Kaffebrennereit with only twenty outlets and 200 employees. The other main players are traditional bakeries which also operate as cafés, the biggest of which is Baker Hansen with twenty-eight stores. Most cafés prepare high quality sandwiches on-site and there is some evidence of an increased demand for quality coffee (Euromonitor International 2013). Foreign companies have made a few inroads, such as the Swedish brand, Wayne's Coffee, and a small presence of Subway in the lower cost segment.

The market in France is significantly smaller, as coffee products continue to be based around the traditional espresso, typically purchased in independent waiter-served bars and cafés. The sandwich sector is growing as some of the traditional lunchtime outlets have closed down reflecting changing consumption patterns, notably the decline of the 'long lunch' and increasing demand for quicker meals. Overall, however, in contrast to Norway and the UK, the market has been contracting, reflecting a stagnating economy and declining purchasing power (Euromonitor International 2014). The sector comprises a large number of independents, including traditional bakeries that have expanded into providing sandwiches and eating space, as well as the growing area of café and bakery chains. French businesses include Paul and Brioche Dorée with over 300 outlets each and around 11,000 employees in total. A particular feature of the French sector is the growing proportion of franchise operations in a number of the large chains, accounting for around 40 per cent of Paul and half of Brioche Dorée outlets. Foreign companies have not been particularly successful, apart from the Subway franchise and the recent expansion of McDonald's into McCafé.

Collective Organization

In the UK, the British Hospitality Association (BHA) represents hotels, restaurants, food service providers, and leisure outlets, acting mainly as an industry lobby group. The sector has something of a reputation for 'hard HRM' and authoritarian management (Head and Lucas 2004). Union density is very low, at around 3.5 per cent, with 3.9 per cent of the workforce covered by collective bargaining (DBIS 2015). In the café sector, despite a number of large employers, union recognition is rare. Greggs—a bakers selling sandwiches—is a notable exception undertaking company-level collective bargaining that is typical of the more organized bakery sector. Most café employers are free to determine pay and conditions subject only to a relatively low national minimum wage and minimum platform of employment rights (see Chapter 4).

In Norway, the main employer organization is the Norwegian Hospitality Association, NHO Reiseliv. The hospitality sector is considered 'an anomaly in the Norwegian context with a relatively weak union presence' (Bergene et al. 2014: 120). Between 15 and 20 per cent of the workforce is unionized, the lowest of any sector in Norway. There is a collective agreement between Fellesforbundet/LO and NHO Reiseliv/NHO, but this is not binding on employer members. Forcing employers to comply, therefore, relies on unions successfully organizing in each company. The agreement sets a minimum pay rate, or 'tariff', for an unskilled worker aged 18 or over at 128.32 kroner (2010–12), a relatively low rate in Norway. Employee survey data put coverage at 58 per cent of workers. In the café sector, union officials from Fellesforbundet stressed the difficulty of establishing collective agreements because of the large number of employers, the small size of workplaces, and the difficulty of recruiting members among students and young workers with short job tenure. Many companies, however, still choose to offer the collectively agreed pay tariff, even though they are not signatories, although they typically fail to follow the wider provisions particularly around pay supplements for working unsocial hours. It has been suggested that Fellesforbundet has been slow to pursue more innovative organizing strategies in low-wage sectors, similar to those adopted by unions in some neo-liberal countries, due to their continued strength at national level (Bergene et al. 2014).

In France, café and sandwich outlets are either assigned to the 'fast food' sector or the 'bakery' sector. Most come under the collective agreement for fast food concluded between the employers' body, SNARR, and the five main trade unions in the sector.[2] Legal extension mechanisms mean that all workers are covered, with pay at entry level broadly in line with the national minimum wage (SMIC), which is substantially higher in France relative to the UK. The bakery agreement is slightly more generous, particularly in relation to payment for unsocial hours. Enforcement, however, remains a problem, given the lack of local union representation in many workplaces, especially small owner-run organizations. Data on union density are not available but, according to a CGT union official, is extremely low at around 0.5 per cent.

Collective bargaining also takes place at company level. Since 2008, around fifty such agreements have been signed covering issues ranging from pay and training to part-time working and the 35-hour week. Unlike the situation in the UK and Norway, there is evidence of union activism at the workplace level, with strikes and occupations having taken place at some of the bigger café companies over the last few years in response to issues such as closures, the spread of franchising, securing 'the 13th month' bonus[3] and pay. These have focused demands at the level of the individual outlet or company rather than the sector collective agreement. At F-Multibrand, a union organized a recent strike in relation to outlet closures and staff relocation, and supported café workers in resisting management attempts to give them additional cleaning tasks.

To summarize, the café subsector has commonalities across the three countries, in terms of low rates of unionization and the difficulties unions face in organizing at workplace level. There remain significant differences, with 100 per cent collective bargaining coverage in France, an apparent tendency to follow the collective tariff in Norway by at least half of employers, and little union or employer association engagement in the sector in the UK (see Table 7.3).

---

[2] The five unions are: FGTA-FO, CGT, INOVA CFE-CGC, CFDT, and Federation CFTC-CSFV.
[3] '13th month' refers to an additional month's pay at the end of the calendar year which is normally paid to salaried workers but less frequently to hourly paid workers. It is included in some sector collective agreements.

Skills in the Age of Over-Qualification

Table 7.3. Employers' organizations and trade unions in the hotels and restaurant sector

	UK	Norway	France
Number of employer organizations	1	2	1 (Fast food)
Employer coordination	Weak	Moderate	High
Number of unions	3	2	5
Union density	3.5%	20%	Below 1%
Collective agreements	Company level	Sector and company level	Sector and company level
Covered by collective agreement	3.9%	30–40%	100%

Source: DBIS 2015, interviews.

The Café Workforce

In all three countries, the café workforce is predominantly a young one in which students and migrant workers have a significant presence. However, the research uncovered variations in workforce composition by company, location, and country, with a hierarchy in working conditions that reflects established patterns of discrimination and disadvantage in the labour market. At the airport cafés, which require transport to work as well as unsocial working hours, and at the franchise stores of Sandwichco, where pay and conditions were at the low end across the three countries, there was a high concentration of black and minority ethnic workers, including recent immigrants, Eastern Europeans, and, in Norway, Swedish students.

The workforce in the UK cafés was the most varied. Some of the major branded coffee shops targeted mainly students (e.g. UK-CoffeeD), although one company had explicitly moved away from student labour in a bid to attract those who wanted a career in cafés, employing older male and female workers (UK-CoffeeA). The café/bakery chains and those in retail stores were, with the odd exception, using a female workforce, comprised of a mix of all ages, and a small number of students. The non-student group typically held low-level qualifications and the older among them had worked in hospitality and retail outlets for most of their working lives. There were few migrant workers in both of these types of organizations, which may reflect the particular local labour market in which these cafés operated.

In the Norwegian capital, Oslo, café workers were predominantly young women, often with relatively high levels of education, working either part-time while studying or full-time between studies. Young female students from Sweden, attracted by higher pay rates in Norway, were popular recruits given the similarities in language and what employers perceived to be their strong 'work ethic'. In contrast to the UK, there appeared to be few school 'drop-outs' or those with low levels of qualification. Interviews with trade unions and employer bodies confirmed that it is rare to find 'mature women' working in cafés in Norway, with the exception of family-run businesses.

In France, the café assistants in the southern city were mainly young, including large numbers of students working part-time. As with the UK, there were many with relatively low-level qualifications, such as the entry level vocational BEP, alongside those working on training contracts as part of their qualifications. Male café workers were less common, although men were more likely to be found at managerial levels, and tended to work for particular types of employers. While the study found few café workers over 30 who had worked in the sector for many years, the exception was at one of the airport cafés (a non-French born black and minority ethnic woman) and women working at the university cafés where they had the status and benefits of civil servants.

Training of Café Workers

The job of a café assistant is to serve customers at a counter, make and/or sell drinks, sandwiches, and snacks in compliance with food hygiene standards, and to clean tables and other areas of the workplace. Qualifications, whether academic or vocational, play little or no role in recruitment and selection in any of the countries. The following comment from the manager of a UK-CoffeeB outlet is fairly typical: 'It doesn't really mean "diddly squat" [nothing] to me if anyone has got a degree or NVQs or anything in customer service.' Instead, the focus is on 'attitude' and 'personality', with managerial accounts emphasizing the ability to interact with customers, alongside the willingness to work hard, do a fair share of work, and 'get on' with co-workers. As one French café manager put it:

> I never ask for qualifications. I am more concerned about their attitude... Are they humble, do they invest totally in the contract that they sign, do they have respect for the job, the manager, and above all their colleagues? Are they on time, move when it's busy, and are they serious? (Andre, F-BakerA)

Without exception, the job involved short initial training, and typically took anything from a few days to one month to learn and to achieve the required speed. Larger companies tended to have more structured approaches to training and development, with the use of work books and signing-off sheets. In the UK coffee chains and the majority of cafés in Norway, some courses were provided off-site, typically a day or half-day of 'barista training' in how to make coffee. For most workers, structured training was focused on food hygiene and learning the product standards. The rest was learnt through 'doubling up' with an experienced worker, who in some cases was a designated trainer, or by being gradually shown over a couple of weeks how to undertake the different tasks by another worker or manager.

A representative with the Norwegian Hospitality Association suggested that 'training is more or less nothing; that means they are shown how to do the coffee...from one of their colleagues and that's about it'. A French union official commented that while large companies had structured provision, among the smaller companies that dominate the sector 'training is catastrophic'. Despite the availability of funds from an industry levy, it was the largest organizations which drew on this to undertake formal off-the-job training and provide development opportunities.

Work Organization, Discretion, and Autonomy

The job of café worker has many elements in common but is not the same everywhere. There are differences with regard to the composition of tasks depending upon the particular café's product and service offer and the extent of delegation of tasks from managers. The hierarchy of a café depends on its size but typically consists of the café manager or owners and the café assistants. In between there may be supervisors, team leaders, and assistant managers. These layers were found in all of the cafés in the UK, but were more selectively used in France and Norway, where it is not unusual to find a manager and café assistants, but no intermediary jobs. The extensive use of supervisors, rewarded with only small increases in pay, was associated with café assistants in the UK rarely being given additional responsibilities.

In both Norway and France, it was typical for café workers to undertake the ordering and receiving of products, and opening and closing the outlet, whereas these tasks were normally assigned to supervisors or managers in the UK. Only the independent café in the UK delegated tasks, with one member of staff being given responsibility for the display and restocking of a particular section of the outlet. In three French outlets, each assistant was responsible for a particular task, for example ensuring a specified piece of equipment was cleaned or managing a window display. In Norway, task delegation was more widespread and typically more extensive, with examples of assistants organizing the flowers, taking money to the bank, or managing the café's Facebook page. Similarly, these café assistants were able to offer refunds to dissatisfied customers, a small element of discretion but one which nevertheless signifies a certain level of trust. This practice was also found in a small number of organizations in France, whereas in all but one outlet in the UK, cash refunds could only be given by authority from the supervisor or manager.

Customization of the Product

Outside of these additional responsibilities, the tasks of the café worker varied in relation to the nature of the production and the extent to which these were standardized or customized. For drinks, the main distinction is between those cafés that use espresso machines and grinders, and where workers are increasingly described as 'baristas', and those who dispense 'instant' coffee at the press of a button. Popular in the UK and Norway are the variety of milk-based coffees, such as cappuccinos and lattes, which are considered to be more difficult to make. It was common for new workers typically in the coffee shops, as opposed to bakery or sandwich outlets, to be sent on 'barista courses' of a few hours to learn how to use the machines and appreciate the company's coffee and methods.

In France, coffee is predominantly served as espressos. Interestingly no worker interviewed had been sent on a coffee-making course or described themselves as a barista. Coffee making was considered a routine part of the job even if using the same type of espresso machines as found in the UK and Norway. A key feature of the coffee chains in the UK was the standardization of coffee drinks. With at least thirty varieties, each one has to be produced in exactly the way specified by the parent company. The aim is for the coffee to taste exactly the same in whichever outlet the customer entered. Although Multibrand also pursued this approach across the three countries, there was no such rigidity among the other organizations in France or in Norway.

A further distinction could be found in the production of sandwiches. In a number of outlets across the three countries, sandwiches arrive pre-prepared. For those cafés where sandwiches are produced on the premises, these may be pre-made, made to customer order, or a combination of the two. In Norway, the preference was to make sandwiches to customer orders, while in France and the UK there was more pre-making of standardized sandwiches. For the chains in the UK and France, the recipe and process for making sandwiches are developed by head office and devolved to outlets through the use of technical sheets that provide rigid instructions. Strict 'formulas' specify the exact 'weighted measure' of cheese or meat and the number of slices of tomato or cucumber that must be used. In a number of cases, each sandwich is allocated a code on the computerized till which allows the detailed calculation of waste and sales. If the rules are applied strictly it can lead to a lack of flexibility in meeting customer demands. An assistant manager at UK-BakerB referred to it as both a system failure and a source of personal frustration; for example she could not even meet a customer request for a jam sandwich because there was no code available.

> I mean you are told you can only do this or you can only do that but when you've got customers coming in and they ask for things and you've got to keep saying 'I'm really sorry, I can't do that'.

Often the only discretion available was when customers asked to remove certain items or not include them in a standardized sandwich. A manager at a French chain explained:

> The complexity, it is complying with the technical specifications and the group standards; for each product, for each sandwich, salad or dessert there is a technical sheet that the preparer must comply with in order to comply with the look of the product, the taste, and the material costs. (F-SandwichA)

Only at independent café F-IndepA, and to a more limited extent at UK-Indep, were sandwiches made on an individualized basis to customer request. Standardization of products and processes was replicated in the multinational company operating across the different countries. Multibrand's units in France and Norway were largely indistinguishable in this respect from those in the UK. As a café worker at one of Multibrand's Norwegian rail units commented, 'It's routine, day-in and day-out, same customers, same food, same order, you can do it blind-folded' (Abdella). A similar standardization process was found at the international chain Sandwichco.

The exception was at the other cafés in Norway where sandwiches were made on-site, and the content was largely at the discretion of the worker. There were some guidelines in some cafés in relation to the weight of expensive items but café assistants could make fairly standard sandwiches, design their own, or respond to customer requests for advice on what to order. At the two units of one such company, N-BakerA, café assistants were encouraged to come up with new sandwich ideas and to put forward suggestions for improving customers' experience, something that was not possible in the UK and French chains. One café assistant (Sofia) commented: 'If there is something that I have seen in other places and that I want to try . . . I will just say let's try it and see how it goes.' Similarly at N-BakerC, workers were encouraged to taste all the food:

> You can chose whatever you like so it's not a menu that I have to learn it's just the customers who want this and this, and sometimes they ask for a recommendation. (Sara, café assistant)

While these approaches did not require much in the way of additional skills or knowledge, as with the ability to give refunds, they did provide some scope to input ideas and make decisions at the level of the task that was appreciated by workers.

Service Delivery

Across France and Norway, many organizations provided little in the way of guidance or rules as to how staff should interact with customers beyond the general requirement to be polite and congenial and, in some cafés, to 'upsell'. While none of the cafés scripted the interaction, there were certain organizations that directed the phrases to be used and those that were 'banned'. At F-SandwichA directives from head office instructed assistants to 'smile all the time, say thank-you, hello, goodbye' (Nicholas, café assistant). In Norway, only at Multibrand were there written guidelines provided by company head office, and a requirement that customers should wait no longer than three minutes to be served:

> We've got a list hanging up of what you have to do, you've got to smile and say hello, and then ask them 'how can I help you?', and then always try upselling or selling more so if they order a coffee we ask them 'which cake do you want?' (Assistant manager)

By contrast in the UK, considerable attention was focused on the interaction with the customer and how to ensure 'good customer service', as well as maximizing customer purchases. Examples included the 'six steps to service' at UK-CoffeeA:

> 'Smile and greet, serve, sell, stamp and pay, sugar and say goodbye'. In the induction book it says positive body language, there's a whole section about it's not necessarily about what you say it's how you say it so you've got to have a smile on your face. (Ryan, café assistant)

Another café assistant explained how 'you have to call them by name if they are really regular, and then have a chat with them, ask them how their day is' (Lauren, UK-CoffeeA). At UK-CoffeeB, there was an 'eight kick start' which included 'three minutes from door to daily cup, guests greeted in a warm, friendly, energetic, welcoming manner, four of each of the products to tempt guests, every order called loudly' (Jack, supervisor).

In addition, there was far more direction from head office in the UK chains as to how to organize customer service. In most cases, when the café is busy, the bar is operated as a line, with one member of staff taking the order and serving food items, another preparing drinks, and someone else taking the final payment at the till. In some cases, head office had simply determined that this is the way service must be delivered on grounds of speed and efficiency (UK-CoffeeB, UK-CoffeeC, and UK-CoffeeD). Staff were only allowed to switch to one-to-one service during quieter periods. As one manager commented, 'it originally came from head office. I know when I was trained that was the way I was trained and it was in the manual that we had' (UK-CoffeeB). In one of the other branded chains (UK-CoffeeA), the model was for a member of staff to serve the customer throughout the entire process. The expectation was that they would serve 'two customers at once' by taking the next order while finishing up the previous one, thereby offering an efficient but 'more personal' service; the problem was that short staffing had created highly intense work routines. In the French and Norwegian chains, there appeared to be less direction from head office and the organization of customer service was the responsibility of individual managers and, in a few cases, decided by the staff themselves.

Managing Staff: Control

The research indicates that there are also some cross-country differences in the way that workers are managed. In France, outlet managers normally allocated staff to tasks and decided how to organize workers, which in some cases included rotating them between tasks and in others appointing each team member to a specified role. Depending on the size and type of organization, most managers were active in the shop, and were involved in the direct monitoring of staff, while the tills could be used to ensure pricing was correct and staff were not stealing. 'On my part, there is an almost constant presence, which means there is a virtually constant visual control and in addition there are means of control with are linked to the till, with all the sales, losses and returns' (manager, F-SandwichA). In two other French cafés, these forms of monitoring were considered to be overbearing by the staff, with pressure to speed up: 'he [manager] is always looking at the turnover, he is always pushing us to do more, more, more... we know the work but it is never good, whether it is the cleaning, the service, the relation with the customer, it is never good enough' (Lara, café assistant, F-SandwichB). Another explained: 'If there is a lot of people and you are with the bosses... they are going to always be there and saying "quicker, quicker, quicker"' (Emilie, F-IndepD).

Where managers were not constantly on site, controls were less prevalent. A café worker employed at an airport explained how managers visited the various outlets a couple of times a day to check on them: 'they ask us often if it is busy, for the figures... if we say yes... they are very happy because they have to make a huge amount without too many staff' (Elodie, F-SandwichD). Overall relationships between café workers and managers in France tended to be more distant than in the UK and Norway. Outside of small family firms, there was little attempt to involve employees, for example by asking them for their opinions on products or processes. As a café assistant (Lara, F-Sandwich B) explained: 'We don't make suggestions as we know we won't be listened to.'

Prevalent among the French chains was the use of 'mystery shoppers' and hygiene controllers, typically taking place every three months. Half of the employers provided bonuses that were either linked to high scores from the mystery shopper or directly related to meeting specified group sales targets. These were small sums paid to all workers and worth up to 100 euros per individual over three months. In some cases, these bonuses had been negotiated with trade unions at the company level. There were no specified individual targets, and outlet targets were reported in terms of overall sales to café workers. There was also little evidence of the use of individual performance reviews or appraisal.

In Norway, some managers worked alongside their staff, while others were frequently 'not there', and much of the organization of work was decided by the staff themselves. There was a widespread view among workers that their managers trusted them to organize tasks among themselves and to work with little supervision. It was also fairly common for the manager to ask workers for their views on the products, organization, and running of the café. Staff described their manager at one of the franchise stores of N-BakerA as 'more like a friend', detailing how he had recently treated them all to a trip to Germany as a reward for good performance. At another store in the same chain, workers described how their manager gave them 'the opportunity to contribute and be creative' and had 'trust and faith' in their abilities (Eva, café worker).

While the use of mystery shoppers was widespread across the larger organizations, they were rarely a source of concern, and in a few cases were linked to small bonuses for the team or individual concerned. As in France, the use of individual appraisals or performance management reviews was rare, with only Multibrand in Norway using regular 'staff chats'. In most cases, there were no targets, although the same company had introduced an upselling bonus as well as competitions with prizes for staff, such as an iPod, while N-BakerA provided prizes, such as trips, to staff at successful franchises.

These more open relationships partly reflected the way companies managed their outlets which often meant less pressure on managers to enhance performance. The two franchise owners at NBaker-A described the relationship with their parent company as being largely supportive and responsive. Although prices and store layout were determined centrally, the company held regular meetings with franchisees who could feed back information and influence decisions. Surprisingly even one of the managers at Norway's international Multibrand explained that if they were not meeting targets, there was some pressure 'but we are talking very nice together and it's no problem' (Olav). Stress was more likely to emanate from the customers and managing staff rather than targets from head office. Another manager (N-BakerB) emphasized her autonomy: 'I cannot have too many workers but if... it's a busy day on Friday, I take one in. I can do whatever I want actually... they [owners] trust me so much so I get very free hands to do actually anything I want.'

It may be that in a country like Norway with a strong egalitarian tradition, managers even in the café sector are more inclined to be inclusive in their approach and to provide such opportunities. A union official explained her perspective on the different approaches of managers:

> We see the difference with people from Austria, Germany and when they become managers you know they had a completely different culture of how to be a manager. They think they should raise their voice and be tough and show them who is the boss but if a Norwegian is doing it like that there will become a conflict because they [workers] will not put up with that.

In the UK, the allocation of individuals to tasks was generally undertaken by the manager or supervisor. Most store managers spent considerable periods working alongside café assistants and supervised them through direct observation. The personality of the manager and how they interacted with staff made a difference to workers, and many spoke of how they valued those who were fair, supportive, and willing to work as part of the team. The use of individual worker targets was not widespread, but the way companies managed their outlets exerted intense pressure on managers. Managers were expected to deliver to a range of targets, the most important being staffing costs, turnover, and quality standards, and workers were acutely aware of these pressures on unit managers. In some cafés, each worker had a code for the till so that sales, and any errors, could be tracked back to individuals. At one company (UK-CoffeeA), the sales figures of each individual were placed on a notice board. As Brandon, an assistant manager stated, 'It's good for encouragement for the staff, it's competitive.' While this example was on the extreme side, most companies conducted regular individual performance reviews and appraisals.

Varying working hours was a particular feature by which managers in the UK sought to reduce staffing costs. Weak regulation of working time and employment contracts means that workers can be offered 'zero hours' or short part-time contracts while regularly working full-time hours. Seven of the eleven UK cafés varied the hours of staff on a regular basis; typically employing them on 15- or 20-hour contracts but increasing hours up to 35 or 40. While many workers were not particularly concerned as they regularly worked longer hours than their contracts, in four cases, issues were raised about being sent home early or the insecurity associated with the lack of guaranteed hours. Reflecting broader evidence on the use of these type of employment practices (Brinkley 2013), at UK-CoffeeC it was claimed that the manager had 'favourites' and used hours as a means to control workers. Two café assistants reported that if they made any complaint to their manager, it would lead to their hours being cut: 'nobody has a say, we have to do as we are told and get on with it' (Laura). Amber explained that 'keeping in' with the manager was crucial: 'I couldn't get the sack, but she will do it in a kind of way of minimizing my hours, that's how it works here.'

As in France, the use of mystery shoppers was prevalent. Four organizations provided small bonuses or rewards for high scores, the largest being an additional 50 pence per hour for a month for the whole team and £25 for the individual members of staff at UK-Multibrand, and the smallest being a box of chocolates at UK-RetailA. Poor results, on the other hand, could result in formal disciplinary procedures at three cafés. At UK-RetailA, following just one poor mystery shopper score, the manager formally disciplined the individual worker concerned causing resentment about the process and response. Only one café (UK-BakerA) provided any other form of incentive or bonus. Here there were regular head office promotions where stores with the top sales on certain items could win chocolates, wine, or £100 for the group.

While workers were in most cases positive about their local manager, the relationship with external managers and head office was often a source of dissatisfaction and frustration. In five of the organizations, staff, and some managers, felt they were simply not valued by senior management or the store owners (UK-CoffeeB, UK-CoffeeC, UK-RetailA, UK-Multibrand, UK-Sandwichco). The inability to praise staff, thank them for their efforts, or simply provide a Christmas bonus or present (beyond a cheap box of chocolates) was particularly galling for many employees: 'I think head office think that we are drones... you toe the line then it's fine... just following everything that they say you have to do... even if it is stupid' (Jack, supervisor, UK-CoffeeB). In one case (UK-BakerB), the lack of trust placed in staff (including the manager) by head office was graphically illustrated by the assumption that if their 'cogs were out' (i.e. the alignment of sales, supplies, and waste figures) this was because staff had stolen the ingredients!

The small size of the workplace and the sheer physical proximity of manager–worker relations mean that the individual style and personality of the manager (or franchisee) is highly significant for how workers experience the job in all of these countries. Nevertheless, there remain significant differences across the countries in levels and forms of managerial control. In the UK, tight controls and intense forms of performance management emanate in part from the way companies manage their outlets through a range of targets. Café workers in France are also subject to direct monitoring of their work but are not faced with individual targets nor is there much evidence of participation in workplace decisions. In Norway, managers appear to give their staff more autonomy and, in a number of cases, provide them with opportunities to be involved in decision-making.

Where is Work Better?

While levels of autonomy and discretion are somewhat higher in Norwegian cafés, does the same apply to other dimensions of job quality? While job quality matters for workers, it also raises the issue of whether higher standards in employment, such as pay, have helped motivate organizations to move up the value chain and adopt better forms of work organization.

Pocock and Skinner (2012: 61) note that workers' perceptions of job quality vary 'according to their circumstances—for example, their health, household situation and life stage'. Café workers are no exception, with different responses depending on whether the individual was a student, a 25-year-old trying to support themselves, a single woman with childcare responsibilities, or a secondary wage earner within a family unit. Nevertheless, some general observations can be made about how workers viewed these jobs. Many cited positive aspects in terms of the variety of tasks and the interaction with customers. Rotation between different tasks on a shift, along with the general 'busyness' of a café, could help to alleviate the boredom and monotony associated with a routine job. Nevertheless, café work is hard, physical labour, involving cleaning, bending, as well as carrying heavy items, with staff on their feet throughout their shift. Being *too* busy can also be stressful. 'You just stand and walk all day long and your back is hurting when you come out', commented Eva, a young café worker at N-BakerA. A café worker in the UK in her mid-40s commented: 'Some nights I go home from work and I'm absolutely exhausted' (Laura UK-CoffeeC). Her remarks echo those of a manager at F-Univ: 'We see our work getting worse. It becomes more physical and we are getting older.'

It is not just the physical nature of the role that makes it demanding. Café workers are also expected to perform 'emotional labour' (Hochschild 1983) and remain polite and congenial, even when customers are abusive. The levels and types of interaction with customers varied depending on the nature of the café and the customer base. However, most workers stated they enjoyed the interaction with customers, especially those who had 'regulars' and were given some space to chat. The most prominent cause for complaint in the UK and France was over low pay and, for some workers in the UK, over contract and hours instability, as noted earlier. The routine and repetitive aspects of the job tended to be mentioned more frequently in France, possibly reflecting higher expectations on the part of workers doing these jobs. The next subsections examine the main similarities and differences in objective features of job quality across the three countries, focusing on pay, contracts and working time, and progression opportunities.

Pay

In all three countries, café work is one of the lowest paid jobs in the labour market. However, levels of pay differ significantly, reflecting the impact of national pay-setting institutions (Table 7.4). In the UK, in all but one unionized company (UK-BakerA), employers determined pay unilaterally, subject

Table 7.4. Café assistant pay and benefits in the case study workplaces

	Norway (NOK)	France (€)	UK (£)
Starter rate 2011 (median)	95–143 (125)	9–9.42 (9)	5.80–6.30 (5.80)
Highest rate (median)	95–150K (130)	9–10.28 (9)	5.80–6.53 (5.80)
Equivalent in euro (30 January 2011)	16.24	9	6.94[1]
PPP ($) equivalent[2]	14.25	10.66	8.47
Proportion of median national wage	56%	63%	52%
Meals provided by employer	Sandwich/drink (most)	Meal (all)	Sandwich/drink (5) 20–50% discount (5) None (1)
Other benefits	Unsocial hours including weekends (5)	Allowance for uniform washing (all) 13th month (3) Extra pay Sundays (2) Extra pay night work (all)	

[1] Uses £5.93 as UK minimum wage (Oct. 2010–Sept. 2011) rather than 2010 minimum wage
[2] Calculated using OECD 2011 PPP Benchmarking results, OECD.Stat.

Note: In the UK some companies used youth wage rates which are lower than the adult minimum wage but data were not consistently collected. Norway youth rates were paid in a number of organizations—lowest 100 NOK.

only to the national minimum wage. In ten of the sixteen outlets, café assistants were employed at the minimum wage, which then stood at £5.80 an hour. Pay was slightly higher in the other cafés, increasing to £6.50 for an experienced worker at UK-CoffeeD and the unionized café was towards the higher end. Additional pay premiums for working weekends and unsocial hours have largely disappeared from the sector.

In France, the collectively agreed pay minimum in the fast food and bakery sectors is at the level of the SMIC, with the vast majority of workers paid at this rate. Set substantially higher than the UK minimum wage, it ensures that café workers in France are better paid, even though, as many pointed out, pay is still 'miserable' given the cost of living. The collective agreements also ensure additional payments for meals, washing uniforms, and public holidays. Only at F-Univ, where workers were civil servants and subject to a different payment system, was pay found to be above this level. Four companies also had their own company-level agreements on top, which added extra bonuses and 13th month payments.

In Norway, where there is no national minimum wage, the collective agreement for hospitality in 2010–11 included a basic rate of 128 NOK for over 20s. Adult worker pay was more varied than in the UK and France, with the lowest at N-Sandwichco (NOK 95) rising to NOK 150 at N-Multibrand, reflecting age and experience. Most companies paid at least the industry tariff for adult workers as stipulated by the collective agreement, irrespective of whether they were signatories. All provided a free lunch for staff and around half (normally those who had signed the collective agreement) paid premiums for weekend working. Starting salaries for café assistants are the highest both in absolute and real terms in Norway. Calculated in purchasing power parity, workers in France typically receive 25 per cent and those in Norway nearly 70 per cent more than their equivalents in the UK. The jobs in Norway are still, however, considered low paid and the tariff as a proportion of the median wage is somewhat less than in France, where wage structures at the lower end are more compressed.

Contracts and Working Time

A central feature of the café sector is that demand fluctuates throughout the week and the working day. In a highly labour-intensive sector, being able to match staff numbers to variation in customer demand is an important way to control labour costs. Relatively weak regulations in the UK enable employers to use working time and contractual flexibility to a far greater extent than in Norway and France. In the UK, full-time posts were reserved mainly for assistant managers and managers, with only two organizations (UK-RetailB and UK-Indep) providing full-time contracts for the majority of staff. While part-time work has always been a feature of the sector, 'loose' labour market conditions, in recent years, have allowed employers to increasingly use 'core hour' or 'variable hour' contracts.

These contracts specify a certain number of hours per week, such as twelve, sixteen, or twenty, with staff offered additional hours according to business need. In a number of cases, this meant that employees were effectively working full-time hours on a regular basis even though they were employed on a part-time contract. For some workers, these contracts were not considered problematic, particularly students who wanted shorter hours. However, others noted widespread problems around financial insecurity, managerial control as identified earlier, and the claiming of in-work benefits.[4] A number stated that they would have preferred more guaranteed hours and had even been recruited believing that they were being offered a full-time job. Recently UK-Multibrand had forced through reductions in contractual hours so that all café workers at the airport were required to be on twenty-hour contracts. Malika explained that although she still often worked full-time, hours fluctuated from week to week: 'I wasn't happy at all because you've got bills to pay and stuff like that and then you have to start looking for another job.'

---

[4] A number of women with younger children were claiming working tax credits which is an in-work benefit aimed at boosting the incomes of working families on low wages. There is a requirement to work a minimum of fifteen hours per week and to report any changes in income.

In France and Norway, there was also extensive use of part-time employment. However, in both cases these workers were students provided with fairly regular hours and shifts. Other workers in the cafés were generally full-time and only in a couple of individual cases in Norway were issues raised about working hours. In both countries, the law requires that the hours worked have to reflect contracted hours. There still, however, remains the issue of enforcement, as union officials noted, although these are more likely to arise in smaller owner-run workplaces. One case of 'non-declared' additional hours was reported by a café assistant in France, and a worker at N-Multibrand in Norway was employed on a fractional 0.2 contract while as a student only to remain on that contract when becoming full-time. These were both, however, isolated examples from the workplaces in the study.

A further issue concerns notice periods for work scheduling. In the UK, there are no legal regulations requiring employers to provide advance notice of changes in work schedules. The research found that most café managers tried to accommodate workers' preferences with regard to rotas and shift arrangements, similar to Lambert and Henly's (2012) study of US clothing retailers, while a few showed scant regard for individual circumstances. At UK-RetailA, for example, the manager was widely criticized for failing to take account of the needs of employees with young children when deciding shift arrangements. Her assistant manager described how this had led to frustration among staff and a 'dip in morale': 'They have all got families, kids, and she's not caring about what days she puts them on.' In France and Norway, there are regulations that specify notice periods for work rescheduling of between ten days and two to four weeks respectively.[5] Although these may not be enforced due to lack of union presence, working hours generally appeared to be relatively stable, although unions in both countries stressed there were problems across the sector.

Progression

Is being a café assistant a 'dead-end' job or can it provide opportunities for progression to better paid work? In all three contexts, the vast majority of workers interviewed stated that they had no wish to pursue a career in cafés. Many were students or former students, who saw the job as a form of temporary employment before embarking on their 'real career'. With the exception of the owner-managed independents and most franchises, all companies offered

---

[5] The fast food collective agreement in France requires ten days' notice before a change, while the hospitality collective agreement in Norway states that there should be agreement between managers and employees four weeks prior to changes, and the Environmental Work Act has a two-week notice period.

some form of progression route from café assistant through to supervisory and managerial level positions. The growing use of franchises, which effectively creates a mass of small companies and allows the parent organization to transfer labour management to the franchisee, generally diminishes progression opportunities and access to more formalized personnel processes. The larger chains, due to their size, are generally better able to accommodate progression aspirations, with positions also available at regional manager level as well as functional roles within head office in areas such as marketing and training.

Some of these companies have quite structured systems of training and development to support progression and actively seek to develop internal labour markets. Multibrand across the three countries was particularly well organized in relation to training provision and routes through into management. Qualifications, whether academic or vocational, however, were found to have little bearing on who gets progression in the café sector in any of the three countries. There is evidence that those with caring responsibilities, in particular women with younger children, encounter barriers to progression linked to the way in which jobs have been designed. Such issues were particularly prominent in the UK, where several workers spoke of the difficulties they faced owing either to the long working hours or the unsocial hours required in higher level jobs. Such barriers appear less prominent in France and Norway, although this may reflect the small number of older women working in these types of jobs.

In larger companies, high levels of labour turnover mean that supervisory positions tend to come up with reasonable frequency. However, there are issues around the quality of the positions on offer. In some cases, workers were reluctant to apply because of the additional demands involved and the small pay increments available, which were typically less than £1 per hour in the UK, 1 euro in France and 10 NOK in Norway. The normally somewhat higher paid manager jobs are rarely available as job holders tend to stay in post owing to few positions higher up.

While there are progression opportunities in the café sector, there are also indications that for some individuals these jobs can become a 'trap'. Ethnic minorities and recently arrived immigrants with limited proficiency in the country's language appear particularly vulnerable. In addition, in the UK, and to a limited extent in France, there were a number of younger workers (non-students) who had been in these jobs for at least three years and who intended to find 'better' employment in a different sector but had made little effort to secure such a change.

For most, café work is not a long-term career choice in any of the three countries. The evidence from this study suggests that the dominance of students in Norway has rendered café work a short-term job for the overwhelming majority, potentially crowding out 'drop outs' from the education system. Indeed, the availability of students to do this type of work could be seen as a central reason as to why low-wage work continues to exist in this sector and why there is little pressure for change. While in France and the UK, students are also an important source of labour, jobs are available for those with limited qualifications. For those looking to pursue a career in the sector, there are indications that opportunities exist particularly in the larger organizations in France and the UK. However, evidence suggests that workers in the UK are also more likely to find themselves stuck in these jobs; the primary group being women with few qualifications and primary responsibility for childcare. In addition, a growing group are those who have been unable to find higher paid jobs commensurate with their qualifications and who have been working in the sector for a number of years.

What Makes a Difference?

The evidence indicates that there are some national differences in work organization for café workers. In Norway, products were found to be less standardized and managers generally provide workers with more opportunities to exercise discretion in tasks, such as making sandwiches and serving drinks. Additional responsibilities, such as ordering, opening and closing stores, and giving refunds, are also more likely to take place. France and the UK are more similar in the standardization process and lack of worker discretion but in the UK workers appear to be subject to more extensive systems of control and monitoring. Despite these differences, the extent to which the job makes additional skill demands in Norway is fairly limited. This section reviews the factors that may explain the differences that are observable but also considers why there may not be more systematic variation.

The first is the role of trade unions. In all three countries this is a sector where unions are weak and have found it difficult to organize. France is the only country where a substantial proportion of workers are covered by collective agreements, but even so they have not been successful at raising pay levels above the SMIC. Beyond this key national difference, across the countries where unions signed a workplace agreement with employers, pay rates tended to be higher or there were some additional benefits, such as unsocial hours payments or company bonuses. However, unions appeared to play little role in relation to work organization, beyond one case of resisting work intensification at F-Multibrand. Cafés are small workplaces and there is little likelihood of a union representative being on site. In France, where works councils exist at company level, there has also been little activity in this area. It is unlikely, therefore, that direct union engagement over issues of work organization are key to explaining the differences observed.

What about the role of labour market factors such as pay or regulations relating to working time or employment security which can also be linked in part to the strength of trade unions at national level? In Norway in particular, but also in France, pay is higher than in the UK and workers also have more employment and hours security. Employer social charges at these lower pay rates are fairly similar in the UK and Norway but are somewhat higher in France in larger organizations. There is no evidence that these higher labour costs and more rigid forms of labour regulation directly impact on work organization, although it may have an influence on the viability of different product market strategies as discussed later. Despite the UK's lightly regulated labour market, long tenure was more of a feature here, with some workers having been in the same job for over ten years. Again, there was no indication that differences in tenure had any impact on the way that jobs were designed.

Education levels also seem to make little difference either within or across countries, with no suggestion, for example, that lack of skills impeded managers in devolving responsibilities or that more qualified workers encouraged broader job design. High out-of-work benefits, low unemployment, and the general 'accepted' minimum pay rates in Norway helps explain why most employers in the café sector abide by the collectively agreed industry tariff, even if they are not signed up to collective agreements. The ability of workers to find alternative employment may also contribute to a more relaxed attitude to performance management by employers and greater attentiveness to the overall attractiveness of their employment offer. However, this is difficult to separate out from other effects, such as embedded social norms around how workers expect to be treated and how managers in turn view their role. Relatively high unemployment in the UK, the limited alternative employment opportunities for lower qualified women with young children, and a ready supply of student and migrant labour ensure that employers have little difficulty filling jobs under existing terms and conditions.

Different management styles are observable in all countries which reflect both the personalities of individual managers and the approach of the company. However, there also appear to be national societal factors in play which shape a more general pattern in terms of the way managers manage and what is deemed to be acceptable behaviour on their part. There are some indications that in Norway an autocratic approach is held at bay by norms around how one relates to one's fellow citizens and how workers in turn expect to be treated. Many factors may feed into this ethos, such as socialization through the education system in a relatively egalitarian society where norms of equality and citizenship are strongly rooted. The data, however, necessitate an element of caution and the need for further research.

Finally, as with the fitness industry (see Chapter 6), it is important to consider the role of product market strategy in relation to work organization. In Norway, small chains and independents have been able to retain their position within the market through a strategy of customization, that is to say a higher quality product, which is relatively expensive, with workers involved in creating and preparing products to order and afforded more discretion in their dealing with customers. High levels of taxation and high labour costs are reflected in high price consumer products and services throughout Norway. As a result, price competition in the sector is restricted such that the differential between a quality product and a pre-packed standardized sandwich or vending machine coffee is relatively small.

In the UK and France, there is far more price competition but also a strategy pursued by the chains (also noted in Multibrand and Sandwichco outlets in Norway) of strict brand uniformity, consistent with Ritzer's (1993) view of McDonaldization and which plays out in terms of highly standardized products and modes of service delivery. As a result of this drive for uniformity of experience for the customer, it is not surprising that there is little potential for discretion in product design and delivery for individual café workers or even outlet managers (see Lloyd and Payne 2014). Furthermore, it is brand marketing which has enabled many of these chains to command a price premium for a standardized product, where quality is defined as consistent delivery to specification (Del Bono and Mayhew 2001). Notwithstanding the presence of some larger chains, the French café sector remains relatively small and continues to include a large number of independent providers. In the UK, the branded chains have a much bigger presence and constitute a highly successful and expanding sector of the market. Company pressures to drive up profitability can be seen as an important factor in imposing a range of demanding financial targets on individual outlets. The use of controls over managers and café workers reflects this relentless drive to cut costs, while maintaining the position and recognizability of the brand.

Across the three countries, there has been limited pressure upon employers to push for improvements in work organization and job design. This returns us to the question posed at the start of the chapter, namely whether there is actually scope to upgrade this type of job. It may be that the nature of the product and delivery makes it improbable that café work could ever be transformed into the type of intermediate level jobs seen in the retail sector in Germany. The competitive model, based on standard products and consistency of the brand, limits the discretion afforded to managers and provides limited opportunities for job upgrading at any level. With a more customized approach, an expanded role for workers could be envisaged encompassing aspects such as the creation of new drinks and sandwiches, purchasing, sourcing, and marketing. Nevertheless, the substantive part of the job would still involve the production, serving, and selling of a set range of fairly simple products.

In terms of performance, the UK has been particularly successful at developing a mass market in the sector, with large chains delivering standardized products with low-skill forms of work organization. Most companies have continued to expand and are achieving healthy profits, although the sandwich outlets and UK-Multibrand had seen downturns during the recession. For workers outcomes are poor, while for consumers they offer 'reliability' at low-to-mid cost, albeit with limited choice on many high streets and retail parks as independents are progressively squeezed out of the market.

In France, many companies had faced a substantial downturn during the recession and had lost customers. The market is highly competitive, and prices are generally lower than in the UK, despite much of the food being prepared on site or to order. As a result, some of the franchise owners and owner-managers have found it difficult to maintain their businesses. The market position lies part way between the Norwegian high quality model and the UK standardized one, with a large number of independents continuing to offer customers variety. Quality of work for café assistants, largely due to the higher national minimum wage and regulations of working time, sits somewhere in between the UK and Norway.

In Norway, the high cost of labour and taxes greatly reduces the price differentials between those cafés focusing on high quality and 'kiosk' chains providing standardized sandwiches and 'push-button' coffee. This, along with a broad affluent customer base, has helped shape a market in which the majority of cafés are situated towards the top end and are not markedly under-cut by lower cost rivals with mass economies of scale. Cafés within traditional bakeries remain popular and many customers expect both a high-quality product and a more individualized service from staff. The ability to customize does require a little more knowledge of products and takes more time but is still not particularly demanding in terms of skills. Overall, most organizations reported healthy profits, while talk of the recent recession that dominates the UK and France has little relevance in Norway.

Conclusions

The job of café worker is essentially a low-skilled position that requires no formal qualifications, and which can be learnt primarily 'on the job' in anything from a few days to a month. On the whole, Norwegian café chains would appear to provide a slightly broader job role and afford workers more discretion, while there is also evidence to suggest that managers may involve workers more and adopt a managerial style that is more inclusive and trusting of their staff. A combination of factors to do with industry structure, the nature of consumer demand, and wider social norms appear to play a role. Union organization and power at a broader societal level certainly influences some of these factors, but there is no evidence of a direct engagement with work organization at sector or workplace level. If there is an employment logic or societal effect it would seem to account for only relatively minor differences in work organization compared to the other countries.

While these differences are still of some importance for those working in cafés, these jobs in Norway remain low skilled, even where firms focus on a higher priced, higher value-added product. There seems little potential to raise the technical knowledge and skill requirements or the interaction with customers in these jobs to levels that might equate to intermediate skilled employment (see Chapter 6). Some improvements to café job design could be made in France and the UK, and to a lesser extent in Norway, but there is a lack of any pressure either from unions or labour market conditions, and certainly few signs of any concern or interest on the part of employers. The dominance of large chains, and the associated standardization of products and processes, is also a strong constraint on progress.

Café work is, therefore, likely to remain a relatively low-skilled job, and many of those engaged in this work are likely be over-qualified. For those who do this work for a short period of time, this may not matter so much but for others such jobs may become a trap. In France, mobility out of these jobs is relatively high, and it is rare to find workers older than 30. In Norway, the widespread use of students operates in the context of low unemployment and a relatively small proportion of young people with low qualifications. These findings reflect broader data which indicate that the percentage of adult workers in Norway and France in low-wage work is extremely small (Chapter 4). In France and the UK, with relatively high levels of youth unemployment, the widespread use of part-time student labour may restrict access to these jobs for younger workers with lower qualifications. At the same time, student labour is likely to place a downward pressure on wages and conditions in all three countries. In the UK, a similar squeeze has arisen from the influx of young, often highly educated, migrant workers into the sector. A further particularity of the UK situation is the presence of middle-age women working in these jobs, a feature that highlights the lack of upward mobility for many with family responsibilities.

If fundamental skill upgrading seems unrealistic and progression opportunities for some are limited, what can be done to improve wider aspects of job quality? Across the board, café jobs are low paid, although how low and where the bottom is reflects national pay setting institutions. In France and Norway, rates are higher, both in absolute and real terms, than in the UK but are still below what would be considered a reasonable income for an independent adult. For example, café workers are paid well below the legal minimum wage in the cleaning industry in Norway, where pay is set at 164 NOK per hour in 2014. For many of those working in café jobs in Norway, this situation is not unacceptable; they are overwhelmingly young students, including those taking a year or two out from education.

The research raises important questions in terms of how far one can speak of a Nordic 'employment logic' that influences jobs across an economy. While café jobs in Norway can be said to provide workers with more autonomy and discretion, those differences are not substantial. At the same time, the research further problematizes the relationship between product strategy and skill in services. Shifting firms up the value chain in this sector is only likely to bring about relatively small changes to skill demands. It is difficult to escape the conclusion that this is a job that is quite difficult to substantially upskill, even outside the model of standardization and routinization characteristic of big chains. That said, national institutions and regulations can and do play a vital role in relation to pay and working time. Improvements in pay and conditions are likely to depend upon the ability of trade unions and other social groups to pressure for stronger forms of employment regulation at national level as well as proactive and innovative approaches to union organizing in hard-to-reach sectors. In the concluding chapter that follows, we turn our attention more broadly to the prospects for developing 'better jobs' in service-dominated economies confronted with rising levels of education.

Table 7.5. Key features of the case study organizations

UK	Size[1]	Main focus of the unit	Market[2]	Number of staff in unit	Café assistant pay £ per hour[3]	Collective agreement
UK-CoffeeA	Large chain	Coffee shop	Mid-market standardized	6 (unit 1) 7 (unit 2) 7 (unit 3)	5.80–6.10	No
UK-CoffeeB	Large chain	Coffee shop	Mid-market standardized	11	5.80–6.10	No
UK-CoffeeC	Medium chain and franchise	Coffee shop Directly managed	Mid-market standardized	8	5.80	No
UKCoffeeD	Large chain	Coffee shop	Mid-market standardized	12 (unit 1) NA (unit 2)	5.85–6.50	No
UK-Multibrand	MNC large chain and contractor	Airport coffee shop and sandwich bar Directly managed	Mid-market standardized	10 (unit 1) 13 (unit 2)	5.80	No
UK-Sandwichco	MNC large franchise chain	Sandwich bar	Low cost standardized	12 (two units same owners)	5.80	No
UK-BakerA	Large chain	Bakery	Lower–mid market standardized	24	6.20	Yes
UK-BakerB	Medium chain	Bakery	Lower–mid market standardized	6	5.80	No
UK-Indep	Independent	Coffee shop and food	Upmarket customized	7	5.80	No
UK-RetailA	Large retail chain	Coffee shop and food Directly managed	Mid-market standardized	7	6.20–6.53	No
UK-RetailB	Medium catering contractor	Food Contractor in retail outlet	Mid-market standardized	14	5.80	No

(Continued)

Table 7.5. Continued

Norway	Size	Main focus of unit	Market	Number of staff in unit	Café assistant pay (NOK per hour)	Sector collective agreement	Collective agreement covering unit
N-CoffeeA	Small chain	Coffee shop	Upper–mid market	5	123		No
N-Multibrand	MNC large chain and contractor	Airport/station coffee shop and sandwich bar Directly managed	Mid-market standardized	48 (two units) 6 (station)	131–150		Yes
N-Sandwichco	MNC large franchise chain	Sandwich bar	Low cost standardized	9	95		No
N-BakerA	Small chain and franchise	Bakery franchises	Upmarket customized	10 (unit 1) 12 (unit 2)	125–130 120–125		No
N-BakerB	Small chain	Bakery	Upmarket some variety	14	130		Yes
N-BakerC	Small chain	Bakery	Upmarket customized	20	115		No
N-BakerD	Small chain	Bakery and sandwiches	Upper–mid market some variety	15	114–140		No
N-BakerE	Small chain	Bakery	Upmarket standardized	15–20	125		No
N-Indep	Independent	Coffee shop	Upmarket some variety	7	120		No

France	Size	Main focus	Market	Number of staff in unit	Café assistant pay (€ per hour)[4]	Sector collective agreement	Company collective agreement
F-SandwichA	Large chain and franchise	Sandwich bar franchise	Mid-market standardized	4	9	Fast food	No
F-SandwichB	Medium chain and franchise	Sandwich bar franchise	Mid-market standardized	12 (two units)	9	Fast food	No
F-SandwichC	Medium chain and a few franchises	Sandwich bar	Mid-market standardized	6	9	Fast food	Yes
F-SandwichD	Large contractor	Airport coffee and sandwiches	Mid-market standardized	9	9	Fast food	Yes

Case	Organization	Product	Market position	Outlets/Units	Wage	Sector	Union
F-Multibrand	MNC large chain and contractor	Coffee shop	Mid-market standardized	8	9	Fast food	Yes
F-Univ	Public sector	University coffee and sandwiches	Low cost standardized	8 (two units)	9.42–10.28	Civil service	Yes
F-BakerA	Large chain and franchise	Bakery franchise contractor	Upmarket standardized	13 Franchise 36 (two contractor units)	9	Franchise: Bakers Contractor: Fast food	No Yes
F-BakerB	Independent	Bakery	Up-market, some variety	4	10	Bakery	No
F-IndepA	Independent	Sandwich bar	Mid-market customized	3	9	Fast food	No
F-IndepB	Independent	Sandwich bar	Lower–mid market standardized	5	9	Fast food	No
F-IndepC	Independent	Sandwich bar	Mid-market standardized	3	9	Fast food	No
F-IndepD	Independent	Bread and sandwiches	Mid-market some variety	5	9	Fast food	No
F-IndepE	Independent	Bread and sandwiches	Mid-market standardized	12	9	Fast food	No

[1] Large chain refers to over 250 outlets, medium chain 50–250, small chain under 50.
[2] 'Standardized' refers to the same products produced in each outlet or pre-prepared for the customer on the basis of standard ingredients and quantities. 'Customized' indicates that products are varied and can be individualized for customers or are designed by the café assistant. 'Some variety' denotes some customization takes place although standard products were frequently sold.
[3] National minimum wage was £5.80.
[4] SMIC was €9.

8

Towards Better Jobs

Possibilities and Prospects in the Age of Over-Qualification

Introduction

Contemporary discussions of the future of work have been dominated by the idea of a globalized knowledge-based economy, where advanced nations fend off competitive threats from low-cost developing countries by adding value to goods and services and 'knowledge workers' enjoy autonomy, control, and 'authorship' over their work (Brown et al. 2010). More broadly, intensifying competition, new technologies, and increasingly sophisticated consumers were said to be transforming work in ways which demanded increasing levels of skill across the workforce. Skills came to be seen by many as a primary mechanism for delivering economic competitiveness and productivity growth, and the means by which individuals could maintain their 'employability' as well as secure good, well-paid jobs. Consequently, education and training has become an increasingly important area of policy intervention.

However, the *economic* argument for universal upskilling confronts a powerful counterfactual in rising wage inequality and the persistence, if not growth in many countries, of low-skill, low-wage jobs (Gautié and Schmitt 2010). Evidence of over-qualification, the under-utilization of skills and work intensification has mounted, issues often seen as particularly problematic in neo-liberal economies but which are not confined to them (Green 2006). While many low-skilled jobs are in place-based services not subject to international competition, there is a broader concern about work intensification, tightening managerial controls, and deskilling further up the occupational ladder among professional and managerial workers (Konzelmann et al. 2007; Thompson 2013).

Towards Better Jobs

It is against this backdrop that the question of how to develop 'more and better jobs', to borrow the phraseology of the European Union (European Commission 2001), has come to exercise a number of academic commentators (see Carré et al. 2012). The 2008 financial crisis, economic recession, and entrenchment of neo-liberalism, however, have ushered in a period of austerity in the majority of European countries leaving many pessimistic about future prospects for work, employment, and society. Some point to a more globalized and financialized capitalism, with a process of 'liberalization' (Baccaro and Howell 2011; Jackson and Deeg 2012) that is weakening the protective web of institutional and regulatory constraints established during the post-war years to protect society from the market (Streeck 2011b), the consequences of which are deepening inequality and rising insecurity. As Streeck (2014b: xii) argues, 'the parallels and interactions among capitalist countries far outweigh their institutional and economic differences'. Hyman (2015b: 273, 275) refers to the 'cancer stage of capitalism' (McMurtry 1998), with the central overarching question being whether a 'more humane, more solidaristic, and more plausible alternative to neoliberalism' can be articulated and advanced.

Why conduct cross-national comparative studies of work organization at this particular juncture? There are two broad responses. First, it can shed light on whether there remain differences both in institutions and the way that they affect work and skills, and in doing so offer an empirical test of the extent, depth, and variability of current trends. Second, it allows us to probe what is possible and what states can do to develop more skilled and better jobs, issues expanded upon in this chapter. However, this book has argued that any attempt to do so has to include a focus on the increasing number of service sector jobs that remain wedded to the national, if not local, economy. The primary focus, therefore, has been the organization of work and the skill content of service sector jobs across different countries and sectors.

This concluding chapter begins by drawing together the main findings from the studies of vocational teachers, fitness instructors, and café workers in Norway, France, and the UK. It then moves on to explore the central explanations for the differences and similarities observed and considers the broader question of 'who benefits?' The following section assesses the contribution of this research to comparative studies of skills and work organization before returning to the complex questions surrounding future prospects for improving job quality.

The View from the Sectors

In comparing service sector jobs across countries, the main focus has been on the organization of work taking into account the knowledge, training, and

Skills in the Age of Over-Qualification

learning required, the complexity of work tasks, and the level of worker autonomy (see Chapter 2). While the relationship with the customer/user is an important part of many service jobs, the book has not directly engaged with the 'emotional labour' element of work that has increasingly dominated discussion of service work 'skill' in the labour process tradition (Bolton 2004; Payne 2009). Instead, as argued in Chapter 2, the focus is on the technical and knowledge requirements of the tasks, and the extent of discretion and control within the job *as a whole*. While employees' experience of the customer varies greatly according to context (Korczynski 2009), it is the design of the job which forms that context. The primary aim was to compare objective aspects of job design and management practice, although our approach draws heavily upon workers' own accounts of their job.

Figures 8.1, 8.2, and 8.3 represent, in pictorial form, various dimensions of work organization for each of the three jobs in Norway, France, and the UK. One difficulty is that many of the elements have different aspects which become more complex as we move up the occupational hierarchy. Take autonomy for example. A teacher may have discretion over what is taught but not over the assessment process, while a café worker may have some choice over the words used to serve a customer but not over how to make a cup of coffee. It should be stressed that the diagrams are intended only as broad thumbnail sketches of the main differences; they do not seek to measure or quantify the precise magnitude of such differences by ascribing numerical

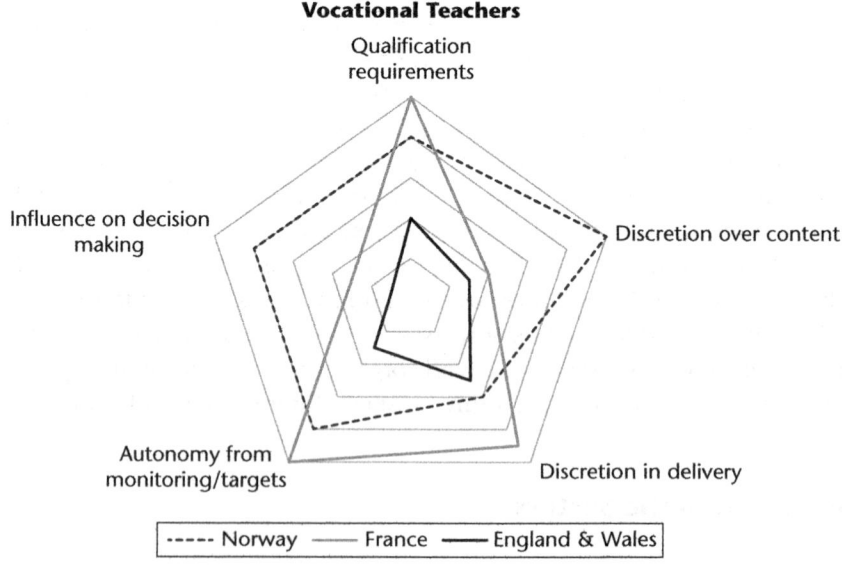

Figure 8.1. Differences in job design: vocational teachers

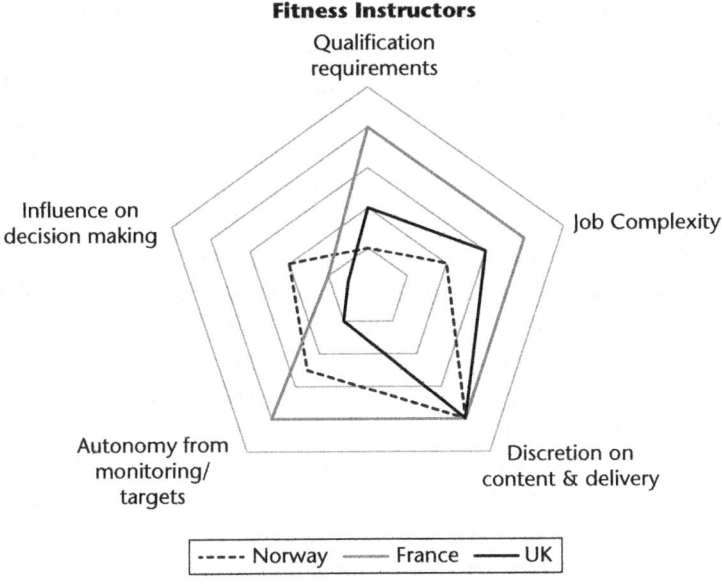

Figure 8.2. Differences in job design: fitness instructors

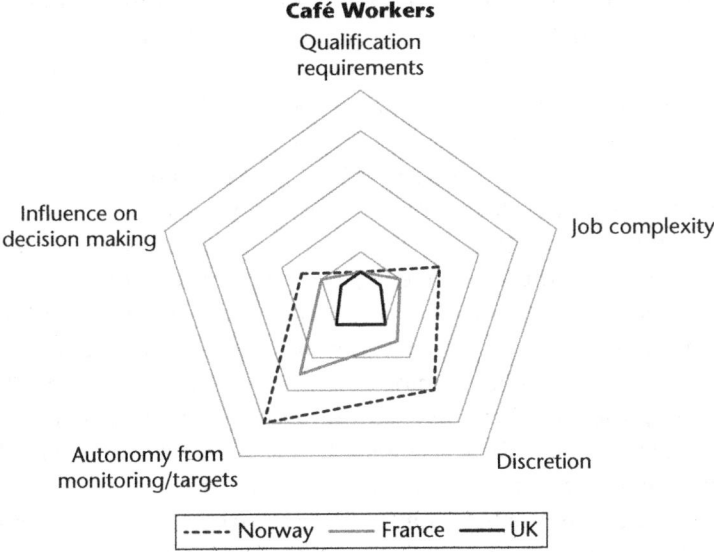

Figure 8.3. Differences in job design: café workers

values. Each diagram should be considered separately, with relatively low values at the centre, moving to higher values towards the outside of the chart.

The most distinctive cross-country differences are found at the top of the occupational ladder in the case of vocational teacher, while the least variation occurs at the bottom with café workers. Norwegian and French vocational teachers have substantially higher levels of discretion and autonomy than those in England and Wales. There are, however, noticeable differences. Norwegian teachers have more control over what is taught and also have substantial influence in decision-making at national policy level and in individual colleges. French teachers are almost completely free from targets and monitoring and have more discretion in how, although not what, they teach given a highly centralized curriculum. Qualification demands are highest in France, a country well known for regulating occupational entry, followed by Norway. Vocational teachers in England and Wales have lower qualification requirements, confront widespread constraints in terms of the curriculum, and are subject to extensive monitoring and targets. Their situation also stands out in terms of the frenetic pace of top-down policy churn, partly reflecting the absence of institutions for social dialogue within the sector. The picture is of a more professionalized workforce in Norway and France, compared to an increasingly casualized and part-time one in England and Wales. There are variations within each country, reflecting locality, regional policy approaches, and managerial style, but differences between the countries stand out sharply.

The direction of change is important too. Norway has seen some shifts towards greater monitoring of school performance and a more directive approach to pedagogic practice in recent years. Yet, there has also been a substantial loosening-up of the curriculum, placing more of the design of vocational programmes in the hands of local teachers. France has not witnessed similar trends towards the performance management of colleges or teachers, but there have been interventions in the teaching process through, for example, cross-curriculum project requirements. The main change, however, has been in relation to teachers' education and qualifications, which has affected all levels of the French education system and remains subject to ongoing revision and contestation. In England and Wales, there has been a long-term trend towards more intense performance management of the sector and, as a result, greater college monitoring of teachers' work. While moves were made to professionalize the workforce by requiring FE teachers to obtain teaching qualifications, albeit at a level below those in France and Norway, these requirements were revoked for England in 2013.

Turning to the 'intermediate' job of fitness instructor, the pattern changes substantially as there are fewer clear-cut differences between the countries as well as more internal variation reflecting organizational strategies and approaches. Whether this can be considered an intermediate job is a central question as there are significant differences in qualification requirements and the way the job is regulated. In France, instructors must possess a one-year or two-year, post-upper secondary school qualification ensuring that it is officially classified as an intermediate-level position. In the UK, a voluntary system of industry registration requires only a minimum vocational qualification at level two (deemed equivalent to successful completion of lower secondary school) and for senior instructors a level three qualification (equivalent to upper secondary). In Norway, there are no minimum standards, and it is seen as a more temporary or casual position situated at the lower end of the occupational ladder.

Overall, French instructors had more complex jobs, for example instructors wrote individual exercise programmes, whereas in the UK and Norway some instructor roles had been downgraded to a basic advice function. Nevertheless, French instructors were also required to teach standardized exercise classes, a role that was often performed by freelancers in the other two countries. Despite lower entry qualification requirements in Norway and the UK, some instructors undertook very similar tasks to those in France, including writing exercise programmes and undertaking individual instructing of those with additional risk factors such as health conditions. The picture of the relationship between qualifications, skills required in the job, and task complexity is, therefore, quite complex.

Are French instructors 'over-qualified' or are some UK and Norwegian workers 'under-qualified'? French instructors were generally considered to be suitably prepared for their positions, whereas in the UK widespread concerns were voiced about the rigour of many vocational qualifications as well as the extent of on-the-job learning required once in post. Again the picture is complicated as many instructors in the UK held qualifications at substantially higher levels, for example degrees in related subjects such as sports science, and many of the Norwegian instructors also held relevant qualifications. In Norway, the demands of the job, however, are often more limited, although again issues were raised about whether some instructors had acquired sufficient knowledge given the potential safety risks involved in giving the wrong advice to gym users.

As with vocational teachers, instructors in France and Norway have more job autonomy and are less subject to targets and monitoring than in the UK. However, the extent of choice over content and delivery method tends to be fairly similar, with French workers having more constraints when it comes to the delivery of standardized exercise classes, but often greater freedom when dealing with individual clients in the gym. Across the board, instructors had little influence over broader sector policies and workplace decisions. Recent years have seen some downgrading of qualification requirements in France and an increase in qualification demands from UK employers. Nevertheless, there is evidence of declining job autonomy in the UK with the more widespread use of monitoring and targets, alongside the deskilling of instructor roles in the private sector towards an increasingly 'meet and greet' function, following the expanded use of personal trainers.

The lower end job of café worker reveals greater similarities both across and within countries in terms of qualification demands and skill use.

Notwithstanding the widespread use of student labour, there are no qualification prerequisites and training is short and predominantly on-the-job. Task complexity and discretion are generally low, although there are some country differences. Workers in Norway and France tend to have slightly more responsibility in their jobs, often reflecting the lack of team leader or supervisor positions typically found in the UK. In Norway, workers also had more discretion in making products as opposed to the often extreme standardization prevalent in the larger UK chains. Workers in the UK are subject to more target-driven approaches and monitoring than the other two countries, particularly Norway. Café workers in Norway were generally consulted and engaged more actively by their managers than workers in the other two countries, although there was no evidence of formal union involvement. Decision-making influence is limited at sector level in the three countries, although unions play a greater role in France and Norway.

The change in the structure of the industry, particularly in the UK and France with the growth in large chains, has been associated with further standardization of the work process and reduced levels of worker discretion. In Norway, the growth of chains has been more limited and even where medium-sized companies exist there has not been a similar shift towards uniformity of products and processes. While larger organizations in all countries provide more opportunities for progression by virtue of their size and functional departments, they also tend to impose more managerial controls over unit managers and their staff in accordance with rigid budgetary controls and pressures for brand uniformity. In France and the UK, there was a perception of increased work intensity among many cafe workers which was not evident in Norway.

Overall, the evidence indicates a complex and rather differentiated picture on work organization and skill requirements when comparing the three jobs across Norway, France, and the UK. There is evidence of some national differences in work organization but these are not always extensive, nor are they necessarily associated with substantial variations in skill demands. Norway emerges as providing more involvement in decision-making and higher levels of autonomy, while the UK experience is of more extensive monitoring and targets than in both Norway and France. France offers an example of a more differentiated approach to autonomy and task complexity depending on the job's position in the occupational hierarchy.

Explanations

The three data chapters sought to explain why there are differences in work organization across countries as well as similarities in some cases. This section examines a number of central factors that can be seen to directly affect skills and work organization and which help to shape the way workers are managed. A number of factors emerge here, namely national sector specificities, the education and training system, the relative power of workers and their unions, and employment regulations and local labour market conditions.

Sector Specifics

For vocational teachers, there is a dual and direct relationship with government policy through the state's role as both employer and as a provider of publicly funded education. In England and Wales, new public management (NPM), in the form of marketization and centralized control via funding, targets, directives, and inspections, has resulted in intensive state and managerial monitoring of teachers' work. In Norway, NPM has made few inroads with only light auditing of quality and performance outcomes. In France NPM is absent, with a public service tradition that provides teachers, as professional civil servants, with considerable autonomy, outside of the curriculum. These differences reflect historically rooted state administrative traditions and, as discussed in a later section, the extent to which teacher professionals and unions are able to exert influence over policy decisions.

National sector composition also explains some of the differences in the fitness industry. Public sector provision, which is central to the UK sector, is rarely found in the fitness industries of France and Norway. UK local authority gyms, with their agenda of inclusiveness and commitment to the public health agenda, provided some of the most demanding instructor roles across the three countries, notwithstanding concerns over the adequacy of some of the instructors' qualifications. The industry in Norway, with its relatively low-cost membership and focus on a more fitness-oriented clientele, has been associated with more limited roles for instructors. If we look across the countries at the effects of individual organizations' positioning within the product market, however, there is little evidence of any consistent link between more expensive gyms competing on 'quality' and fitness instructor qualifications or the skill content of the job, reflecting the earlier work of Lloyd (2005) on UK gyms.

In the café sector, each country's product market has distinctive features which again impact on the organization of work. The rapid expansion of large chains in the UK, and increasingly in France, has been associated with a high degree of product and service standardization. The result has been a routinization of the café worker's role, allowing limited opportunities for discretion or involvement in local decision-making. In Norway, a combination of factors appears to have enabled independents and small chains to protect and expand their market whilst restricting the opportunities for those organizations selling standardized products. Key aspects include the small scale of the domestic market and the high level of affluence and relatively egalitarian income distribution among consumers, which reflects the wider Norwegian social model. In addition, relatively high labour costs limit the cost advantages to organizations of producing standardized, lower quality products. The resulting predominance of independents and relatively small chains focusing on higher quality and more customized products enables café workers to have more discretion within the job, although it is still within the boundaries of a series of low-skilled tasks.

The configuration of the sector, therefore, can be seen to have some links with the organization of work. However, the relationship is neither consistent nor straightforward. There is little evidence, for example, to support a direct link between a higher priced, higher quality offer and higher skilled jobs. However, there is a clear indication that social norms, consumption patterns, and expectations vary between countries and that they have some influence on the way that jobs are designed.

Skill Formation Systems

What about the role of the skill formation system? The higher qualifications required of vocational teachers in France and Norway in part reflects the organizational strength of the teaching profession in these countries and also helps to underpin claims to professional status. In contrast, low teacher qualification standards in England and Wales can be linked to union weakness and the low status of vocational education which, at the same time, acts to further undermine teachers' bargaining power through enabling the use of casual workers often employed in restricted job positions. However, qualifications are only one part of the explanation for differences in levels of discretion and autonomy. There is little evidence to suggest that simply raising the qualification requirements would have any substantive effect in England and Wales without wider changes to governance regimes, performativity demands, and collective voice mechanisms.

Similarly, for fitness instructors in France, the requirement to undertake post-BAC qualifications in combination with the restrictions on the number of students limits the pool of potential instructors and gives workers greater occupational status and *potentially* more power in the labour market. This status and higher knowledge base creates certain expectations among instructors in terms of what the job should involve and, in particular, how they are managed. In England and Wales, the learner-driven approach to education and training provision, where there is no attempt to match labour supply with actual demand, has led to a surplus of qualified individuals (from entry level to degree level) keen to pursue a career in sports and fitness. The low level of minimum entry qualifications, however, contributes to a weakening of instructors' position, limits potential power in the workplace, and depresses wages across the industry. In Norway, fitness instructors lack the status of a 'skilled' occupation—there is no recognized apprenticeship—which contributes to its positioning as a temporary, low-paid job that requires few skills and offers little in the way of a career path.

For café workers, the jobs are disconnected from the VET system in every country in that vocational qualifications related to hospitality or customer service appear to have little influence on employers' recruitment and selection decisions. There was no evidence that managers in the UK or Norwegian gyms (where weak or non-existent qualification regulation respectively means workers have highly variable qualifications), or in cafés across the three countries, redesigned their jobs in accordance with the vocational or academic qualifications of the individual worker or group of workers.

Union Organization and Influence

There is certainly good reason to believe that the power and influence wielded by organized labour is important in explaining country differences in work organization experienced by vocational teachers. In Norway, teacher unions have near universal membership and are powerful actors in a national policy-making process which affords considerable influence to the social partners, depending to some extent upon the political complexion of government (Helgøy and Homme 2007). Teacher unions also play an important role at school level, where there are legally backed channels for union participation in decision-making. The institutional embeddedness of strong teacher unions and their ability to mobilize members across the education sector limits what governments can do without encountering strong collective opposition and helps to explain why NPM has made fewer inroads and has acquired a different character in Norway.

In France, policy influence is exerted through a myriad of consultative bodies, which offer weaker forms of social partnership to Norway, but also more directly through strike action targeted at unpopular reforms that are seen as a threat to teachers' work and professionalism. However, lack of power and organization in the workplace can leave French teachers subject to school heads' unilateral decision-making in relation to local issues, such as student behavioural policies or resource allocation. In England, and to a lesser extent in Wales, teacher unions are marginalized from the state-controlled policy process, where social partnership is noticeably absent. The decline in union strength among further education teachers is reflected in the 'balkanization' of the workforce and growing employment insecurity as well as their seeming inability to influence policy, teacher qualification requirements, or inspection regimes.

In the fitness and café industries, trade unions are weak in all three countries, with low density rates that are significantly below the national average. Sector-level collective bargaining covers all organizations in both industries in France, most public sector gyms in the UK, and a minority of gyms and café outlets in Norway. These agreements tend to provide better pay and conditions for workers in the UK and Norway compared with those organizations that are not included. The most extensive union influence at sector level is in France where unions are involved in a broader range of institutional bodies created for social dialogue. Although French trade unions are weak at workplace level, there was more evidence of activism in the café sector than was the case in either Norway or the UK. In all three countries, where unions were organized at company or workplace level, there was evidence of a union effect when it came to improving pay and conditions but little influence over issues such as job design and skills use.

Employment Regulations, Labour Supply, and Workforce Composition

Differences in employment regulation did not appear to have a substantial *direct* impact on the way work was organized, notwithstanding its relevance for other aspects of job quality and the potential to exert indirect influence. The main observable effect was in the UK in relation to less regulation of self-employment and contractual hours which enabled employers to use more casual employment. The rapid expansion in the use of self-employment contracts for personal training in the private fitness industry and the widespread use of casual contracts and small part-time jobs for vocational teachers were often associated with a process of workforce segmentation creating narrower positions with fewer responsibilities. In cafés, the ease of hire-and-fire, along with variable hours contracts, allowed managers more scope to control and discipline workers than would have been possible if workers were harder to dismiss or had fixed hours.

Another factor to be considered is labour supply and workforce composition. In the café case studies, migrant workers were more extensively employed in Norway than in the UK and France, although in Norway's case these were predominantly young women from neighbouring Sweden. This finding may partly be due to the regions where the research was undertaken, which in the case of France and the UK did not include the capital cities. There are, however, important national differences in workforce composition which lend some support to Carré and Tilly's (2012) argument that factors in the 'reproductive sphere', such as the affordability of childcare and the education system, can play an important role in shaping who does low-end jobs. In the

UK café sector, the presence of substantial numbers of working-class mature women with low or no qualifications, who have worked in the sector for many years, is not found in Norway, where the job is overwhelmingly undertaken by female students and migrants. In France, those working in cafés are mainly young men and women who are passing through these jobs either as students or as a step on the ladder to better positions in the industry or wider labour market.

Students and those taking a break from their studies are important sources of labour for the café sector in all three countries as well as for the fitness industry in Norway. A plentiful supply of student labour undermines pressure on employers to raise pay levels in France and the UK, where there also remains a substantial non-student workforce in these sectors. In Norway, café worker and fitness instructor are jobs dominated by students looking for temporary employment. As a result, there is little pressure to pay a higher wage, join a trade union, create qualification standards, or develop career paths. This deployment of young people in what they consider to be temporary positions creates problems in terms of union organization and appears to limit both individual and wider societal concerns about the quality of employment. This position contrasts with other low-end jobs, such as cleaning in Norway, where full-time, older, mostly female workers are employed, and unions have successfully campaigned for improvements (Torvatn 2011).

Central Factors

Comparing these three service sector jobs across Norway, France, and the UK suggests a complex picture of country-level differences and similarities in respect of work organization, knowledge, and skill. In the case of vocational teachers, governance regimes, initial teacher education, and the extent to which teacher professionals exert collective influence explain substantive differences between countries. In the fitness industry, the regulation of qualifications, the distinctive role of public provision in the UK, and the weakness of unions across the board, shape a more complex pattern of between-country and within-country differences. In the café sector, where qualifications play no role and organized labour is again universally weak, country differences are relatively small. The explanation for such differences that do exist appears to relate mainly to product market factors, such as the size of chains and consumption patterns, alongside national differences in management styles. The next two sections examine, first, how differences in work organization impact on workers and second, the relationship with 'performance'.

Job Quality

Do workers benefit from broader and more demanding roles and how do these jobs fare across other dimensions of job quality? The evidence indicates that for employees the context is important when expanding job roles or increasing the complexity of tasks. Adding more complexity and responsibility to what is already a stretched position is not necessarily appreciated, especially where this is accompanied by targets and tighter managerial controls. However, providing jobs that are more demanding of skills and knowledge in the context of adequate time and space to exercise enhanced responsibilities was generally seen as positive among those working as teachers and fitness instructors. Studies have long drawn attention to the health problems often associated with work where individuals have limited control or discretion (Marmot 2004; Chandola 2010).

Lower down the occupational ladder, it would appear that issues of pay and conditions figure far more prominently in workers' evaluations of job quality, with workers often displaying low expectations in relation to work organization. Managerial approach is crucial too, with dissatisfaction voiced in relation to high levels of monitoring and control, and workers valuing managers who are fair and treat them with dignity. The social context of work also has a significant bearing on how workers feel about their jobs, including relationships with co-workers, and with students, clients, or customers. In addition, workers' own evaluation of a job often varies according to personal circumstance and across their life course, adding further complexity (Pocock and Skinner 2012).

What about the relationship between work organization and other job quality measures? Workers in all three jobs in Norway are substantially better paid than their counterparts in France and the UK, even when taking into account cost of living differences. This applies irrespective of differences in qualification and skill demands compared to the other countries, and reflects Norway's relative flat income distribution and high wage economy. In contrast, UK fitness instructors and café workers receive the lowest pay, reflecting weak collective organization and a lower national minimum wage than in France.

Some interesting differences can be noted in terms of positioning in the national pay hierarchy. In Norway, vocational teachers receive an average wage, whereas in England and Wales they are close to the top quartile despite having lower qualification demands, less autonomy, and weaker teacher unions. French teachers, with the highest level of qualification, are also near the top quartile. These outcomes are indicative of the relatively compressed occupational wage structures in Norway, which position skilled manual workers' pay much closer to that of public sector professionals. Again, national differences in where jobs sit in the pay structure apply in the case of fitness instructors. Instructors in France are positioned slightly higher than in the other two countries which in this case does appear to reflect higher qualification requirements and their associated status. Fitness instructors in Norway and the UK are located towards the bottom end of their respective national pay hierarchy, regardless of the differences in qualification requirements or forms of work organization. In all three countries, café workers are amongst the lowest paid.

In relation to other job quality outcomes, being a vocational teacher in Norway and France is far more likely to offer secure employment than in England and Wales, and is also built around a model that emphasizes full-time employment. This approach is partly due to the wider support in the two countries for the employment of women on a full-time basis which includes a range of leave entitlements and childcare provision. In England and Wales, part-time employment was often a product of managerial cost imperatives rather than the individual preferences of teachers. Other benefits for teachers, such as holidays and pensions, are fairly comparable across the three countries, although various leave arrangements (parental, training, etc.) are significantly higher in Norway, followed by France. In the UK, fitness instructors and café workers were also more likely to face insecure employment and lack of guaranteed hours. In addition, workers have to rely on much lower levels of state support than in Norway and France, for example in relation to pensions, leave arrangements, training, and unemployment payments. The exception is fitness instructors working in the public sector who receive more comparable employment benefits.

There is evidence of higher levels of stress and longer working hours among teachers in England and Wales than in Norway. French teachers also faced similar issues, indicating that autonomy and discretion do not necessarily protect against intensive work patterns. These experiences of work reflect broader concerns about the expansion of temporal demands and excessive workloads in professional jobs (Pocock and Skinner 2012). Occupational ill-health was raised as a significant issue among fitness instructors in France, resulting from teaching an excessive number of group exercise classes. Physical injury among instructors in Norway and the UK was not common, although it may be something that affects freelance teachers who undertake the majority of these activities, a group not included in this study. Work intensification was also an issue for café workers in France and the UK, a reminder that intensive working regimes are not necessarily related to workers taking on greater responsibilities or broader job roles.

The research confirms that for lower level jobs, where individuals have limited labour market power by virtue of a high degree of labour substitutability and weak collective organization, workers remain particularly reliant on national pay setting institutions and employment regulations for their pay and conditions (Carré and Tilly 2012). For example, in relation to pay, higher wages for lower earners in Norway are achieved through a combination of high out-of-work benefits and employers opting to abide by collectively agreed pay rates even if they are non-signatories to these agreements. In both France and the UK, national minimum wages (although at very different rates) have a substantial impact on raising the pay of those at the lower end of the labour market.

Performance Outcomes

Do differences in the organization of work affect performance? This is a tricky question to answer for several reasons, not least the issue of 'what is performance?' As the comparative chapters indicate, there are problems in terms of the measures one might adopt (e.g. turnover, employment, profit, productivity, quality), some of which, like quality, are difficult to pin down. Where definitional issues appear less problematic, in the case of productivity or turnover for example, the lack of data at organization or sector level renders cross-country comparison difficult.

Such problems are particularly acute in public services. A performance outcome, such as the number of students achieving qualifications at certain levels, is a far from perfect measure of the quality of the teaching and learning, let alone the breadth or depth of knowledge and skills acquired by learners themselves. In England and Wales, vocational programmes, for example, do not provide the broad platform of general education that is available to vocational learners in France, Norway, and indeed much of continental Europe that is seen as forming the basis for citizenship and future learning (Brockmann et al. 2011). Take the training of hairdressers for example. While in England and Wales, the aim is primarily to produce competent practitioners with the skills and knowledge to do the job, in France and Norway it is to produce good hairdressers who *also* have the potential to undertake further learning within or outside the profession and who are equipped to take their part in society as active and informed citizens.

With this in mind, what does this research have to tell us about the relationship between work organization and performance? For professional workers, one question might be whether performance is best secured through top-down controls and targets or by allowing expert labour the scope to make local judgements and to experiment and innovate with new ways of doing things from the bottom up (Lipsky 1980). The decision to allow a profession to take greater responsibility for outcomes or quality is often considered to be an issue of trust but it is also about the power of professional groups and their collective organizations to carve out and defend their professional autonomy. Of course, many other factors impact on teaching quality besides the space to share new ideas and approaches, such as resources and opportunities for continuing professional development (see Lloyd and Payne 2012).

What this research can shed light on is the degree to which vocational teachers had time and capacity to undertake what Høyrup et al. (2012) might term 'employee-driven innovation'. In Norway, teachers were less weighed down with bureaucracy and paperwork, and had more time to experiment with their colleagues when it came to finding innovative ways of improving students' experience. How far the variation in the availability of time and space across countries affected the actual process of teaching and learning requires further research. Nevertheless, it was clear that in England and Wales, audit demands and unremitting policy changes have severely reduced the opportunities available to collectively share ideas, with many teachers trying to squeeze this in as best they can (see Ertl and Kremer 2010).

If the relationship between work organization and performance is complex for vocational teachers, how does this play out in the other two jobs? For the fitness industry and the café sector, the relationship between workers' skills, the way the job is designed, and performance outcomes is also complex. Some fitness organizations favour approaches that emphasize high-quality instruction and/or demand higher qualifications, whereas others aim for only minimum service and very basic advice. There is no evidence that those organizations offering the former are necessarily more successful in relation to the 'bottom line'. However, this is *not* to imply that qualifications and the quality of instruction do not matter for performance. Again, the issue turns on what is meant by performance. If performance extends to guaranteeing the safety of gym users, including those with injuries or health-related conditions, then the depth of instructor knowledge and its consistency across the sector and individual instructors matters. Such assurance and consistency is questionable in the UK and Norway, and is best achieved by the French occupational licensing model which ensures all instructors hold a rigorous, high-level qualification. At sector level, there is also the question of whether the industry can contribute to broader social goals (another measure of performance) by accommodating the needs of poorer members of society and helping with public health issues, such as obesity. Here, the role of public sector provision, notably in the case of UK local authority gyms, is important.

In the café sector, large coffee chains have emerged quite rapidly in the UK and France, and have been successful in developing a business model based upon standardized products using workers undertaking low-skill, low-discretion jobs. These chains have squeezed out smaller businesses, particularly in the UK. In Norway, the market is skewed more towards smaller cafés and chains offering higher quality products, with limited availability of lower priced, standardized products. While both approaches restrict the 'choice' available to consumers, the implications for workers are somewhat different because the degree of standardization and brand uniformity required by the big chains reduces scope for both managerial and worker discretion (see Lloyd and Payne 2014). The UK and French chains embrace a model of employment that limits the opportunities for even the kind of worker discretion or involvement at the level of the work task observed in Norway. Looking at performance data across the hospitality sector as a whole, the UK appears to use high volumes of relatively cheap labour, has low levels of productivity, but obtains profit margins that are substantially higher than companies in France and Norway. While productivity typically figures prominently as an objective of government policy, it may not be a priority for companies who continue to profit despite low productivity.

Two general points emerge from this discussion. First, the issue of performance can be approached and understood in different ways and in relation to different interests. Second, there is no simple or necessary 'win–win' connection between better jobs and organizational performance, a point that is picked up in the next section when considering the contribution of this research to current debates around work organization and skill.

Research Contribution

In terms of broad discussions about the future of work, this research questions any inevitable or universal trend towards jobs becoming more skilled, whether we are looking at those towards the top of the hierarchy or those at the bottom. At the same time, there is little support for any 'technological imperative' that routinizes jobs in the middle of the labour market while raising the skill content of those at the top (Goos et al. 2014). The picture is undeniably more variable and complex. Many jobs are fixed within national or even local labour markets and have a more direct relationship with local patterns of service provision and consumption. The research also questions the idea of cross-national convergence in terms of work organization and job design highlighting significant national differences in the way some jobs are designed as well as similarities.

What does this research have to contribute to cross-national comparative studies of skill and work organization and the broader question of what can be done to improve work organization in respect of place-based service sector jobs? As discussed in Chapter 3, the dominant theoretical template for the study of national differences has been provided by varieties of capitalism (Hall and Soskice 2001), an approach derived from the manufacturing sector and subject to widespread criticism. Power resource theory, with its emphasis on the societal power and political influence of organized labour, has been offered as a better explanation for why Scandinavian countries achieve higher levels of task discretion than other types of economies (Gallie 2007, 2011).

The research outlined in this book offers some support for the view that Scandinavia is distinctive, with higher levels of task discretion across a 'whole spectrum of jobs' (Dobbin and Boychuk 1999: 261). However, Dobbin and Boychuk's contention that jobs in Scandinavia are characterized by a 'skills-governed' employment logic, while those in neo-liberal economies tend to be 'rule-governed', requires some qualification. The three jobs in Norway do afford higher levels of discretion and autonomy compared with the UK, although not always with those in France. These differences are not extensive in all cases, nor are they necessarily associated with higher skill demands. For example, if one compares fitness instructor jobs in Norway and the UK, many of these jobs look quite similar in terms of skill content, although managerial approaches differ. The same applies when comparing café jobs in these two countries.

The three UK jobs suggest that a 'rule-governed' logic might apply across a broad range of occupations, given the prevalence of targets and other mechanisms for performance monitoring. Insofar as one might speak of national employment logics, this would seem to relate to distinctive ways of managing workers, with workers generally afforded greater scope for discretion and autonomy in Norway (even where this remains relatively limited) compared with the UK, rather than to skill levels. While some institutional and power-related factors are important in shaping managerial norms, broader issues of how citizens relate to each other and how workers in turn expect to be treated are also of relevance, reflecting different societal norms around equality and citizenship. France, which does not appear in Dobbin and Boychuk's work, has often been associated with an autocratic managerial approach (Lane 1989), and there was evidence of this in the case of café workers. However, vocational teachers and fitness instructors experienced similar levels of autonomy to comparable workers in Norway, though the precise nature of such autonomy varied across the two countries. Again, this suggests that some modification is required to generalized notions of a French employment logic or managerial approach.

The limited distinctiveness of the Norwegian jobs at intermediate level and at the lower end may reflect the chosen sectors which lack the core institutional supporting blocks that are often put forward as explanations for high average levels of skill and discretion, such as strong trade unions, good quality apprenticeships, and legally backed mechanisms of co-determination. The findings from the French fitness sector also indicate that alternative supports to these types of jobs may be found in strong occupational regulation, although, as noted earlier, this is not necessarily a protection against high levels of work intensity. These findings further underscore the internally variegated nature of national models, particularly in terms of industrial relations and skill formation systems, the heterogeneity of the service economy, and the corresponding dangers of over-generalization (Crouch 2005). In accounting for differences, the research also highlights the importance of coming to grips with specific *national* sector dynamics, which have a particular relevance for non-traded service sector jobs. More attention needs to be placed on factors such as public service traditions as well as broader social norms and consumption patterns that show few signs of global convergence.

Comparative studies of work organization going back many years have emphasized the role played by the skill formation system in accounting for country differences, particularly when comparing manufacturing jobs (Maurice et al. 1986; Streeck 1992; Hall and Soskice 2001). Our research questions, first, the extent to which we can talk about a 'national system' of skill formation and, second, the problematic relationship between skill formation and usage. The research in this book emphasizes the variety of ways in which higher and intermediate level skills are developed. There are differences in content, place of delivery, and length of initial education provided to vocational teachers and fitness instructors both within and across countries. At the same time, many lower level jobs are separated from the national VET system in areas where qualifications play little or no role in employers' recruitment and selection decisions.

What of the relationship between skills supply and usage? At the national level, all three countries have undertaken a range of initiatives designed to boost the supply of qualified labour. In the UK, a greater emphasis has been placed on skills supply as the lever for improved economic and social outcomes than in France and Norway, given that other policy levers are either lacking or have been rejected on ideological grounds by UK policy-makers. The sector studies find little evidence to support the view that boosting skills supply on its own can have a significant impact on the way that organizations design jobs and make use of skills (see also Keep and Mayhew 2014). Few difficulties were cited in relation to skill shortages in recruitment, while over-qualified workers in the café and fitness industries were undertaking the same jobs as their less qualified colleagues and were on the same pay rates. Unlike the earlier tentative findings of Mason (2002) and Elias and Purcell (2004), there was no evidence that managers restructured tasks to utilize the higher skills offered by graduates in any of the countries.

Nevertheless, regulations that require job entrants to hold a higher level qualification *may* have an impact on status, pay, and potentially work organization, depending on the wider context. Where qualifications are associated with specific pay rates in the collective bargaining system (for example apprenticed skilled workers in Norway) or with a status in the occupational hierarchy (as in France), then there may be knock-on effects. The example of fitness instructors in France indicates that having a recognized qualification and associated status as a *professeur* has some influence on the way the job is designed and how instructors are subsequently managed. In the UK, however, the links between qualification, pay, and status are much more tenuous and such outcomes far less assured. These findings suggest that the impact of qualification regulation is likely to vary depending on the broader institutional and social structures within a country.

What does this research have to say about the role of organized labour in developing better designed jobs? The evidence broadly supports Gallie's (2007) argument that high *average* levels of task discretion in the Nordic countries reflect strong national labour movements which have been able to embed encompassing employment regimes that constrain employer behaviour. These findings from the three jobs are supported by a small number of comparative studies of low-wage jobs indicating that work organization is often better in more organized or regulated European economies compared with the UK or USA. In some of these studies, evidence also points to the ability of trade unions to directly influence job design decisions at workplace level, operating in conjunction with other supporting institutions, such as works councils and employment protection legislation, which again vary depending upon country and sector (Doellgast 2010; Gautié and Schmitt 2010). These studies, from a 'power resource' perspective, point towards the need to understand trade union influence at *multiple levels*—national, sector, and workplace—which is also reflected in our research.

Identifying the role of unions in explaining country differences in work organization is perhaps more straightforward than when it comes to understanding why some jobs look quite similar. In the case of café work, unions are relatively weak in all three countries. Does this weakness explain low levels of job complexity and skill demands or are there other more important factors? Might some jobs simply have limited potential for skill upgrading? Would a strong union in Norway push for apprenticeships in fitness instructing and seek to place pressure on managers to redesign work as a 'skilled' position? Do sector dynamics mean that union weakness is simply inscribed or written into *certain* sectors anyway? If union organization is a key element in realizing the potential of better work organization and job design in the service sector, not to mention improved terms and conditions, then the prospect for union organization, particularly outside the public sector, assumes a vital significance, a point that is returned to later.

It may be that some lower end jobs in sectors such as retail, hospitality, and cleaning offer little scope for significant skill upgrading, café work being a case in point. However, some caution is needed. The extensive use made of apprenticeships in broad job roles in German retailing indicates that substantial progress can be made in some areas, even supermarkets, if broader job design is part of the agenda (Voss-Dahm 2008). There is also some potential even in those sectors where it might appear impossible at first sight, such as contract cleaning in Norway (Torvatn 2011). Moreover there is no reason why workers in low-skilled jobs could not be provided with higher levels of discretion and autonomy. That said, it is very difficult to envisage how many lower end jobs could be transformed into intermediate level jobs that required two to three years of education or training.

What seems important is the scope for job redesign and the degree to which trade unions are able to organize within the particular sector, as well as draw upon institutional supports, to directly influence work organization decisions. In the absence of trade unions, employers have considerable latitude in terms of how they design jobs. Might employers still be persuaded to adopt better approaches, where such scope exists, despite union weakness and gaps in the regulatory framework? Is there a role still for organizational strategy? Referring to low-wage jobs, Carré and Tilly (2012) argue that one advantage of international sector comparisons is that they can help to highlight variation within any given country or sector which can result from product market 'niching' and employers adopting a 'high road' approach. As discussed in the previous section, however, any purported link between product market positioning, the management of workers, skill, and pay would appear to be highly contingent in services. While supporting the view that particular market positioning *might* allow for better work organization and improved job quality, the evidence from our research shows that more 'upmarket' employers need not necessarily adopt such an approach.

Even in the absence of what Streeck (1997b) terms 'beneficial constraints' on employer actions which foreclose 'low road' strategies, we are still likely to find some organizations opting to pursue competitive advantage through a 'high road' product market approach, of which a number may also adopt an associated 'high road' employee strategy. The danger, however, is that without robust constraints on employer choice, these organizations will remain 'islands of excellence' (Streeck 1989: 94), with the potential to be undercut by others that either adopt a 'low road' approach to their workforce or a more generalized low-cost, low-quality strategy.

As we have argued before (Lloyd and Payne 2002), broader improvements in skills and work organization require a combination of national institutional supports, more quality-based product market strategies, and increased power resources in the workplace. The use of high intensive work regimes for workers at intermediate and professional level also points to the importance of focusing on issues of autonomy, discretion, and work intensity towards the higher end of the occupational ladder. In addition, to ensure a public sector governance regime founded on professional autonomy and trust, there is the requirement for strong collective organization and an institutionalized voice for social partners within national policy arrangements. Trust and power form *two sides of the same coin*.

The findings lend further support to other studies (see Gallie 2007; Gautié and Schmitt 2010) which have highlighted the kind of 'beneficial constraints' or institutional supports that can make a difference to skills and work organization. These include systems of tripartite policy formation; extensive collective bargaining and high minimum wages; strong forms of initial education and training; a high reservation wage; institutionalized channels for worker/union voice in organizational-decision making; regulations governing employment protection, working time, contractual status, and outsourcing; and macro-policies which support union organization, full employment, and tight labour markets. These factors have been used to explain why Nordic countries have proportionally more jobs with higher levels of task discretion and skill at the macro-level (Gallie 2007), but many of these features also appear in specific sectoral studies highlighting differences between countries (e.g. Gautié and Schmitt 2010; Doellgast 2010).

The research also indicates that these factors are likely to make the *most significant* differences in terms of job design to workers in the middle and upper ends of the occupational ladder, where the scope for both upskilling and deskilling is likely to be greater. However, many of these factors may still play a part in improving work organization and skill in lower level jobs, where there is sufficient scope to do so. For many service sector workers in cleaning, hospitality, and retail, however, the potential for change in skills levels is likely to be relatively limited, notwithstanding far greater scope to make improvements in terms of pay and conditions, for which many of these institutional supports also remain central.

When it comes to developing better forms of work organization it is easier to identify what needs to be done than to grapple with the issues of how progressive change can be achieved and what can be learnt from other countries. Many of the key elements required, such as strong unions and regulatory constraints on employer action, run counter to neo-liberal arguments that economic performance is about flexibility and further deregulation, a position which is increasingly advanced at national and European level (see Heyes 2013; Meardi 2014). As noted in the introduction to this chapter, the current juncture makes thinking about such a question incredibly difficult, but no less important. It is to this question that we now turn.

Prospects for Progress

It is well known that simplistic 'policy borrowing'—in the sense of dragging specific policies from one country to another regardless of context—rarely works (Noble 1997). Learning from other countries whose institutional structures are the product of historical and contemporary struggles involving the state, capital, and labour is a highly complex undertaking. Does this mean that comparative research is a detached academic exercise with little practical utility? One of the main values of comparative research resides in its ability to question what can be presented within the national discourse as unchangeable, to stretch the parameters of possibility, and, in doing so, wrest it from the jaws of inevitability. In England and Wales, for example, it is increasingly difficult for teachers who work within the further education sector to even envisage a system where they are managed without targets, inspections, and corresponding grading of colleges and departments. How can it be that a fitness instructor in France is a regulated occupation or that café workers in Norway are paid nearly twice as much as those in the UK? The research reported in this book suggests that there are possibilities to improve work organization and job quality across a diverse range of sectors and at different levels of the labour market and occupational hierarchy. Even where jobs are difficult to upgrade substantially in terms of their skill content, they can certainly be improved along broader dimensions of job quality.

Making better use of workers' skills means finding ways by which policy can impact on work organization and job design. In the private sector, this involves considering the institutional and regulatory context which shapes employer behaviour as well as developing targeted forms of support to help organizations within particular sectors to upgrade their product market strategy, job redesign, skills development, and wider managerial approaches. In the public sector, forms of governance which are founded on trust in professional judgement within a broad framework which provides for public accountability is one of the starting points for enhancing job skills, autonomy, and discretion in countries where NPM currently holds sway.

As noted earlier, the Nordic countries benefit from a range of supportive macro-institutional conditions which help to achieve a relatively high proportion of jobs with forms of work organization that involve high levels of discretion and learning intensity (Holm et al. 2010). Scandinavian commentators have also emphasized the role played by national workplace innovation programmes whereby research experts help organizations to develop new and better ways of working (Gustavsen 2007). The evidence, however, indicates that changing employer behaviour through projects of this kind is not easy and requires long-term policy commitment. Therefore, while these programmes may be part of the story (OECD 2010a), it is hard to escape the conclusion that it is the wider institutional context which is the *main* driver of better forms of work organization.

What progress might be made through workplace innovation programmes, skill ecosystem initiatives, or skills utilization projects in countries with unsupportive institutional environments remains unclear but the evidence to date suggests that this is likely to be akin to 'grinding through granite' (Buchanan et al. 2010: 34–5; see also Payne 2012). This is not to suggest that no progress could be made but the steps are likely to be very small and may not necessarily prove sustainable. To move beyond small gains requires robust regulatory institutions and social constraints that can foreclose 'low road' routes to competitive success, policies designed to grow the share of firms competing successfully on the basis of high-skilled work, and institutionalized voice mechanisms that afford labour a strong say in national policy and workplace decision-making within both the public and private sectors.

As British-based researchers, we feel it necessary to consider the steps needed to advance a 'more and better jobs' agenda in the UK. The one lever of labour market regulation that has become embedded in the UK is the national minimum wage. Using a relatively high minimum wage to foreclose the low road, and business support and workplace development programmes to help organizations develop new and better ways of working, would offer an initial starting point. A willing government could attempt to shift the public sector governance regime away from NPM towards an approach that emphasized professional expertise and collective improvement, while at the same time using public procurement to encourage better quality jobs, in terms of both skills and pay and conditions. Substantive progress, however, would require a fundamental break with neo-liberalism to make possible a more effective policy agenda. This would encompass rebuilding collective labour organization and influence, including a central role in the management of the economy and workplace, and a strong platform of employment and social rights as part of an alternative growth strategy focused on jobs, high wages, and decent work.

Ultimately, this struggle for *better jobs* is the struggle for economic and industrial democracy, to manage capital in the interests of labour, and to develop a protective shell of regulatory and social constraints that can insulate the economy and society from the destabilizing effects of the market (Coates 2013: 50; Hyman 2015a). As Streeck (2010: 37) notes, such a project requires a 'resisting society' with 'enough political muscle' to face down opposition. It is one thing to attempt this in conditions when labour movements are strong and capital has limited exit options, such as existed in the post-war years, and quite another when capital is more mobile, economies are increasingly financialized, and organized labour is being weakened. The challenge is particularly acute in countries like the UK, given the extent of trade union decline and marginalization from public policy.

The question facing other countries with more socially embedded economies is whether their models are sustainable. What concerns many commentators is that globalization, financialization, and a resurgent neo-liberalism are unravelling historic 'social compromises' through which advances were made in the past, as the balance of power shifts further towards capital and away from organized labour. Some point to a complex process of 'liberalization' that plays out differently in different contexts but with a common direction of travel, whereby social and regulatory institutions are eroded or weakened and employers' ability to shape pay and conditions is extended (Streeck 2011b; Baccaro and Howell 2011).

There is no doubt that the weakening of organized labour in many European countries is a major problem, given the historic role played by national labour movements in imposing constraints on capital. The shift to services is often seen as contributing to union decline, confronting unions with major organizational challenges in sectors where they are currently weak, and where workplaces can be small and the workforce transient. Streeck (2014a: 64) goes further, arguing that contemporary capitalism has disorganized labour to such an extent that there may now be no viable agency left to defend society against the market, thereby condemning capitalism to a 'long and painful period of cumulative decay'. If so, then the prospects for advancing better jobs look incredibly bleak.

As Streeck (2011c: 18) notes elsewhere, however, 'The capacity of the social sciences to make predictions is limited if it exists at all'. The current economic crisis and push towards austerity is highly variable across nation states, but in many countries the economic and social consequences are real and painful, the effects of which cannot be predicted with any certainty (Hyman 2015b: 272). High unemployment, not least youth unemployment, continues to haunt many European countries, while many graduates also confront underemployment and in the UK increasing student debt. Excessive executive pay and bank bonuses, rising social inequality, corporate tax avoidance, and cuts to public services and social supports provide an agenda around which a broad-based progressive opposition to neo-liberalism can mobilize. While protests have already erupted in many countries, as neo-liberal austerity tears at the social fabric, it remains impossible to predict if or how these may evolve.

Unions have a vital role to play in this agenda. Union assertiveness and influence continues to differ greatly between countries and union decline is not inevitable as Norway shows. However, unions everywhere face the problem of building their organizational strength and extending their reach to new areas of the service sector. While revitalizing the union movement is certainly a major challenge for reasons outlined earlier, it is not impossible. Unions have had some success in organizing in private services, even in seemingly unpromising areas such as call centres, the fast food sector in the USA, and retail parcel delivery sectors in Germany (Gold and Artus 2015). After a number of years of deregulation and a dramatic growth in low-waged work in Germany, political pressure and union campaigns have led to the introduction of a national minimum wage, albeit at a relatively low level.

There is no doubt that innovative organizing strategies are required. But the challenge for unions, as Hyman (2015b: 273–5) argues, also remains broader: to be a 'sword of justice' (Flanders 1970), to engage as 'outsiders' in 'contentious politics', and to join with other progressive social movements to offer a *real* alternative to neo-liberalism.

Education

Any book concerned with skills needs to consider carefully the role and purpose of education and training. Skills, on their own, are certainly not a panacea for addressing contemporary economic and social problems (Keep and Mayhew 2010). Their contribution to the development of skilled jobs and decent work is partial, contingent, and conditional on many other factors. Furthermore, 'education and training have functions other than the transmission of the skills necessary for work. They are also a powerful means for ensuring personal development and the full realisation of human capabilities' (Ashton and Green 1996: 191).

Who 'wins' and 'loses' in the struggle for 'good' jobs in any country will partly reflect the extent to which the education system serves to mitigate the advantages afforded by parental wealth and cultural capital. However, as Bernstein (1970) noted many years ago, 'Education cannot compensate for society'. The greater the inequality in income and wealth and the higher the levels of poverty in a country, the more intense the fight to secure good jobs and to avoid the lower reaches of the labour market, a competitive struggle for which inevitably the wealthier are more equipped to succeed. A good example is the expansion of higher education in the UK, which many commentators argue has only served to reproduce and deepen class-based inequalities within the university system (Trow 2006). As Reay (2011: 2) notes, 'educational systems are only as good as the societies they emerge out of. Capitalist, neoliberal societies beget capitalist neoliberal education systems.'

'Meritocracy' is itself an unattainable, or even dystopian, ideal and one frequently invoked by the privileged and the powerful to legitimize inequality (Young 1958; Tawney 1964a). Ultimately, the supply of jobs, the quality of jobs, rights at work, and the social protections available if one is without work are not in the power of education and training to alter, only respond to. This is the major flaw in the neo-liberal depiction of individuals as self-reliant economic actors protecting themselves from social risks by dint of their human capital, something which applies only to those with scarce, marketable skills. As Colin Crouch observed,[1] for all the talk of new social risks and

---

[1] 'Reintegrating industrial relations and social policy', Plenary Session, BUIRA 2015 Conference, De Montfort University, 26 June.

an enabling role for the state in empowering opportunity and protection for individuals through education and training, the 'old' social risks of low wages, insecure work, and unemployment have not gone away.

Finally, while we have stressed the possibilities for better designed jobs, there is likely to remain in all advanced economies a significant stratum of service sector jobs in areas such as personal and protective services, hospitality, and retail which are both difficult to upgrade substantially in terms of their skill content and are unlikely to be swept away by technological change and international competition. The persistence of such jobs in the context of expanded education systems means that over-qualification and the under-utilization of skills look set to remain an ongoing challenge for all countries, albeit to differing extents depending upon the structure of their labour markets. This represents a continuing challenge to economistic and instrumentalist approaches to education and training, and the whole 'learning for earning' discourse which may leave many feeling disillusioned (Brown et al. 2010).

In an age of over-qualification, the case for educating people to live more fulfilling lives, irrespective of what job they do, becomes all the more salient. This is not to deny that many low-end jobs, in addition to performing vital social and economic functions, are meaningful to many of those who undertake them. However, it would be equally wrong to deny that many offer little in the way of personal fulfilment. This adds further weight to arguments that all forms of initial education and training should be a preparation not only for work but for life.

As noted earlier, the broader component of general education provided to vocational learners in many European countries as a foundation for citizenship and future learning is certainly an advance on the situation in the UK where such an element remains weak (Brockmann et al. 2011). But the challenge goes far beyond this. A more equal society and the democratization of the economy require both an inclusive school system where all social groups are educated together and a fully democratic education that can nurture critical knowledge, challenge social injustice, and, crucially, build a collective sense of responsibility for others, as Dewey (1916), Tawney (1964b), and others (e.g. Reay 2012) have long argued. The challenges to develop such a democratic education remain just as difficult as those involved in transforming the workplace and needs to be seen as part of an integrated struggle, with the Nordic countries again having gone furthest in this respect.

An Optimism of the Will

These are hard times to be thinking about the prospects for better jobs, 'good capitalism', 'post-capitalism', 'socialism', or whatever other label one might choose to apply to such a project (Hyman 2015b: 275), and it is all too easy to slide into hopeless pessimism (Streeck 2014a). The challenge for the left, as Hyman (2015b: 275) reminds us, is to be optimistic, to put forward a 'persuasive vision of a different and better society and economy'. In that sense, the vision needs to be 'utopian', in order to go beyond existing constraints and to challenge what is presented by proponents of neo-liberalism as unarguable 'common sense'. It was the Italian Marxist Antonio Gramsci (1971) who from the dark confines of Mussolini's prisons, famously observed that the 'pessimism of the intellect' requires an 'optimism of the will'.

While there are undeniably common pressures bearing down on all advanced capitalist countries, it is important to avoid collapsing these into a crude convergence perspective and to recognize the considerable diversity in national capitalisms that still exists and the way these pressures play out differently. While some forms of capitalism are better than others, we do not suggest that any model is without its own problems, tensions, and contradictions; capitalism may come in a huge variety of forms but *it is still capitalism*. As Coates (2000: 234) observes, the problem with picking any model is that its future success cannot be vouchsafed. Besides, no country can rewrite its own history and become another. Cross-national comparative research can, however, provide valuable insights into what is possible and what would be required to realize progressive change.

In emphasizing progressive possibilities, we are acutely aware that this does not mean that change will happen. In many countries, job quality is not even on the political radar. Forging a credible alternative to neo-liberalism in an era of financialized capitalism requires intellectual effort as well as mass mobilization. At a time of crisis, it is perhaps more important than ever to assert what is possible, if the political will existed. States act in the context of inherited institutional structures, development paths, and social orders where the balance of power between social actors and the contours of political struggle are highly variable. While this undoubtedly renders progressive possibilities easier to pursue in some contexts than others, nothing is inevitable. Gains still have to defended, and progressive change is always possible where there is a collective demand. The shockwaves currently reverberating throughout Europe as austerity policies bite, social inequality rises, and everyday life becomes increasingly subject to the market, bring new challenges, contradictions, and possibilities. It is from this reality, and the necessity of change, that hope springs.

Appendix 1

The appendix gives additional information regarding the interviews undertaken as part of the main research project underpinning the book, and is intended to supplement the material presented in Chapters 5, 6, and 7. Organizations and individuals identified here have been given pseudonyms to ensure anonymity. All interviews were recorded and transcribed.

Vocational Teachers

For vocational teachers, the sector bodies contacted and interviewed related to the education and training of teachers, union representatives, and relevant government officials. Secondary source materials were also consulted, depending on their availability, to help build a picture of the sector and its challenges. With far more information available in England and Wales, this reduced the necessity to gather so much of this material through interviews, whereas in France and Norway these interviews proved far more important in this respect.

In order to provide systematic comparative data, research focused on one group of vocational teachers—those teaching hairdressing. Hairdressing was chosen as the subject area, as it was taught in public colleges and schools across all three countries as part of initial VET. Schools and colleges were selected in different localities to take account of any effects of the particular socio-economic profile of the student population. In England and Wales, where inspections are a central part of the institutional landscape, colleges were also selected on the basis of inspection ratings, with two colleges graded highly and two at the lower end.

In terms of research access, approaches were made directly to either the head of the school or college or the hairdressing department. In each institution, the aim was to interview the head, the departmental manager or coordinator, and a range of hairdressing teachers. In each case, a day was spent at the school, with tours provided of teaching rooms, staff areas, and other student facilities. In many cases, the teachers selected for interview were all those in work on the day of the study visit or a selection based on staff availability. Interviews typically lasted between thirty minutes and one hour, and followed a standard schedule of questions. In three schools (Norway1, Norway2, and France3), a group interview was held with teachers lasting around

Appendix 1

two hours. Teachers interviewed also completed a one page tick-box questionnaire which covered standard measures of job satisfaction, job autonomy, and work intensity. The small sample size, however, meant that these did not form a substantive part of the data analysis. In all countries, all hairdressing teaching staff were female which may have provided a different perspective on how they viewed and experienced their jobs than male teachers or teachers in departments which are mixed or predominantly male (e.g. engineering). In total, fifty-four individuals were interviewed at school/college level. All interviews were undertaken between 2009 and 2011.

Sector Interviews (16 Interviews)

ENGLAND AND WALES

Lifelong Learning UK, the sector skills council for the learning and skills sector
The Institute for Learning (the compulsory membership body for teachers in English FE colleges between 2007 and 2012)
The Association of Colleges (England's employers' association)
Senior national official UCU, the main teachers' union
University lecturer coordinating an FE teacher training course, England

NORWAY

Directorate of Education and Training (the executive arm of the Ministry of Education and Research)
Senior national official, Union of Education, the main teachers' union
Education Department, County
Two lecturers, university providing teacher education programmes
Researchers, FAFO (independent research foundation)

FRANCE

Lecturer, coordinator for training hairdressing teachers, IUFM
Two national inspectors of vocational teachers
Regional senior officer, Department of Education and Sports
Teaching coordinator and hairdressing teacher, private college

Workplace Interviews

ENGLAND AND WALES (25 INTERVIEWS)

England1

Human resources manager
Head of quality
Head of department, Hair, Beauty, and Hospitality
Janet, full-time hairdressing teacher
Sandra, part-time (50 per cent) hairdressing teacher (typically works 30 hours per week)
Lynne, full-time hairdressing teacher
Sharon, full-time hairdressing teacher

Appendix 1

England2
    Human resources administrator
    Jan, head of hairdressing team and teacher
    Liz, part-time (60 per cent) hairdressing teacher
    Sarah, part-time (50 per cent) hairdressing teacher
    Cheryl, full-time hairdressing teacher
    Lisa, full-time hairdressing teacher instructor (lower grade)

Wales1
    Staff development manager
    Personnel officer
    Susan, deputy faculty head (includes hairdressing) and previously hairdressing teacher
    Julie, faculty quality manager and hairdressing teacher
    Rachael, part-time (80 per cent) hairdressing teacher
    Maria, full-time hairdressing teacher

Wales2
    College principal
    Head of Services to People department
    Linda, full-time hairdressing teacher (curriculum leader)
    Debbie, part-time, temporary hairdressing teacher (14 hours of teaching per week, hourly paid)
    Donna (80 per cent contract) hairdressing teacher
    Tina, full-time hairdressing teacher

NORWAY (15 INTERVIEWS)

Norway1
    School principal
    School vice-principal and head of Arts and Crafts department (covers hairdressing)
    Laura, full-time hairdressing teacher (group interview)
    Anna, full-time, temporary hairdressing teacher (group and individual interview)
    Helga, full-time hairdressing teacher (group interview)
    Inger, full-time hairdressing teacher (group interview)

Norway2
    Head of Arts and Crafts department (covers hairdressing)
    Anya, full-time hairdressing teacher (group interview)
    Eva, full-time hairdressing teacher (group interview)
    Jan, full-time hairdressing teacher (group interview)

Norway3
    School head
    School deputy head
    Linda, part-time (20 per cent) hairdressing teacher; full-time, vocational teacher training student
    Heidi, full-time hairdressing teacher
    Kristine, full-time hairdressing teacher, teaching coordinator

Appendix 1

FRANCE (14 INTERVIEWS)

France1
   Principal
   Head of works (assistant head)
   Corinne, full-time hairdressing teacher
   Catherine, full-time hairdressing teacher and teaching coordinator
   Marie, full-time hairdressing teacher

France2
   Head of works (assistant head)
   Brigitte, full-time hairdressing teacher
   Martine, full-time hairdressing teacher
   Nadine, full-time hairdressing teacher, hairdressing coordinator

France3
   Corinne, full-time hairdressing teacher (group interview)
   Nicole, full-time hairdressing teacher (group interview)
   Agnes, full-time hairdressing teacher (group interview)
   Nathalie, full-time hairdressing teacher (group interview)
   Jocelyn, full-time hairdressing teacher (group interview)

Fitness Instructors

The sector study of the fitness industry was partly limited by the lack of substantive secondary data available in France and Norway. In contrast for the UK, documentary sources and previous research by Caroline Lloyd on the industry provided extensive background data and contextual information. Interviews were undertaken at industry level in the three countries with representatives from training providers and employers' associations where they existed. Lack of union organization in the fitness industry meant that it was not possible to find a relevant individual at national level to interview in any of the countries.

Gyms were selected to include those located in different market positions, with some emphasizing quality and others focusing more on lower prices. The aim was also to select those types of organizations that dominate the market in each country. In the UK, gyms were chosen to include two which were part of large chains and two from the public sector. In Norway, a larger chain, a small chain, and a not-for-profit provider offered a useful reflection of the industry. In France, a larger chain was included, along with a range of gyms from smaller organizations within one particular locality. Access was arranged through a variety of means, including approaches to head office, contacting local gym managers, and through walk-ins (France).

As far as possible, semi-structured interviews were undertaken with the gym manager, fitness instructors, and, where they existed, gym supervisor and personal trainers. Interviews typically lasted for an hour with managers and around thirty to sixty minutes for instructors. Interviewees were selected by managers but were typically instructors who were on duty that day. All interviews took place at the gym and tours were provided of the fitness areas, changing rooms, and general facilities. Fitness

Appendix 1

instructors also completed a one-page tick-box questionnaire which covered standard measures of job satisfaction, job autonomy, and work intensity. They also completed a job task sheet, which asked whether and how often they undertook forty-one specified tasks. The small sample size, however, meant that these did not form a substantive part of the data analysis. In total, forty-nine people were interviewed at workplace level. All interviews were undertaken between 2009 and 2011.

Sectoral Interviews (15 Interviews)

UK
   Representative of the Register of Exercise Professionals
   Two representatives from Skills Active (sector skills council for fitness and leisure)
   Private training provider
   FE college training provider

NORWAY
   Private training provider
   Four lecturers, university training provider
   Independent researcher
   Representative from HSH (employers' association)

FRANCE
   Representative from the National Observatory of Sport and Employment
   Public training provider
   French representative of employers on European Fitness Association

Workplace Interviews

UK (19 INTERVIEWS)

UKgym1
   Gym manager
   Jack, instructor (30 hours), supervisor and self-employed personal trainer at UKgym1
   Anna, instructor full-time and self-employed personal trainer at UKgym1

UKgym2
   General manager
   Fitness manager
   Dan, instructor, full-time
   Kelly, personal trainer, self-employed at UKgym2

UK-LA1
   Local authority programme development manager
   Duty manager
   Jamie, instructor, part-time casual, 12 to 20 hours per week (full-time job in another sector)
   Thomas, instructor, full-time
   Andrea, instructor, part-time, 20 hours per week
   Joe, instructor, full-time

Appendix 1

UK-LA2
    Centre general manager
    Gym manager
    Rachel, gym supervisor and instructor, full-time
    Scott, instructor, 26 hours per week
    Jessica, instructor, part-time, 24 hours per week
    David, instructor, part-time, 24 hours per week and casual hours

NORWAY (15 INTERVIEWS)

Ngym1
    Gym manager
    Anders, instructor, 3 hours per week, personal trainer part-time at Ngym1 (full-time student)
    Kristine, full-time, personal trainer (previously instructor)
    Luke, full-time, personal trainer (previously instructor)
    Martin, full-time, personal trainer
    Thomas, full-time, personal trainer

Ngym2 (2 gyms)
    Female Gym A, manager and instructor
    Male Gym B, manager and instructor
    Maria, instructor, full-time
    Camilla, instructor, part-time varied hours
    Jonas, instructor, part-time varied hours (full-time student)

Ngym3
    Sports manager
    Gym manager, instructor
    Artur, instructor, 20 per cent contract (full-time student)
    Ole, instructor, 20 per cent contract (full-time job in another sector)

FRANCE (15 INTERVIEWS)

Fgym1 (2 gyms)
    Chief executive
    Director of training and human resources
    Henri, Gym A manager
    Nicole, Gym B manager
    Fabian, full-time head of fitness team (just promoted from fitness instructor)
    Mathieu, fitness instructor, full-time

Fgym2
    Gym manager
    Nicolas, fitness instructor, 30 hours per week

Fgym3
    Michelle, manager
    Laura, fitness instructor, 24 hours per week

Fgym4
  Antoine, fitness instructor, full-time

Fgym5
  Owner and fitness instructor
  Vincent, fitness instructor, full-time
  Axel, fitness instructor, 21 hours per week (full-time student)

Fgym6
  Manager and fitness instructor, full-time

Café Workers

Interviews were undertaken at industry level, the balance of which once again reflected the lack of secondary data available on France and Norway and the need to gather more background information in these countries using interviews. The definition of a café was kept relatively broad and was defined as those outlets selling sandwiches and non-alcoholic beverages with a seated area for consumption. Due to the wide variety of outlets, the small numbers of workers in each outlet, and, on a number of occasions, the difficulty in obtaining multiple interviews, it was decided to include a larger selection of outlets within the study. In France, a café (the definition of café used in this study) is not as common and interviews were also conducted in some outlets that did not include 'sit down' areas as well as a larger number of independents.

The choice of cafés was based primarily on locality, but also with the aim of ensuring that the larger chains were included and that there was a good reflection of the general market. One company head office (Multibrand) organized access to units across the three countries, while 'walk-in' requests enabled interviews to be undertaken at units of Sandwichco in the UK and Norway. Although access was occasionally arranged via direct contact with head offices, in most cases it was negotiated with local managers through 'walk-in' requests. In the UK and Norway, there was generally a willingness to participate. In France, there were a substantial number of rejections from managers, making the interview process more difficult. While in the UK and Norway, all interviews were held with workers in the workplace, in France a number of café assistants were interviewed outside of work and without the permission of their employer. Semi-structured interviews with café managers typically took between forty-five and sixty minutes and those with café assistants between twenty and thirty minutes. The interviews were supplemented with unstructured observation prior to, and in between, interviews. Over 100 interviews were conducted at workplace level. The research was carried out between April 2010 and 2011.

Sectoral Interviews (8 Interviews)

UK
  Representative, sector skills council People First

Norway
  Representative, NHO Employers Association
  Representative, HSH Employers Association

Appendix 1

Senior official, *Fellesforbundet* (largest private sector union in Norway)
Two union officials, HK union (commerce and offices)

France
SNARR Employers Association
CGT Trade union official

Workplace Interviews

UK (51 INTERVIEWS)

UK-CoffeeA (3 outlets)
Manager, full-time
Amanda, assistant manager, full-time
Brandon, assistant manager, full-time
Danielle, supervisor, 30 hours per week (regularly works more)
Liz, supervisor, full-time
Lauren, café assistant, 30 hours per week (regularly works more)
Ryan, café assistant, 30 hours per week (regularly works more)
Jasmine, café assistant, unclear contract (regularly works full-time)

UK-CoffeeB
Manager, full-time
Jack, supervisor, part-time (20 to 25 hours)
Christina, café assistant, 20 hours per week (works around 30 hours)

UK-CoffeeC
Manager, full-time
Jacob, supervisor, full-time
Laura, café assistant, 30 hours per week (works 20 to 30 hours per week)
Amber, café assistant, 30 hours per week (works around 20 to25 hours per week)

UK-CoffeeD (2 units)
Rebecca, supervisor, part-time (typically works full-time)
Heather, supervisor, 32 hours per week (works regular extra hours)
Sarah, café assistant, 20 hours per week (works regular extra hours)
Adam, café assistant, 16 hours per week (works regular extra hours)

UK-Multibrand (2 units)
HR director
Operations director
Manager, full-time
Melissa, supervisor, full-time
Angela, supervisor, part-time (16 hours per week).
Lisa, café assistant, 25 hours per week (typically works full-time)
Aisha, café assistant, 20 hours per week (typically works full-time)
Malika, café assistant, 20 hours per week (typically works full-time)

Appendix 1

UK-Sandwichco (2 outlets)
    Manager, full-time
    Nicole, supervisor, full-time
    Sue, supervisor, full-time
    Amira, café assistant, 16 to18 hours per week
    Chaya, café assistant, part-time
    Nabila, café assistant, 20 hours per week

UK-BakerA
    Manager, full-time
    Megan, supervisor, full-time
    Katherine, café assistant, part-time (20 hours per week)
    Monica, café assistant, part-time (16 hours per week)

UK-BakerB
    Manager, full-time
    Katie, assistant manager, full-time
    Julie, café assistant, part-time

UK-Indep
    Manager, full-time
    Sian, café assistant, full-time
    Tess, café assistant, full-time

UK-RetailA
    Manager, full-time
    Alison, assistant manager, full-time
    Karen, café assistant, part-time (20 hours per week)
    Jess, café assistant, part-time (20 hours per week)

UK-RetailB
    Richard, supervisor, full-time
    Anna, café assistant, full-time
    Tara, café assistant, full-time
    Kelly, café assistant, full-time

Norway (26 Interviews)

N-Multibrand (2 units)
    Operations manager
    Camilla, manager, unit 1, full-time
    Olav, manager, unit 2, full-time
    Linn, assistant manager, full-time
    Silje, café assistant, part-time and holidays (full-time student)
    Ida, café assistant, full-time
    Abdella, café assistant, full-time
    Lisa, café assistant, full-time
    Kristin, café assistant, 20 per cent contract (currently works full-time)

Appendix 1

N-BakerA (2 units)
    Manager/franchise owner, unit 1
    Manager/franchise owner, unit 2
    Sofia, café assistant, full-time
    Johanna, café assistant, full-time
    Hanna, café assistant, full-time
    Eva, café assistant, full-time

N-BakerB
    Manager
    Silvana, café assistant, part-time contract (typically works full-time)

N-CoffeeA
    Annette, café assistant, part-time (full-time student)
    Anne, café assistant, part-time (full-time student)
    Ingrid, café assistant, part-time (full-time student)

N-BakerC
    Sara, café assistant, 14 hours per week (full-time student)
    Emma, café assistant, 12 hours per week (full-time student)

N-SandwichCo
    Ivanna, café assistant, 20 hours per week (full-time student)

N-BakerD
    Manager, full-time

N-BakerE
    Thea, café assistant, one day a week and holidays (full-time student)

N-Indep
    Manager, 30 to 40 hours per week (part-time student)

France (25 Interviews)

F-Multibrand
    Director of resources and training
    Training director
    Manager, full-time
    Christelle, café assistant, full-time

F-SandwichA
    Manager/franchise owner
    Nicolas, café assistant, 30 hours per week

F-SandwichB
    Manager
    Lara, café assistant, 20 hours per week (full-time student)
    Aurelie, café assistant, 30 hours per week (typically work 35 hours undeclared)

Appendix 1

F-SandwichC
  Manager
  Thomas, team leader, full-time

F-SandwichD
  Jeremy, team leader, full-time
  Julien, café assistant, full-time
  Carole, café assistant, 16 hours per week (full-time student)

F-BakerA (3 outlets)
  Louis, manager, franchise, unit 1
  Andre, manager, contractor, unit 2
  Jean, manager, contractor, unit 3

F-BakerB
  Noelle, café assistant, full-time

F-Univ (2 units)
  Manager, full-time
  Sylvie, supervisor, full-time

F-IndepA
  Owner

F-IndepB
  Owner

F-IndepC
  Female, part-time (18 hours per week)

F-IndepD
  Emilie, café assistant, 20 hours per week (full-time student)

F-IndE
  Marie, café assistant, part-time (10.5 hours per week)

Appendix 1

Bibliography

Alvarez, I. (2015) 'Financialization, non-financial corporations and income inequality: the case of France', *Socio-Economic Review*, 13(4): 449–75.

Amossé, T. and Pignoni, M.-T. (2006) 'La transformation du paysage syndical depuis 1945', in *Données Sociales—La Société française*. Paris: Insee, pp. 405–12.

Anderson, P. (2009) 'Intermediate occupations and the conceptual and empirical limitations of the hourglass economy thesis', *Work, Employment and Society*, 23(1): 169–80.

Andersson, T., Kazemi, A., Tengblad, S., and Wickelgren, M. (2011) 'Not the inevitable Bleak House? The positive experience of workers and managers in retail employment in Sweden', in I. Grugulis and O. Bozkurt (eds.), *Retail Work*. New York: Palgrave Macmillan, pp. 253–77.

Andolfatto, D. and Labbé, D. (2012) 'The future of the French trade unions', *Management Revue*, 23(4): 341–52.

Appelbaum, E., Bailey, T., Berg, P., and Kalleberg, A. (2000) *Manufacturing Advantage: Why High-Performance Work Systems Pay Off*. Ithaca, NY: Cornell University Press.

Arbeidstilsynet (2015) 'Is there a minimum wage in Norway?' <http://www.arbeidstilsynet.no/fakta.html?tid=240068>, accessed 8 December 2015.

Arrowsmith, J. (2010) 'Industrial relations in the private sector', in T. Colling and M. Terry (eds.), *Industrial Relations: Theory and Practice*. Chichester: John Wiley, pp. 178–206.

Arrowsmith, J. (2012). Book review: 'The role of collective bargaining in the global economy: negotiating for social justice', *Industrial Relations Journal*, 43(4): 370–1.

Ashton, D. and Green, F. (1996) *Education, Training and the Global Economy*. Cheltenham: Edward Elgar.

Ashton, D. and Sung, J. (2006) 'How competitive strategy matters? Understanding the drivers of training, learning and performance at the firm level'. Oxford and Warwick Universities, SKOPE Research Paper 66.

Ashton, D. and Sung, J. (2011) *Productivity and Skills, Skills in Focus*. Glasgow: Skills Development Scotland.

Attewell, P. (1990) 'What is skill?' *Work and Occupations*, 17(4): 422–48.

Autor, D., Levy, F., and Richard, M. (2003) 'The skill-content of recent technological change: an empirical investigation', *Quarterly Journal of Economics*, 118: 1279–333.

Avis, J. (2003) 'Re-thinking trust in a performative culture: the case of education', *Journal of Education Policy*, 18(3): 315–32.

Avis, J., Canning, R., Fisher, R., and Simmons, R. (2013) 'State intervention in vocational teacher education in Scotland and England: 1999–2012', in J. Stephenson and L. Ling (eds.), *Challenges to Teacher Education in Difficult Economic Times*. London: Routledge, pp. 127–41.

Bibliography

Baccaro, L. and Howell, C. (2011) 'A common neoliberal trajectory: the transformation of industrial relations in advanced capitalism', *Politics & Society*, 39(4): 521–63.

Bach, S. (2010) 'Public sector industrial relations: the challenge of autonomy', in M. Terry and T. Colling (eds.), *Industrial Relations: Theory and Practice*, 3rd edn. Chichester: John Wiley, pp. 151–77.

Bach, S. and Bordogna, L. (2011) 'Varieties of new public management or alternative models? The reform of public service employment relations in industrialized democracies', *International Journal of Human Resource Management*, 22(11): 2281–94.

Bailey, T. R. and Bernhardt, A. D. (1997) 'In search of the high road in a low-wage industry', *Politics & Society*, 25(2): 179–201.

Barroso, J. M. (2008) 'Inspiring future generations', speech to the European Round Table of Industrialists, Brussels, 2 October. <http://europa.eu/rapid/press-release_SPEECH-08-481_en.htm>, accessed 14 December 2015.

Batt, R. (2000) 'Strategic segmentation in front-line services: matching customers, employees and human resource systems', *International Journal of Human Resource Management*, 11(3): 540–61.

Bechter, B., Brandl, B., and Meardi, G. (2012) 'Sectors or countries? Typologies and levels of analysis in comparative industrial relations', *European Journal of Industrial Relations*, 18(3): 185–202.

Becker, B. and Huselid, M. (1998) 'High performance work systems and firm performance: a synthesis of research and managerial implications', *Research in Personnel and Human Resources Management*, 16: 53–101.

Becker, G. (1964) *Human Capital*, 2nd edn. New York: Columbia University Press.

Bélanger, J. and Edwards, P. (2013) 'The nature of front-line service work: distinctive features and continuity in the employment relationship', *Work, Employment and Society*, 27(3): 433–50.

Belfield, C. (2010) 'Over-education: what influence does the workplace have?' *Economics of Education Review*, 29(2): 236–45.

Bell, D. (1973) *The Coming of Post-Industrial Society*. New York: Basic Books.

Bentham, J. et al (2013) 'Manifesto for the Foundational Economy'. CRESC Working Paper No 131, University of Manchester and the Open University.

Bergene, A. N., Jordhus-Lier, D., and Underthun, A. (2014) 'Organizing capacities and union priorities in the hotel sector in Oslo, Dublin, and Toronto', *Nordic Journal of Working Life Studies*, 4(3): 119–36.

Berggren, C. (1992) *Alternatives to Lean Production: Work Organization in the Swedish Auto Industry*. Ithaca, NY: Cornell University Press.

Bernstein, B. (1970) 'Education cannot compensate for society', *New Society*, 26 February, pp. 344–7.

Berrebi-Hoffmann, I., Grimshaw, D., Lallement, M., and Miozzo, M. (2010) 'Employment challenges facing the knowledge economy in Europe: the case of IT services', *Work Organisation, Labour & Globalisation*, 4(1): 24–40.

Bevir, M., Rhodes, R., and Weller, P. (2003) 'Traditions of governance: interpreting the changing role of the public sector in comparative and historical perspective', *Public Administration*, 81: 1–17.

Bibliography

Bieler, A. (2012) 'Small Nordic countries and globalization: analysing Norwegian exceptionalism', *Competition and Change*, 16(3): 224–42.

Blair, T. (1998) 'Foreword', in DTI White Paper, *Fairness at Work*. London: HMSO.

Blauner, R. (1964) *Alienation and Freedom: The Factory Worker and His Industry*. Chicago: University of Chicago Press.

Bolton, S. (2004) 'Conceptual Confusions: emotion work as skilled work', in C. Warhurst, I. Grugulis, and E. Keep (eds.), *The Skills That Matter*. Basingstoke: Palgrave Macmillan, pp. 19–38.

Bordogna, L. and Neri, S. (2011) 'Convergence towards a NPM programme or different models? Public service employment relations in Italy and France', *International Journal of Human Resource Management*, 22(11): 2311–30.

Bosch, G. and Kalina, T. (2008) 'Low-wage work in Germany: an overview', in G. Bosch and C. Weinkopf (eds.), *Low-Wage Work in Germany*. New York: Russell Sage Foundation, pp. 19–112.

Bosch, G. and Lehndorff, S. (2005) *Working in the Service Sector: A Tale from Different Worlds*. London: Routledge.

Bosch, G. and Weinkopf, C. (eds.) (2008) *Low-Wage Work in Germany*. New York: Russell Sage Foundation.

Bowman, J. (2005) 'Employers and the politics of skill formation in a coordinated market economy: collective action and class conflict in Norway', *Politics & Society*, 33(4): 567–94.

Boxall, P. and Purcell, J. (2007) *Strategy and Human Resource Management*. Basingstoke: Palgrave Macmillan.

Braverman, H. (1974) *Labor and Monopoly Capital*. New York: Monthly Review Press.

Brinkley, I. (2013) *Flexibility or Insecurity? Exploring the Rise in Zero Hours Contracts*. London: The Work Foundation.

Brinkley, I., Fauth, R., Mahdon, M., and Theodoropoulou, S. (2009) *Knowledge Work and Knowledge Workers*. London: The Work Foundation.

Briscoe, G., Pill, M., Davies, R., and Drinkwater, S. (2011) 'Stay, leave or return? Understanding Welsh graduate mobility'. Cardiff University, WISERD/SKOPE Paper.

Brockmann, M., Clarke, L., and Winch, C. (2011) *Knowledge, Skills and Competence in the European Labour Market*. London: Routledge.

Brown, G. (2008) 'We'll use our schools to break down class barriers', *The Guardian*, 10 February. <http://www.guardian.co.uk/commentisfree/2008/feb/10/gordonbrown.education>, accessed 10 December 2015.

Brown, P. and Hesketh, A. (2004) *Mismanagement of Talent: Employability and Jobs in the Knowledge Economy*. Oxford: Oxford University Press.

Brown, P., Lauder, H., and Ashton, D. (2008) 'Education, globalisation and the future of the knowledge economy', *European Educational Research Journal*, 7(2): 131–56.

Brown, P., Lauder, H., and Ashton, D. (2010) *The Global Auction: The Broken Promises of Education Jobs and Incomes*. New York: Oxford University Press.

Brugård, K. (2013) 'Does school choice improve student performance?' Trondheim: Department of Economics, Norwegian University of Science and Technology, Working Paper No. 7.

Bibliography

Brynin, M., Lichtwardt, B., and Longhi, S. (2006) 'Overqualification: Major or Minor Mismatch?' ISER Working Paper 2006–17.

Bryson, A. and Forth, J. (2006) 'The theory and practice of pay setting'. London: Manpower Human Resources Laboratory, Centre for Economic Performance.

Buchanan, J., Scott, L., Yu, S., Schutz, H., and Jakubausakas, M. (2010) *Skills Demand and Utilisation: An International Review of Approaches to Measurement and Policy Development*. Paris: OECD.

Busemeyer, M. R. and Trampusch, C. (eds.) (2012) *The Political Economy of Collective Skills Formation*. Oxford: Oxford University Press.

Cabral Vieira, J. (2005) 'Skill mismatches and job satisfaction', *Economics Letters*, 89(1): 39–47.

Callaghan, G. and Thompson, P. (2002) '"We recruit attitude": the selection and shaping of routine call centre labour', *Journal of Management Studies*, 39(2): 233–54.

Caroli, E. and Gautié, J. (2008) *Low-Wage Work in France*. New York: Russell Sage Foundation.

Caroli, E., Gautié, J., Lloyd, C., Lamanthe, A., and James, S. (2010) 'Delivering flexibility: contrasting patterns in the French and the UK food processing industry', *British Journal of Industrial Relations*, 48(2): 284–309.

Carré, F., Findlay, P., Tilly, C., and Warhurst, C. (2012) 'Job quality: scenarios, analysis and interventions', in C. Warhurst, F. Carré, P. Findlay, and C. Tilly (eds.), *Are Bad Jobs Inevitable? Trends, Determinants and Responses to Job Quality in the Twenty-First Century*. Basingstoke: Palgrave Macmillan, pp. 1–22.

Carré, F. and Tilly, C. (2012) 'A framework for international comparative analysis of the determinants of low-wage job quality', in C. Warhurst, F. Carré, P. Findlay, and C. Tilly (eds.), *Are Bad Jobs Inevitable? Trends, Determinants and Responses to Job Quality in the Twenty-First Century*. Basingstoke: Palgrave Macmillan, pp. 78–92.

Carré, F., Tilly, C., van Klaveren, M., and Voss-Dahm, D. (2010) 'Retail jobs in comparative perspective', in J. Gautié and J. Schmitt (eds.), *Low Wage Work in the Wealthy World*. New York: Russell Sage Foundation, pp. 211–69.

Castells, M. (1996) *The Rise of the Network Society, The Information Age: Economy, Society and Culture*. Oxford: Blackwell.

Chandola, T. (2010) *Stress at Work*. London: British Academy.

Clark, T., Sweet, R., Heinz Gruber, K., Lourtie, P., Santiago, P., and Sohlman, A. (2009) *OECD Review of Tertiary Education: Norway*. Paris: OECD.

Clarke, L. (2011) 'Trade? Job? Or occupation? The development of occupational labour markets for bricklaying and lorry driving', in M. Brockmann, L. Clarke, C.and Winch (eds.), *Knowledge, Skills and Competence in the European Labour Market*. London: Routledge, pp. 102–19.

Clarke, L. and Winch, C. (2006) 'A European Skills Framework? But what are skills? Anglo-Saxon versus German concepts', *Journal of Education and Work*, 19(3): 255–69.

Coates, D. (2000) *Models of Capitalism: Growth and Stagnation in the Modern Era*. Cambridge: Polity Press.

Coates, D. (2013) 'Labour after New Labour: escaping the debt', *British Journal of Politics and International Relations*, 15(1): 38–52.

Cockburn, C. (1983) *Brothers: Male Dominance and Technological Change*. London: Pluto.

Bibliography

Coffield, F. (2007) *Running Ever Faster Down the Wrong Road: An Alternative Future for Education and Skills*. London: Institute of Education, University of London.

Coffield, F. (2008) *Just Suppose Teaching and Learning Became the First Priority...* Dorset: Learning and Skills Network.

Coffield, F., Edward, S., Finlay, I., Hodgson, A., Steer, R., and Spours, K. (2008) *Improving Learning, Skills and Inclusion: The Impact of Policy*. London: Routledge.

Connolly, H. (2010) *Renewal in the French Trade Union Movement: A Grassroots Perspective*. Bern: Peter Lang.

Côté, J. (2014) 'The decline in study time in British and American universities', in S. Pickard (ed.), *Higher Education in the UK and the US: Converging University Models in a Global Academic World*. Leiden and Boston: Brill, pp. 197–224.

Cowell, D. (1988) 'New service development', *Journal of Marketing Management*, 3(3): 296–312.

Cribb, A. and Gerwitz, S. (2007) 'Unpacking autonomy and control in education: some conceptual and normative groundwork for comparative analysis', *European Education Research Journal*, 6(2): 203–13.

Cros, F. and Obin, J. P. (2003) *Attracting, Developing and Retaining Effective Teachers: Country Background Report for France*. Paris: OECD.

Crouch, C. (2005) *Capitalist Diversity and Change: Recombinant Governance and Institutional Entrepreneurs*. Oxford: Oxford University Press.

Crouch, C., Finegold, D., and Sako, M. (1999) *Are Skills the Answer?* Oxford: Oxford University Press.

Crouch, C., Schröder, M., and Voelzkow, H. (2009) 'Regional and sectoral varieties of capitalism', *Economy and Society*, 38(4): 654–78.

Culpepper, P. (1999) 'The future of the high-skill equilibrium in Germany', *Oxford Review of Economic Policy*, 15: 43–59.

Culpepper, P. (2003) *Creating Cooperation: How States Develop Human Capital in Europe*. Ithaca, NY: Cornell University Press.

Culpepper, P. and Finegold, D. (eds.) (1999) *The German Skills Machine: Sustaining Comparative Advantage in a Global Economy*. New York: Berghahn Books.

Cutler, T. (1992) 'Vocational training and British economic performance: a further instalment of the "British labour problem"?' *Work, Employment and Society*, 6(2): 161–83.

Czerniawski, G. (2013) 'Professional development for professional learners: teachers' experiences in Norway, Germany and England', *Journal of Education for Teaching*, 39(4): 383–400.

Daly, A., Hitchens, D., and Wagner, K. (1985) 'Productivity, machinery and skills in a sample of British and German manufacturing plants', *National Institute Economic Review*, 111: 48–61.

D'Arcy, C. and Hurrell, A. (2014) *Escape Plan: Understanding Who Progresses from Low Pay and Who Gets Stuck*. London: Resolution Foundation.

DBIS (Department for Business Innovation and Skills) (2015) *Trade Union Membership 2014: Statistical Bulletin*. London: DBIS.

Del Bono, E. and Mayhew, K. (2001) 'The specification and quality of British products'. University of Warwick, Coventry, SKOPE Research Paper 19.

Bibliography

Dewey, J. (1916) *Democracy and Education*. New York: Macmillan.

Dobbin, F. and Boychuk, T. (1999) 'National employment systems and job autonomy: why job autonomy is high in the Nordic countries and low in the United States, Canada and Australia', *Organisation Studies*, 20(2): 257–91.

Doellgast, V. (2009) 'Still a coordinated model? Market liberalization and the transformation of employment relations in the German telecommunications industry', *Industrial and Labor Relations Review*, 63(1): 3–23.

Doellgast, V. (2010) 'Collective voice under decentralized bargaining: a comparative study of work reorganization in US and German call centres', *British Journal of Industrial Relations*, 48(2): 375–99.

Doellgast, V., Batt, R., and Sørensen, O. H. (2009) 'Introduction: institutional change and labour market segmentation in European call centres', *European Journal of Industrial Relations*, 15(4): 349–71.

Dølvik, J. and Stokke, T. (1998) 'Norway: revival of centralised concertation', in A. Ferner and R. Hyman (eds.), *Changing Industrial Relations in Europe*. Oxford: Blackwell, pp. 118–45.

Dølvik, J. and Stokland, D. (1992) 'Norway: the "Norwegian model" in transition', in A. Ferner and R. Hyman (eds.), *Industrial Relations in the New Europe*. Oxford: Blackwell, pp. 143–67.

Drucker, P. (1969) *The Age of Discontinuity*. New York: Harper & Row.

Drucker, P. (1993) *Post-Capitalist Society*. Oxford: Butterworth Heinemann.

Duru-Bellat, M. and Kieffer, A. (2008) 'From the Baccalauréat to higher education in France: shifting inequalities', *Population* 63(1): 119–54.

EFILWC (European Foundation for the Improvement of Living and Working Conditions) (2007) *A Review of Working Conditions in France*. Dublin: EFILW.

Elias, P. and Bynner, J. (1997) 'Intermediate skills and occupational mobility', *Policy Studies*, 18(2): 101–24.

Elias, P. and Purcell, K. (2004) 'Is mass higher education working? Evidence from the labour market experiences of recent graduates', *National Institute Economic Review*, 190(1): 60–74.

Elias, P. and Purcell, K. (2013) 'Classifying graduate occupations for the knowledge society'. Futuretrack Working Paper 5. Warwick: Institute for Employment Research.

Emery, F. E. and Thorsrud, E. (1976) *Democracy at Work: The Norwegian Industrial Democracy Program*. Leiden: Martinus Nijhoff Social Sciences Division.

Ertl, H. and Kremer, H. (2010) 'Educational change and innovative teaching practice: a study of the impact of reforms on the work of lecturers in vocational education and training in England and Germany', *ORBIS SCHOLAE*, 4(2): 133–47.

Esping-Andersen, G. (1990) *Three Worlds of Welfare Capitalism*. Cambridge: Polity Press.

Esser, I. and Olsen, K. (2012) 'Perceived job quality: autonomy and job security within a multi-level framework', *European Sociological Review*, 28(4): 443–54.

Estevez-Abe, M., Iverson, T., and Soskice, D. (2001) 'Social protection and the formation of skills: a reinterpretation of the welfare state', in P. A. Hall and D. Soskice (eds.), *Varieties of Capitalism: The Institutional Foundations of Comparative Advantage*. Oxford: Oxford University Press, pp. 145–83.

Bibliography

Estyn (2006) *The Annual Report of Her Majesty's Chief Inspector of Education and Training in Wales 2005–2006*. Estyn.

Euromonitor International (2013) 'Coffee in Norway'. Country report.

Euromonitor International (2014) 'Coffee in France'. Country report.

European Commission (2001) *Employment in Europe 2001*. Luxembourg: Office for the Official Publications of the European Communities.

European Commission (2010) 'An agenda for new skills and jobs: a European contribution towards full employment' COM (2010) 682 final.

European Commission (2013) *Innovation Union Scoreboard*. Luxembourg: Publications Office of the European Union.

European Parliament (2000) 'Lisbon European Council 23 and 24 March 2000, Presidency Conclusions'. <http://www.europarl.europa.eu/summits/lis1_en.htm>, accessed 10 December 2015.

Eurydice (2008) *Levels of Autonomy and Responsibilities of Teachers in Europe*. Brussels: Eurydice.

Felstead, A., Fuller, A., Jewson, N., Kakavelakis, K., and Unwin, L. (2007) 'Grooving to the same tunes? Learning, training and productive systems in the aerobics studio', *Work, Employment and Society*, 21(2): 189–208.

Felstead, A., Gallie, D., and Green, F. (2004) 'Job complexity and task discretion: tracking the direction of skills at work in Britain', in C. Warhurst, I. Grugulis, and E. Keep (eds.), *The Skills That Matter*. Basingstoke: Palgrave Macmillan, pp. 148–70.

Felstead, A., Gallie, D., Green, F., and Inanc, H. (2013a) *Skills at Work in Britain: First Findings from the Skills and Employment Survey 2012*. Centre for Learning and Life Chances in Knowledge Economies and Societies, Institute of Education, London.

Felstead, A., Gallie, D., Green, F., and Inanc, H. (2013b) *Work Intensification in Britain: First Findings from the Skills and Employment Survey 2012*. Cardiff: LLAKES, University of Cardiff.

Felstead, A., Gallie, D., Green, F., and Zhou, Y. (2007) *Skills at Work, 1986–2006 Project Report*. Oxford: ESRC Centre on Skills, Knowledge and Organisational Performance.

Ferlie, E. and Geraghty, K. (2005) 'Professionals in public services organizations: implications for public sector "reforming"', in E. Ferlie, L. Lynn and C. Pollitt (eds.), *The Oxford Handbook of Public Management*. Oxford: Oxford University Press, pp. 422–45.

Ferner, A. and Hyman, R. (eds.) (1998) *Changing Industrial Relations in Europe*. Oxford: Blackwell.

Fernie, S. (2011) 'Occupational licensing in the UK: the case of the private security industry', in D. Marsden (ed.), *Employment in the Lean Years: Policy and Prospects for the Next Decade*. Oxford: Oxford University Press, pp. 102–18.

Fevre, R., Rees, G., and Gorard, S. (1999) 'Some sociological alternatives to human capital theory and their implications for research on post-compulsory education and training', *Journal of Education and Work*, 12(2): 117–40.

Fine, B. (1998) *Labour Market Theory: A Constructive Reassessment*. London: Routledge.

Finegold, D. (1991) 'Institutional incentives and skills creation: preconditions for high skill equilibrium', in P. Ryan (ed.), *International Comparisons of Vocational and Educational Training for Intermediate Skills*. London: Falmer Press, pp. 93–116.

Finegold, D. (1999) 'Creating self-sustaining, high-skill ecosystems', *Oxford Review of Economic Policy*, 15(1): 60–81.

Bibliography

Finegold, D. and Soskice, D. (1988) 'The failure of training in Britain: analysis and prescription', *Oxford Review of Economic Policy*, 4(2): 21–53.

Flanders, A. D. (1970) *Management and Unions: The Theory and Reform of Industrial Relations*. London: Faber and Faber.

Fligstein, N. and Byrkjeflot, H. (1996) 'The logic of employment systems', in J. N. Baron, D. Grusky, and D. Treiman (eds.), *Social Differentiation and Social Inequality*. Boulder, CO: Westview, pp. 11–35.

Florida, R. (2004) *The Rise of the Creative Class*. New York: Basic Books.

Forth, J., Bryson, A., Humphris, A., Koumenta, M., and Kleiner, M. (2011) 'A review of occupational regulation and its impact'. UKCES Evidence Report 40. Wath-Upon-Dearne: UK Commission for Employment and Skills.

Frenkel, S. (2005) 'Service workers: in search of decent work", in S. Ackroyd, R. Batt, P. Thompson, and P. Tobert (eds.), *A Handbook of Work and Organization*. Oxford: Oxford University Press, pp. 356–75.

Friedman, A. (1977) *Industry and Labour: Class Struggle at Work and Monopoly Capitalism*. London: Macmillan.

Frontier Economics (2014) *Further Education Workforce Data for England: Analysis of the 2012–2013 Staff Individualised Record Data*. London: Frontier Economics.

Froy, F. (2013) 'Global policy developments towards industrial policy and skills: skills for competitiveness and growth', *Oxford Review of Economic Policy*, 29(2): 344–60.

Fuller, A. and Unwin, L. (2003) 'Creating a "modern apprenticeship": a critique of the UK's multi-sector, social inclusion approach', *Journal of Education and Work*, 16(1): 5–25.

Fuller, A. and Unwin, L. (2012) 'What's the point of adult apprenticeships?' *Adults Learning*, 23(3): 8–13.

Gadrey, J. (2000) 'Working time configurations: theory, methods, and assumptions for an international comparison', in C. Baret, S. Lehndorff, and L. Sparks (eds.), *Flexible Working in Food Retailing: A Comparison between France, Germany, the UK, and Japan*. London: Routledge, pp. 21–30.

Gallie, D. (1994) 'Patterns of skill change, upskilling, deskilling or polarization', in R. Penn, M. Rose, and J. Rubery (eds.), *Skill and Occupational Change*. Oxford: Oxford University Press, pp. 41–76.

Gallie, D. (2003) 'The quality of working life: is Scandinavia different?' *European Sociological Review*, 19(1): 61–79.

Gallie, D. (2007) 'Production regimes and the quality of employment in Europe', *Annual Review of Sociology*, 33: 85–104.

Gallie, D. (2011) 'Production regimes, employee job control and skill development'. LLAKES Research Paper 31. London: LLAKES.

Gallie, W. B. (1956), 'Essentially contested concepts', *Proceedings of the Aristotelian Society*, 56: 167–98.

Gatta, M., Boushey, H., and Applebaum, E. (2009) 'High-touch and here-to-stay: future skill demands in low wage US service occupations', *Sociology*, 43(5): 968–89.

Gautié, J. (2015) 'France's social model: between resilience and erosion', in D. Vaughan-Whitehead (ed.), *The European Social Model in Crisis: Is Europe Losing its Soul?* Geneva: ILO, pp. 121–74.

Bibliography

Gautié, J. and Schmitt, J. (eds.) (2010) *Low-Wage Work in the Wealthy World*. New York: Russell Sage Foundation.

Géhin, J. P. (2007) 'Vocational education in France: a turbulent history and peripheral role', in L. Clarke and C. Winch (eds.), *Vocational Education in International Context: Philosophical and Historical Dimensions*. London: Routledge, pp. 34–48.

Gerogiannis, E., Kerckhofs, P., and Vargas, O. (2012) *Employment and Industrial Relations in the Hotels and Restaurants Sector*. Dublin: European Foundation for the Improvement of Living and Working Conditions.

Giddens, A. (1998) *The Third Way: The Renewal of Social Democracy*. Malden, MA: Polity Press.

Giret, J.-F., Nauze-Fichet, E., and Tomasini, M. (2006) 'Le déclassement des jeunes sur le marché du travail', in *Données sociales—La société française*. Paris: Insee, pp. 307–14.

Gleeson, D., Davies, J., and Wheeler, E. (2005) 'On the making and taking of professionalism in the further education workplace', *British Journal of Sociology of Education*, 26(4): 455–60.

Godard, J. (2004) 'A critical assessment of the high-performance paradigm', *British Journal of Industrial Relations*, 42(2): 349–378.

Goetschy, J. (1998) 'France: the limits of reform', in A. Ferner and R. Hyman (eds.), *Changing Industrial Relation in Europe*. Oxford: Blackwell, pp. 357–94.

Gold, M. and Artus, I. (2015) 'Employee participation in Germany: tensions and challenges', in S. Johnstone and P. Ackers (eds.), *Finding a Voice at Work? New Perspectives on Employment Relations*. Oxford: Oxford University Press, pp. 193–217.

Goldfinch, S. and Wallis, J. (2010) 'Two myths of convergence in public management reform', *Public Administration*, 88(4): 1099–115.

Goodson, I. F. and Lindblad, S. (eds.) (2011) *Professional Knowledge and Educational Restructuring in Europe*. Rotterdam: Sense Publishers.

Goos, M. and Manning, A. (2007) 'Lousy and lovely jobs: the rising polarization of work in Britain', *Review of Economics and Statistics*, 89(1): 118–33.

Goos, M., Manning, A., and Salomons, A. (2009) 'The polarization of the European labour market', *American Economic Review Papers and Proceedings* (May): 58–63.

Goos, M., Manning, A., and Salomons, A. (2014) 'Explaining job polarization: routine biased technological change and offshoring', *American Economic Review*, 104(8): 2509–26.

Gospel, H. and Casey, P. (2012) *Understanding Training Levies*. Evidence Report 47. London: UK Commission for Employment and Skills.

Gospel, H. and Lewis, P. (2011) 'Who cares about skills? The impact and limits of statutory regulation on qualifications and skills in social care', *British Journal of Industrial Relations*, 49(4): 601–22.

Gramsci, A. (1971) *Selections from the Prison Notebooks of Antonio Gramsci*. New York: International Publishers.

Gray, J. (1998) *False Dawn: The Delusions of Global Capitalism*. London: Granta.

Green, A. (1998) 'Core skills, key skills and general culture: in search of the common foundation in vocational education', *Evaluation and Research in Education*, 12(1): 23–43.

Green, F. (2006) *Demanding Work: The Paradox of Job Quality in the Affluent Economy*. Oxford: Princeton University Press.

Bibliography

Green, F. (2010) *Unions and Skills Utilisation*. London: Unionlearn.

Green, F. (2011) 'What is skill? An inter-disciplinary synthesis'. LLAKES Research Paper 20. London: LLAKES.

Green, F., Felstead, A., Gallie, D., Inanc, H., and Jewson, N. (2015) 'The declining volume of workers' training in Britain', *British Journal of Industrial Relations*. DOI:10.1111/bjir.12130.

Green, F. and Zhu, Y. (2010) 'Overqualification, job dissatisfaction and increasing dispersion in returns to graduate education'. University of Kent, Department of Economics, Discussion Paper.

Grimshaw, D. and Lehndorff, S. (2010) 'Anchors for job quality: sectoral systems of employment in the European context', *Work, Organisation, Labour & Globalisation*, 4(1): 24–40.

Grimshaw, D. and Rubery, J. (2007) 'Undervaluing women's work'. London: Equal Opportunities Commission, Working Paper Series no 53.

Grollmann, P. and Rauner, F. (2007) 'TVET teachers: an endangered species or professional innovation agents?' in P. Grollmann and F. Rauner (eds.), *International Perspectives on Teachers and Lecturers in Technical and Vocational Education*. Dordrecht: Springer, pp. 1–26.

Groot, W. and Van den Brink, H. M. (2000) 'Overeducation in the labor market: a meta-analysis', *Economics of Education Review*, 19(2): 149–58.

Groshen, E. (1991) 'The structure of the female/male wage differential: is it who you are, what you do, or where you work?' *Journal of Human Resources*, 26(3): 457–72.

Grugulis, I. and Lloyd, C. (2010) 'Skill and the labour process: the conditions and consequences of change', in P. Thompson and C. Smith (eds.), *Working Life: Renewing Labour Process Analysis*. Basingstoke: Palgrave Macmillan, pp. 91–112.

Grugulis, I. and Stoyanova, D. (2011) 'Skills and performance', *British Journal of Industrial Relations*, 49(3): 515–36.

Grugulis, I., Warhurst, C., and Keep, E. (2004) 'What's happening to skill?' in C. Warhurst, I. Grugulis, and E. Keep (eds.), *The Skills That Matter*. Basingstoke: Palgrave Macmillan, pp. 1–18.

Grumbrell-McCormick, R. and Hyman, R. (2006) 'Embedded collectivism? Workplace representation in France and Germany', *Industrial Relations Journal*, 37(5): 473–91.

Gustavsen, B. (1985) 'Workplace reform and democratic dialogue', *Economic and Industrial Democracy*, 6(4): 461–79.

Gustavsen, B. (2007) 'Work, organisation and "the Scandinavian model"', *Economic and Industrial Democracy*, 28(40): 650–71.

Hagen, I. M. and Pape, A. (1997) 'Medspillere eller motspillere? Lederes og tillitsvalgtes erfaringer med Hovedavtalen i staten', Fafo-report 227. Oslo: FAFO.

Hall, P. (1986) *Governing the Economy: The Politics of State Intervention in Britain and France*. Oxford: Oxford University Press.

Hall, P. and D. Soskice (eds.) (2001) *Varieties of Capitalism: The Institutional Foundations of Comparative Advantage*. Oxford: Oxford University Press.

Hancké, B. (1993) 'Trade union membership in Europe 1960–1999: rediscovering local unions', *British Journal of Industrial Relations*, 31(4): 593–613.

Bibliography

Harvey, D. (2010) *The Enigma of Capital and the Crisis of Capitalism*. London: Profile Books.

Hassel, A. (2012) 'The paradox of liberalization: understanding dualism and the recovery of the German political economy', *British Journal of Industrial Relations*, 52(1): 57–81.

Hassenteufel, P. and Palier, B. (2015) 'Still the sound of silence? Towards a new phase in the Europeanisation of welfare state policies in France', *Comparative European Politics*, 13: 112–30.

Hayden, A. (2006) 'France's 35-hour week: attack on business? Win-win reform? Or betrayal of disadvantaged workers', *Politics & Society*, 34(4): 503–42.

Head, J. and Lucas, R. (2004) 'Employee relations in the non-union hotel industry: a case of "determined opportunism"?' *Personnel Review*, 33(6): 693–710.

Heiret, J. (2012) 'Three Norwegian varieties of a Nordic model: a historical perspective on working life relations', *Nordic Journal of Working Life Studies*, 2(4): 45–66.

Helgøy, I. and Homme, A. (2006) 'Policy tools and institutional change: comparing education policies in Norway, Sweden and England', *Journal of Public Policy*, 26(2): 141–65.

Helgøy, I. and Homme, A. (2007) 'Towards a new professionalism in school? A comparative study of teacher autonomy in Norway and Sweden', *European Educational Research Journal*, 6(3): 232–49.

Heyes, J. (2013) 'Vocational training, employability and the post-2008 jobs crisis: responses in the European Union', *Economic and Industrial Democracy*, 34(2): 291–311.

Hochschild, A. (1983) *The Managed Heart: Commercialisation of Human Feeling*. Los Angeles: University of California Press.

Hodkinson, P. (2008) 'Scientific research, educational policy and educational practice in the United Kingdom: the impact of the audit culture on further education', *Cultural Studies—Critical Methodologies*, 8(3): 303–24.

Hollingsworth, J. R. and Streeck, W. (1994) 'Countries and sectors: concluding remarks on performance, convergence and competitiveness', in J. R. Hollingsworth, P. C. Schmitter, and W. Streeck (eds.), *Governing Capitalist Economies: Performance and Control of Economic Sectors*. Oxford: Oxford University Press, pp. 270–300.

Holm, J. and Lorenz, E. (2015) 'Has "discretionary learning" declined during the Lisbon Agenda? A cross-sectional and longitudinal study of work organization in European nations', *Industrial and Corporate Change*, 24(6): 1179–214.

Holm, J. R., Lorenz, E., Bengt-Ake, L., and Valeyre, A. (2010) 'Organisational learning and systems of labour market regulation in Europe', *Industrial and Corporate Change*, 19(4): 1141–73.

Holman, D. and McClelland, C. (2011) 'Job quality in growing and declining economic sectors of the EU'. Work and Life Quality in New and Growing Jobs Working Paper 3, Manchester Business School, University of Manchester.

Holtgrewe, U. and Sardadvar, K. (2012) 'Hard work: job quality and organisation in European low-wage sectors'. <http://www.walqing.eu>.

Holzer, H., Lane, J., Rosenblum, D., And Anderson, F. (2011) *Where Are all the Good Jobs Going?* New York: Russell Sage Foundation.

Bibliography

Hood, C. (1991) 'A public management for all seasons?' *Public Administration*, 69(1): 3–19.

Hood, C. (2006) 'Gaming in Targetworld: the targets approach to managing British public service', *Public Administration Review*, 66(4): 515–21.

Høst, H. (2008) 'Continuity and Change in Norwegian VET'. Oslo: Norwegian Institute for Studies in Innovation, Research and Education. <http://www.udir.no/upload/Rapporter/Fagopplaring/nifu_engelsk.pdf>.

Houtsonen, J., Czaplicka, M., Lindblad, S., Sohlberg, P., and Sugrue, C. (2010) 'Welfare state restructuring in education and its national refractions: Finnish, Irish and Swedish teachers' perceptions of current changes', *Current Sociology*, 58(4): 597–622.

Howell, C. (2005) *Trade Unions and the State: The Construction of Industrial Relations Institutions in Britain, 1890–2000*. Oxford: Princeton University Press.

Howell, C. (2009) 'The transformation of French industrial relations: labour representation and the state in a post-*dirigiste* era', *Politics & Society*, 37(2): 229–56.

Howell, C. and Givan, R. (2011) 'Rethinking institutions and institutional change in European industrial relations', *British Journal of Industrial Relations*, 49(2): 231–55.

Høyrup, S., Bonnafous-Boucher, M., Hasse, C., Lotz, M., and Møller, K. (2012) *Employee-Driven Innovation: A New Approach*. Basingstoke: Palgrave Macmillan.

Huddlestone, P. and Unwin, L. (2007) *Teaching and Learning in Further Education: Diversity and Change*. London: Routledge.

Hurrell, S. A., Scholarios, D., and Thompson, P. (2013) 'More than a "humpty dumpty" term: strengthening the conceptualization of soft skills', *Economic and Industrial Democracy*, 34(1): 161–82.

Huzzard, T. and Bjørkman, H. (2012) 'Trade unions and action research', *Work, Employment and Society*, 26(1): 161–71.

Hyland, T. (1994) *Competence, Education and NVQs: Dissenting Perspectives*. London: Cassell.

Hyman, R. (1988) 'Flexible specialisation: miracle or myth?', in R. Hyman and W. Streeck (eds.), *New Technology and Industrial Relations*. Oxford: Blackwell, pp. 48–60.

Hyman, R. (2003) 'The historical evolution of British industrial relations', in P. Edwards (ed.), *Industrial Relations: Theory and Practice*, 2nd edn. Oxford: Blackwell, pp. 37–57.

Hyman, R. (2015a) 'Three scenarios for industrial relations in Europe', *International Labour Review*, 154(1): 5–14.

Hyman, R. (2015b) 'Making voice effective: imagining trade union responses to an era of post-industrial democracy', in S. Johnstone and P. Ackers (eds.), *Finding a Voice at Work? New Perspectives on Employment Relations*. Oxford: Oxford University Press, pp. 265–77.

Ibsen, C. L., Larsen, T. P., Madsen, J. S., and Due, J. (2011) 'Challenging Scandinavian employment relations: the effects of new public management reforms', *International Journal of Human Resource Management*, 22(11): 2295–310.

IHRSA (2011) 'The IHRSA Global 25', *Club Business International* (July): 36–43.

Insee (2014) 'Contrat de professionnalisation'. <http://www.insee.fr/fr/methodes/default.asp?page=definitions/contrat-professionnalisation.htm>, accessed 17 December 2015.

Jackson, G. and Deeg, R. (2012) 'The long-term trajectories of institutional change in European capitalism', *Journal of European Public Policy*, 19(8): 1109–25.

James, D. and Diment, K. (2003) 'Going underground? Learning and assessment in an ambiguous space', *Vocational Education and Training*, 55(4): 407–22.

James, S., Warhurst, C., Tholen, G., and Commander, J. (2013) 'What we need to know about graduate skills', *Work, Employment and Society*, 27(6): 952–63.

Jany-Catrice, F. and Lallement, M. (2015) 'Conversion through inequality: the transformation of the French social model', in S. Lehndorff (ed.), *Divisive Integration: The Triumph of Failed Ideas in Europe—Revisited*. Brussels: ETUI, pp. 179–94.

Jellab, A. (2008) *Sociologie du Lycée Professionnel: L'expérience des Élèves et des Enseignants dans une Institution en Mutation*. Toulouse: Presses universitaires du Mirail.

Jephcote, M. and Salisbury, J. (2009) 'Further education teachers' account of their professional identities', *Teacher and Teacher Education*, 25(7): 966–72.

Jephcote, M., Salisbury, J., and Rees, G. (2008) 'Being a teacher in further education in changing times', *Research in Post Compulsory Education*, 13(2): 163–72.

Jephcote, M., Salisbury, J., and Rees, G. (2009) 'Learning and working in further education in Wales: an overview and initial findings', *Welsh Journal of Education*, 14(2): 18–28.

Johansson, A. W. and Lindhult, E. (2008) 'Emancipation or workability? Critical versus pragmatic scientific orientation in action research', *Action Research*, 6(1): 95–115.

Johnsen, Å. (2012) 'Why does poor performance get so much attention in public policy?', *Financial Accountability and Public Management*, 28(2): 121–42.

Kalleberg, A. L. (2011) *Good Jobs, Bad Jobs: The Rise of Polarized and Precarious Employment Systems in the United States, 1970s–2000s*. New York: Russell Sage Foundation.

Kasvio, A., Gonäs, L., and Skorstad, E. (2012) 'In search of the Nordic working life model: introduction to the thematic issue', *Nordic Journal of Working Life Studies*, 2(4): 1–19.

Katz, H. C. and Darbishire, O. (2000) *Converging Divergences: Worldwide Changes in Employment Systems*. Ithaca, NY: Cornell University Press.

Keep, E. (2000) 'Creating the knowledge-driven economy: definitions, challenges and opportunities'. University of Warwick, Coventry, SKOPE Policy Paper 2.

Keep, E. (2006) 'State control of the English VET system: playing with the biggest trainset in the world', *Journal of Vocational Education and Training*, 58(1): 47–64.

Keep, E. (2009) 'The limits of the possible: shaping the learning and skills landscape through a shared policy narrative'. University of Warwick, Coventry, SKOPE Research Paper No. 86.

Keep, E. (2015a) 'Governance in English VET: on the functioning of a fractured "system"', *Research in Comparative and International Education*, 10(4): 464–75.

Keep, E. (2015b) *Employer Ownership Explored*. London: Chartered Institute for Personnel and Development.

Keep, E. and James, S. (2011) 'Employer demand for apprentices', in T. Dolphin and T. Lanning (eds.), *Apprenticeships: An Edited Collection*. London: IPPR, pp. 55–65.

Keep, E. and Mayhew, K. (1999) 'The assessment: knowledge, skills and competitiveness', *Oxford Review of Economic Policy*, 15(1): 1–15.

Bibliography

Keep, E. and Mayhew, K. (2004) 'The economic and distributional implications of the expansion of higher education', *Oxford Review of Economic Policy*, 20(4): 298–314.

Keep, E. and Mayhew, K. (2010) 'Moving beyond skills as a social and economic panacea', *Work, Employment and Society*, 24(3): 565–77.

Keep, E. and Mayhew, K. (2014) *Industrial Strategy and the Future of Skills Policy: The High Road to Sustainable Growth*. London: Chartered Institute of Personnel and Development.

Keep, E., Mayhew, K., and Corney, M. (2002) 'Review of the evidence on the rate of return to employer investment in training and employer training measures'. University of Warwick, Coventry, SKOPE Research Paper no. 34.

Keep, E. and Payne, J. (2004) '"I can't believe it's not skill": the changing meaning of skill in the UK context and some implications', in G. Hayward and S. James (eds.), *Balancing the Skills Equation: Key Issues and Challenges for Policy and Practice*. Bristol: Policy Press, pp. 53–76.

Keep, E. and Rainbird, H. (2003) 'Training', in P. K. Edwards (ed.), *Industrial Relations: Theory and Practice*, 2nd edn. Oxford: Blackwell, pp. 392–419.

Kerr, C. (1983) *The Future of Industrial Societies: Convergence or Continuing Diversity?* Cambridge, MA: Harvard University Press.

Kerr, C., Dunlop, J., Harbison, F., and Myers, C. (1960) *Industrialism and Industrial Man*. Cambridge, MA: Harvard University Press.

Kersley, B., Alpin, C., Forth, J., Bryson, A., Bewley, H., Dix, G., and Oxenbridge, S. (2006) *Inside the Workplace: Findings from the 2004 Workplace Employment Relations Survey*. London: Routledge.

Keune, M. (2010) 'Derogation clauses on wages in sectoral collective agreements in seven European countries'. Dublin: Eurofound.

Kickert, W. (2007) 'Public management reforms in countries with a Napoleonic state model: France, Italy and Spain', in C. Pollitt, S. van Thiel, and V. Homburg (eds.), *New Public Management in Europe: Adaptation and Alternatives*. Basingstoke: Palgrave Macmillan, pp. 26–51.

Kjellberg, A. (1998) 'Sweden: restoring the model?' in A. Ferner and R. Hyman (eds.), *Changing Industrial Relations in Europe*. Oxford: Blackwell, pp. 74–117.

Konzelmann, S., Wilkinson, F., and Mankelow, R. (2007) 'Work Intensification and Employment Insecurity in Professional Work'. University of Cambridge, Centre for Business Research, Working Paper 345.

Korczynski, M. (2002) *Human Resource Management in Service Work*. Basingstoke: Palgrave Macmillan.

Korczynski, M. (2005) 'Skills in service work: an overview', *Human Resource Management Journal* 15(2): 3–14.

Korczynski, M. (2009) 'The mystery customer: continuing absences in the sociology of service work', *Sociology*, 43(5): 952–67.

Korczynski, M. (2013) 'The customer in the sociology of work: different ways of going beyond the management-worker dyad', *Work, Employment and Society*, 27(6): 1–7.

Korcznyski, M. and Evans, C. (2013) 'Customer abuse to service workers: an analysis of its social creation within the service economy', *Work, Employment and Society*, 27(5): 768–84.

Bibliography

Korpi, W. (2006) 'Power resources and employer-centred approaches in explanations of welfare states and varieties of capitalism: protagonists, consenters and antagonists', *World Politics*, 58(2): 167–206.

Kosonen, T. and Houtsonen, J. (2007) 'Nurses' life and work under restructuring in seven European contexts: a comparative report', in T. Kosonen and J. Houstsonen (eds.), *European Nurses' Life and Work under Restructuring: Professional Experiences, Knowledge and Expertise in a Changing Context*. ProfKnow Consortium Report No. 5, pp. 12–18. <http://www.profknow.net>.

Krings, B.-J., Nierling, L., and Valenduc, G. (2007) 'Conclusions of the comparative analysis', in G. Valenduc, P. Vendramin, B. J. Krings, and L. Nierling (eds.), *How is Restructuring Changing Occupations? Case Study Evidence from Knowledge-Intensive Manufacturing and Service Occupations*. Final Report of WP 11 WORKS report. Leibniz Information Centre for Economics, pp. 159–92. <http://econstor.eu/bitstream/10419/67055/1/D11.1.pdf>.

Kuczera, M., Brunello, G., Field, S., and Hoffman, N. (2008) *Learning for Jobs: OECD Reviews of Vocational and Educational Training—Norway*. Paris: OECD.

Kvarud Analyse (2011) 'Treningssenterbransjen'. <http://www.trening.no>.

Lafer, G. (2004) 'What is "skill"? Training for discipline in the low wage labour market', in C. Warhurst, E. Keep, and I. Grugulis (eds.), *The Skills That Matter*. Basingstoke: Palgrave Macmillan, pp. 109–127.

Lambert, S. J. and Henly, J. R. (2012) 'Frontline managers matter: labour flexibility practices and sustained employment in US retail jobs', in C. Warhurst, F. Carré, P. Findlay, and C. Tilly (eds.), *Are Bad Jobs Inevitable?* Basingstoke: Palgrave Macmillan, pp. 143–59.

Lane, C. (1989) *Management and Labour in Europe*. Aldershot: Edward Elgar.

Lane, C. and Wood, G. (2014) 'Capitalist diversity, work and employment relations', in A. Wilkinson, G. Wood, and R. Deeg (eds.), *The Oxford Handbook of Employment Relations: Comparative Employment Systems*. Oxford: Oxford University Press, pp. 156–72.

Larré, F., Lloyd, C., and Payne, J. (2013) 'Quel développement professionnel continu pour les enseignants des matières professionnelles? L'exemple de la coiffure. Approche comparée Angleterre, Pays de Galles, France et Norvège', *Revue Française de Pédagogie*, 184: 55–68.

Laurent, L. (2010) 'Gym culture not working out for the French'. <http://uk.reuters.com/article/fitness-france-idUKLDE68M0CV20100927>, accessed 15 December 2015.

Leidner, R. (1993) *Fast Food, Fast Talk: Service Work and the Routinization of Everyday Life*. Los Angeles: University of California Press.

Lemistre, P. (2013) 'Le déclassement, entre mythe et réalité', *Alternatives Economiques*, 59 January).

Lindbeck, A., Molander, P., Persson, T., Peterson, O., Sanmo, A., Swedenborg, B., and Thygesen, N. (1993) 'Options for economic and political reform in Sweden', *Economic Policy*, 8(17): 219–63.

Lingfield, R. (2012) *Professionalism in Further Education: Final Report of the Independent Review Panel*. London: DBIS.

Linsley, I. (2005) 'Causes of overeducation in the Australian Labour Market', *Australian Journal of Labour Economics*, 8(2): 121–43.

Bibliography

Lipowski, K., Jorde, D., Prenzel, M., and Seidel, T. (2011) 'Expert views on the implementation of teacher professional development in European countries', *Professional Development in Education*, 37(5): 685–700.

Lipsky, M. (1980) *Street Level Bureaucracy: Dilemmas of the Individual in Public Services*. New York: Russell Sage Foundation.

Littler, C. (1982) *The Development of the Labour Process in Capitalist Society*. London: Heinemann.

Lloyd, C. (1999) 'Regulating employment: implications for skill development in the aerospace industry', *European Journal of Industrial Relations*, 5(2): 163–85.

Lloyd, C. (2005) 'Competitive strategy and skills: working out the fit in the fitness industry', *Human Resource Management Journal*, 15(2): 15–34.

Lloyd, C., Mason, G., and Mayhew, K. (2008) *Low-Wage Work in the United Kingdom*. New York: Russell Sage Foundation.

Lloyd, C. and Mayhew, K. (2010) 'Skills: the solution to low wage jobs?', *Industrial Relations Journal*, 41(5): 429–45.

Lloyd, C. and Payne, J. (2002) 'On the "political economy of skill": assessing the possibilities for a viable high skills project in the UK', *New Political Economy*, 7(3): 367–95.

Lloyd, C. and Payne, J. (2006) 'Goodbye to all that? A critical re-evaluation of the role of the high performance work organisation within the UK skills debate', *Work, Employment and Society*, 20(1): 151–65.

Lloyd, C. and Payne, J. (2007) 'Tackling the UK skills problem: can unions make a difference?' in S. Shelley and M. Calveley (eds.), *Learning with Trade Unions: A Contemporary Agenda in Employment Relations*. Aldershot: Ashgate, pp. 57–77.

Lloyd, C. and Payne, J. (2009) '"Full of sound and fury, signifying nothing": interrogating the new skill concepts in service work—the view from two call centres', *Work, Employment and Society*, 24(4): 617–34.

Lloyd, C. and Payne, J. (2012) 'Raising the quality of vocational teachers: continuing professional development in England, Wales and Norway', *Research Papers in Education*, 27(1): 1–18.

Lloyd, C. and Payne, J. (2014) '"It's all hands-on, even for management": managerial work in the UK café sector', *Human Relations*, 67(4): 465–88.

Lloyd, C. and Steedman, H. (1999) 'Intermediate level skills: how are they changing?' Skills Task Force Research Paper 9. Sheffield: DfEE.

Lloyd, C., Warhurst, C., and Dutton, E. (2013) 'The weakest link? Product market strategies, skills and pay in the hotel industry?' *Work, Employment and Society*, 27(2): 254–71.

Lloyd, C., Weinkopf, C., and Batt, R. (2010) 'Restructuring customer service: labor market institutions and call center workers in Europe and the United States', in J. Gautié and J. Schmitt (eds.), *Low Wage Work in the Wealthy World*. New York: Russell Sage Foundation, pp. 421–66.

LLUK (2007) 'New overarching professional standards for teachers, tutors and trainers in the lifelong learning sector'. Lifelong Learning UK (LLUK).

Løken, E. and Stokke, T. (2009) 'Labour Relations in Norway'. FAFO Report 33. Oslo: FAFO. <http://www.fafo.no/pub/rapp/20123/20123>.

Bibliography

Løken, E., Stokke, T., and Nergaard, K. (2013) 'Labour Relations in Norway'. Oslo: FAFO.

Lopes, H., Lagoa, S., and Calapez, T. (2014) 'Work autonomy, work pressure, and job satisfaction: an analysis of European Union countries', *Economic and Labour Relations Review*, 25(2): 306–26.

Lorenz, E. (2015) 'Work organisation, forms of employee learning and labour market structure: accounting for international differences in workplace innovation', *Journal of the Knowledge Economy*, 6(2): 437–66.

Lorenz, E. and Valeyre, A. (2005). 'Organisational innovation, HRM and labour market structure: a comparison of the EU-15', *Journal of Industrial Relations*, 47(4): 424–42.

Lyng, S. and Blichfeldt, J. (2003) 'Norwegian Country Background Report for the OECD Project Attracting, Developing and Retaining Effective Teachers'. Oslo: Work Research Institute.

McIlroy, J. (2011) 'Britain: how neoliberalism cut the unions down to size', in G. Gall, R. Hurd, and A. Wilkinson (eds.), *International Handbook on Labour Unions' Responses to Neoliberalism*. Aldershot: Edward Elgar, pp. 122–53.

MacInnes, J. (1987) *Thatcherism at Work*. Milton Keynes: Open University Press.

McKinlay, A. and Smith, C. (eds.) (2009) *Creative Labour: Working in the Creative Industries*. Basingstoke: Palgrave Macmillan.

McLoughlin, I. and Clark, J. (1994) *Technological Change at Work*. Buckingham: Open University Press.

McMurtry, J. (1998) *The Cancer Stage of Capitalism and its Cure*. London: Pluto Press.

Maglen, L. (1990) 'Challenging the human capital orthodoxy: the education–productivity link re-examined', *Economic Record*, 66: 281–94.

Marks, A. and Scholarios, D. (2008) 'Choreographing a system: skill and employability in software work', *Economic and Industrial Democracy*, 29(1): 96–124.

Marmot, M. (2004) *The Status Syndrome: How Social Standing affects our Health and Longevity*. London: Henry Holt.

Marsh, D. (1992) *The New Politics of British Trade Unionism: Union Power and the Thatcher Legacy*. New York: ILR Press.

Mason, G. (2002) 'High skills utilisation under mass higher education: graduate employment in service industries in Britain', *Journal of Education and Work*, 15(4): 427–56.

Mason, G. (2004) 'Enterprise product strategies and employer demand for skills in Britain: evidence from the Employers Skill Survey'. Universities of Oxford and Warwick, SKOPE Research Paper no. 50.

Mason, G., van Ark, B., and Wagner, K. (1994) 'Productivity, product quality and workforce skills: food processing in four European countries', *National Institute Economic Review*, 147(1): 62–83.

Mason, G., van Ark, B., and Wagner, K. (1996) 'Workforce skills, product quality and economic performance', in A. L. Booth and D. J. Snower (eds.), *Acquiring Skills: Market Failures, their Symptoms and Policy Responses*. Cambridge: Cambridge University Press, pp. 177–97.

Mason, G. and Wagner, K. (1994) 'Innovation and the skill mix: chemicals and engineering in Britain and Germany', *National Institute Economic Review*, 148: 61–72.

Bibliography

Mather, K., Worrall, L., and Seifert, R. (2009) 'The changing locus of workplace control in the English further education sector', *Employee Relations*, 31(2): 139–57.

Mattei, P. (2012) 'The French Republican school under pressure: falling basic standards and rising social inequalities', *French Politics*, 10(1): 84–95.

Maurice, M., Sellier, F., and Silvestre, J. (1986) *The Social Foundations of Industrial Power*. Cambridge, MA: MIT Press.

Maurice, M., Sorge, A., and Warner, M. (1980) 'Societal differences in organizing manufacturing units: a comparison of France, West Germany and Great Britain', *Organization Studies*, 1(1): 59–86.

Maynard, D. C., Joseph, T. A., and Maynard, A. M. (2006) 'Underemployment, job attitudes, and turnover intentions', *Journal of Organizational Behavior*, 27: 509–36.

Meardi, G. (2014) 'Employment relations under external pressure: Italian and Spanish reforms during the great recession', in M. Hauptmeier and M. Vidal (eds.), *The Comparative Political Economy of Work and Employment Relations*. Basingstoke: Palgrave Macmillan, pp. 332–50.

Méhaut, P. (2006) 'Key concepts and debates in the French VET system and labour market'. Paper for the seminar 'Developing a European Qualification Framework: Conceptual and Labour Market Questions', King's College, London, June.

Méhaut, P., Berg, P., Grimshaw, D., Jaehrling, K. with van der Meer, M. and Eskildsen, J. (2010) 'Cleaning and nursing in hospitals: institutional variety and reshaping of low wage jobs', in J. Gautié and J. Schmitt (eds.), *Low Wage Work in the Wealthy World*. New York: Russell Sage Foundation, pp. 319–67.

Metcalf, H. (2009) 'Pay gaps across the equality strands: a review'. Research Report 14. London: Equality and Human Rights Commission.

Milner, S. and Mathers, A. (2013) 'Membership, influence and voice: a discussion of trade union renewal in the French context', *Industrial Relations Journal*, 44(2): 122–38.

Mintel (2009) *Health and Fitness Clubs—UK*. London: Mintel.

Mintel (2011a) *Health and Fitness Clubs—UK*. London: Mintel.

Mintel (2011b) *Coffee Shops—UK*. London: Mintel.

Mishel, L. and Davis, A. (2014) 'CEO pay continues to rise as typical workers are paid less'. Economic Policy Institute, Issue Brief Number 380, June.

Misra, P. K. (2014) 'The state of teacher education in France: a critique'. FMSH-WP-2014-58. <http://wpfmsh.hypotheses.org/440>.

Møller, J., Eggen, A., Fuglestad, O. L., Langfeldt, G., Presthus, A. M., Skrøvset, S., Stjernstrøm, E., and Vedøy, G. (2005) 'Successful school leadership: the Norwegian case', *Journal of Educational Administration*, 43(6): 584–94.

Møller, J. and Skedsmo, G. (2013) 'Modernizing education: NPM reform in the Norwegian education system', *Journal of Educational Administration and History*, 45(4): 336–55.

Moss, B. (1988) 'Industrial law reform in an era of retreat: the Auroux Laws in France', *Work, Employment and Society*, 2(3): 317–34.

MTEFD (Ministère du Travail, de l'Emploi, de la Formation professionnelle et du Dialogue social) (2015) *La Négociation Collective en 2014*. Paris: MTEFD.

Müller, J., Hernández, F., Sancho, J., Creus, A., Muntadas, M., Larrain, V., et al. (2007) 'European school teachers' work and life under restructuring: professional experiences,

Bibliography

knowledge and expertise in a changing context'. ProfKnow Consortium Report No. 4. <http://www.profknow.net>.

Nauze-Fichet, E. and Tomasini, M. (2002) 'Diplôme et insertion sur le marché du travail: approches socioprofessionnelle et salariale du déclassement', *Économie et Statistique*, 354: 21–43.

Nergaard, K. (2014a) *Trade Unions in Norway: Coordinated Wage Bargaining and Workplace Level Codetermination*. Berlin: Friedrich Ebert Stiftung.

Nergaard, K. (2014b) 'Organisasjonsgrader, tariffavtaledekning og arbeidskonflikter 2013'. FAFO notat 2014:14. Oslo: FAFO.

Newman, J. (2000) 'Beyond the new public management: modernizing public services', in J. Clarke, S. Gerwitz, and E. McLaughlin (eds.), *New Managerialism, New Welfare?* London: Sage, pp. 45–61.

Noble, C. (1997) 'International comparisons of training policies', *Human Resource Management Journal*, 7(1): 5–18.

Nolan, P. (2001) 'Shaping Things to Come', *People Management*, 7(25): 30–1.

Nolan, P. and Brown, W. (1983) 'Competition and workplace wage determination', *Oxford Bulletin of Economics and Statistics*, 45(3): 269–87.

Nolan, P. and Slater, G. (2010) 'Visions of the future, the legacy of the past: demystifying the weightless economy', *Labor History*, 51(1): 7–27.

Nonaka, I. (1991) 'The knowledge-creating company', *Harvard Business Review*, 69(6): 96–104.

Noram, L. and Uba, K. (2015) 'Austerity measures across Europe', in L. Foster, A. Brunton, C. Deeming, and T. Haux (eds.), *In Defence of Welfare 2*. Bristol: Policy Press, pp. 55–8.

Obama, B. (2009) 'Remarks of President Barack Obama: Address to Joint Session of Congress', 24 February. <https://www.whitehouse.gov/the-press-office/remarks-president-barack-obama-address-joint-session-congress>, accessed 14 December 2015.

O'Mahony, M. and Stevens, P. (2005) *International Comparisons of Performance in Public Services: Outcomes Based Measures for Education*. London: NIESR.

OECD (1996) *The Knowledge-Based Economy*. OCDE/GD(96)102. Paris: OECD.

OECD (2001) 'The characteristics and quality of service sector jobs', *OECD Employment Outlook*, pp. 89–128.

OECD (2005) *Teachers Matter: Attracting, Developing and Retaining Effective Teachers*. Final Report. Paris: OECD.

OECD (2010a) 'An Agenda for New Skills and Jobs'. COM 682/3. Paris: OECD.

OECD (2010b) *Economic Policy Reforms: Going for Growth*. Paris: OECD.

OECD (2011) *Towards an OECD Skills Strategy*. Paris: OECD.

OECD (2012) *Better Skills, Better Jobs, Better Lives: A Strategic Approach to Skills Policies*. Paris: OECD.

OECD (2013) *OECD Skills Outlook 2013: First Results from the Survey of Adult Skills*. Paris: OECD.

OECD (2015a) *Education at a Glance 2014: OECD Indicators*. Paris: OECD.

OECD (2015b) 'Average annual hours actually worked per worker'. <http://stats.oecd.org/index.aspx?DataSetCode=ANHRS>, accessed 16 December 2015.

Ohmae, K. (1990) *The Borderless World: Power and Strategy in the Interlinked Economy*. New York: Harper Business.

Bibliography

Oinas, T., Anttila, T., Mustosmäki, A., and Nätti, J. (2012) 'The Nordic difference: job quality in Europe 1995–2010', *Nordic Journal of Working Life Studies: Changing the World of Work*, 2(4): 135–52.

Okay-Somervill, B. and Scholarios, D. (2013) 'Shades of grey: understanding job quality in emerging graduate occupations', *Human Relations*, 66(4): 555–85.

ONPES (Observatoire National de la Pauvreté et de l'Exclusion Sociale) (2014) *Les Effects d'une Crise Economique de Longue Durée: Rapport 2013–2014*. Paris: ONPES.

Osborn, M. (2006) 'Changing the context of teachers' work and professional development: a European perspective', *International Journal of Educational Research*, 45(4–5): 242–53.

Osterman, P. (2000) 'Work reorganization in an era of restructuring: trends in diffusion and effects on employee welfare', *Industrial and Labor Relations Review*, 53(2): 179–86.

Palier, B. and Thelen, K. (2010) 'Institutionalizing dualism: complementarities and change in France and Germany', *Politics & Society*, 38(1): 119–48.

Palpacuer, F., Seignour, A., and Vercher, C. (2011) 'Financialization, globalization and the management of skilled employees: towards a market-based HRM model in large corporations in France', *British Journal of Industrial Relations*, 49(3): 560–82.

Parsons, D., Hughes, J., Allinson, C., and Walsh, K. (2008) *The Training and Development of VET Teachers and Trainers in Europe*. Thessaloniki: CEDEFOP.

Parsons, N. (2005) *French Industrial Relations in the New World Economy*. London: Routledge.

Payne, J. (2000). 'The unbearable lightness of skill: the changing meaning of skill in UK policy discourses and some implications for education and training', *Journal of Education Policy*, 15(3): 353–69.

Payne, J. (2006) 'The Norwegian competence reform and the limits of lifelong learning', *International Journal of Lifelong Learning*, 25(5): 477–505.

Payne, J. (2008a) 'Skills in context: what can the UK learn from Australia's experiment with skill ecosystem projects?' *Policy and Politics*, 36(3): 307–23.

Payne, J. (2008b) 'Sector skills councils and employer engagement: delivering the employer-led skills agenda in England', *Journal of Education and Work*, 21(2): 93–113.

Payne, J. (2009) 'Emotional labour and skill: a reappraisal', *Gender, Work & Organization*, 16(3): 348–67.

Payne, J. (2012) 'Fronting-up to skills utilisation: what can the UK learn from Scotland's skills utilisation projects?' *Policy Studies*, 33(5): 419–38.

Payne, J. and Keep, E. (2003) 'Re-visiting the Nordic approaches to work re-organization and job redesign: lessons for UK skills policy', *Policy Studies*, 24(4): 205–24.

Perez, J.-P. (2009) 'Fitness 2009: le future est de retour', *Planet Fitness Management*, 2: 16–17.

Perkins, S. J. and White, G. (2010) 'Modernising pay in the UK public services: trends and implications', *Human Resource Management Journal*, 20(3): 244–57.

Phillips, A. and Taylor, B. (1980) 'Sex and skill: notes towards a feminist economics', *Feminist Review*, 6: 78–88.

Piore, M. and Sabel, C. (1984) *The Second Industrial Divide: Possibilities of Prosperity*. New York: Basic Books.

Pocock, B. and Skinner, N. (2012) 'Good jobs, bad jobs and the Australian experience', in C. Warhurst, F. Carré, P. Findlay, C., and Tilly (eds.), *Are Bad Jobs Inevitable?* Basingstoke: Palgrave Macmillan, pp. 61–77.
Pollert, A. (1988) 'Dismantling flexibility', *Capital and Class*, 34: 42–75.
Pollitt, C. (1993) *Managerialism and the Public Services*. Oxford: Blackwell.
Pollitt, C. (2007) 'New Labour's re-disorganization: hyper-modernism and the costs of reform—a cautionary tale', *Public Management Review*, 9(4): 529–43.
Pollitt, C. and Bouckaert, G. (2004) *Public Management Reform: A Comparative Analysis*. Oxford: Oxford University Press.
Porter, M. (1980) *Competitive Strategy*. New York: Free Press.
Prais, S. J., Jarvis, V., and Wagner, K. (1989) 'Vocational qualifications in Britain and Europe: theory and practice', *National Institute Economic Review*, 123: 34–7.
Purcell, J. (2000) 'After collective bargaining? ACAS in the age of human resource management', in B. Towers and W. Brown (eds.), *Employment Relations in Britain: 25 Years of the Advisory, Conciliation and Arbitration Service*. Oxford: Blackwell, pp. 163–80.
Purcell, K., Elias, P., Atfield, G., Behle, H., Ellison, R., and Luchinskaya, D. (2013) 'Transitions into employment, further study and other outcomes'. Futuretrack Stage 4 Report. University of Warwick: Institute for Employment Research.
Purcell, K., Elias, P., and Wilton, N. (2004) 'Higher education skills and employment: careers and jobs in the graduate labour market'. Research Paper 3, University of Warwick: Institute for Employment Research.
Quack, S., O'Reilly, J., and Hildebrandt, S. (1995) 'Structuring change: training and recruitment in retail banking in Germany, Britain, and France', *International Journal of Human Resource Management*, 6(4): 759–94.
Quintini, G. (2011) 'Over-qualified or under-skilled: a review of existing literature'. OECD Social Employment and Migration Working Paper No. 121. Paris: OECD.
Qvale, T. (2002) 'A case of slow learning? Recent trends in social partnership in Norway with particular emphasis on workplace democracy', *Concepts and Transformation*, 7(1): 31–55.
Ramstad, E. (2009) 'Expanding innovation system and policy: an organisational perspective', *Policy Studies*, 30(5): 533–53.
Reay, D. (2011) 'Schooling for democracy: a common school and a common university? A response to "Schooling for Democracy"', *Democracy & Education*, 19(1): 1–4.
Reay, D. (2012) 'What would a socially just education system look like? Saving the minnows from the pike', *Journal of Education Policy*, 7(5): 587–99.
Rees, G. (2007) 'The impacts of parliamentary devolution on education policy in Wales', *Welsh Journal of Education*, 14(1): 8–20.
Regini, M. (1995) 'Firms and institutions: the demand for skills and their social production in Europe', *European Journal of Industrial Relations*, 1(2): 191–202.
Reich, R. (1991) *The Work of Nations: Preparing Ourselves for 21st Century Capitalism*. New York: Vintage Books.
Reich, R. (2002) *The Future of Success: Working and Living in the New Economy*. New York: Vintage Books.
Ringerikes Blad (2009) 'Motarbeidet av Elixia', 24 January. <http://www.ringblad.no/nyheter/motarbeidet-av-elixia/s/1-97-4073893>, accessed 17 December 2015.

Bibliography

Ritzer, G. (1993) *The McDonaldization of Society*. Thousand Oaks, CA: Pine Forge Press.

Robson, J., Bailey, B., and Larkin, S. (2004) 'Adding value: investigating the discourse of professionalism adopted by vocational teachers in further education colleges', *Journal of Education and Work*, 17(2): 183–95.

Rohrbach-Schmidt, D. and Tiemann, M. (2011) 'Mismatching and job tasks in Germany: rising over-qualification through polarization?' *Empirical Research in Vocational Education and Training*, 1(3): 39–53.

Rolfe, H., Taylor, P., Casey, B., Christie, I., and McRae, S. (1994) *Employers' Role in the Supply of Intermediate Skills*. London: Policy Study Institute.

Rosecrance, R. (1999) *The Rise of the Virtual State*. New York: Basic Books.

Royle, T. (2004) 'Low road convergence? The significance of sectoral factors in understanding MNC cross-border behaviour: the case of the Spanish and German quick food service sectors', *European Journal of Industrial Relations*, 10(1): 51–71.

RRS (2015) *Repères et Références Statistiques: Enseignements, Formation, Recherche*. Paris: Ministre de L'Education Nationale de L'Enseignement Supérieur et de la Recherche.

Sandberg, Å. (1995) *Enriching Production: Perspectives on Volvo's Uddevalla Plant as an Alternative to Lean Production*. Aldershot: Avebury.

SATS (2010) *SATS Holding AB: Annual Report 2009*. Sundbyberg: SATS.

Schilling, G. and Vanselow, A. (2011) 'More than co-management: lessons from a research-supported trade union project in German manufacturing'. Presentation to the International Labour Process Conference, Leeds, April.

Schuler, R. and Jackson, S. (1987) 'Linking competitive strategies and human resource management practices', *Academy of Management Executive*, 1(3): 207–19.

Schulze-Marmeling, S. (2014) 'France: changes to wage-setting mechanisms in the context of the crisis and the EU's new economic governance regime'. EurWork. Dublin: Eurofound.

Scottish Government (2007) *Skills for Scotland: A Lifelong Skills Strategy*. Edinburgh: Scottish Government.

Senker, J. and Senker, P. (1994) 'Information technology and skills in manufacturing', in K. Ducatel (ed.), *Employment and Technical Change in Europe*. Aldershot: Edward Elgar, pp. 58–77.

Simmons, R. (2008) 'Golden years: further education colleges under local authority control', *Journal of Further and Higher Education*, 32(4): 359–71.

Simmons, R. (2013) ' "Sorry to have kept you waiting so long, Mr Macfarlane': further education after the Coalition', in M. Allen and P. Ainley (eds.), *Education Beyond the Coalition: Reclaiming the Agenda*. London: Radicaled Books, pp. 82–105.

Simmons, R. and Thompson, R. (2008) 'Creativity and performativity: the case of further education', *British Educational Research Journal*, 34(5): 601–18.

SkillsActive (2008) *Working in Fitness Survey 2008*. London: SkillsActive.

SkillsActive (2010) *Sector Skills Assessment 2011: UK Report*. London: SkillsActive.

SkillsActive/REPs/FIA (2008) *Health and Fitness: REPs Occupational Research 2008, Executive Summary*. London: SkillsActive.

Skule, S., Stuart, M., and Nyen, T. (2002) 'International briefing 12: training and development in Norway', *International Journal of Training and Development*, 6(4): 263–76.

Smith, A. (1776) *An Inquiry into the Nature and Causes of the Wealth of Nations*. London: Methuen & Co.

Smith, P. (2009) 'New Labour and the commonsense of neoliberalism: trade unionism, collective bargaining and workers' rights', *Industrial Relations Journal*, 40(4): 337–55.

Sorge, A. and Streeck, W. (1988) 'Industrial relations and technical change: the case for an extended perspective', in R. Hyman and W. Streeck (eds.), *New Technology and Industrial Relations*. Oxford: Basil Blackwell, pp. 19–47.

Soskice, D. (1993) 'Social skills from mass higher education: rethinking the company-based initial training paradigm', *Oxford Review of Economic Policy*, 9(3): 101–13.

Souto-Otero, M. and Ure, O.-B. (2012) 'The coherence of vocational education and training in Norway and Spain: national traditions and the reshaping of VET governance in hybrid VET systems', *Compare*, 42(1): 91–111.

Spence, A. (1973) 'Job market signalling', *Quarterly Journal of Economics*, 87(3): 355–74.

Sports.gouv.fr (2012) 'Centre de remise en forme ou de fitness'. <http://www.sports.gouv.fr/IMG/archives/pdf/remise.pdf>.

Standing, G. (2011) *The Precariat*. London: Bloomsbury.

Steedman, H. and Wagner, K. (1989) 'Productivity, machinery and skills: clothing manufacture in Britain and Germany', *National Institute Economic Review*, 128: 40–58.

Steen Johnsen, K. and Kirkegaard, L. (2010) 'The history and organisation of fitness exercise in Norway and Denmark', *Sport in Society*, 13(4): 609–24.

Streeck, W. (1989) 'Skills and the limits of neo-liberalism: the enterprise of the future as a place of learning', *Work, Employment and Society*, 3(1): 89–104.

Streeck, W. (1992) *Social Institutions and Economic Performance: Studies of Industrial Relations in Advanced Capitalist Economies*. London: Sage.

Streeck, W. (1997a) 'German capitalism: does it exist? Can it survive?' in C. Crouch and W. Streeck (eds.), *Political Economy of Modern Capitalism: Mapping Convergence and Diversity*. London: Sage, pp. 33–54.

Streeck, W. (1997b) 'Beneficial constraints: on the economic limits of rational voluntarism', in J. Hollingsworth, J. Rogers, and R. Boyer(eds.), *Contemporary Capitalism: The Embeddedness of Institutions*. Cambridge: Cambridge University Press, pp. 197–219.

Streeck, W. (2010) 'E pluribus unum? Varieties and commonalities of capitalism'. MPIfG Discussion Paper 10/12.

Streeck, W. (2011a) 'Skills and politics: general and specific'. MPIfG discussion paper 11/1.

Streeck, W. (2011b) 'Taking capitalism seriously: towards an institutionalist approach to contemporary political economy', *Socio-Economic Review*, 9(1): 137–67.

Streeck, W. (2011c) 'The crisis in context: democratic capitalism and its contradictions'. MPIfG Discussion Paper 11/15.

Streeck, W. (2014a) 'How will capitalism end?' *New Left Review*, 87 (May–June).

Streeck, W. (2014b) *Buying Time: The Delayed Crisis of Democratic Capitalism*. London: Verso Books.

Streeck, W. and Thelen, K. (2005) 'Introduction: institutional change in advanced political economies', in W. Streeck and K. Thelen (eds.), *Beyond Continuity: Institutional Change in Advanced Political Economies*. Oxford: Oxford University Press, pp. 3–39.

Bibliography

Stuart, M., Grugulis, I., Tomlinson, J., Forde, C., and MacKenzie, R. (2013) 'Reflections on work and employment into the 21st century: between equal rights, force decides', *Work, Employment and Society*, 27(3): 379–95.

Sung, J. and Ashton, D. (2015) *Skills in Business: The Role of Business Strategy, Sectoral Skills Development and Skills Policy*. London: Sage.

Tawney, R. H. (1964a) *Equality*. London: Unwin Books.

Tawney, R. H. (1964b) *The Radical Tradition*. London: Allen & Unwin.

Taylor, P. and Bain, P. (1999) ' "An assembly line in the head": work and employee relations in the call centre', *Industrial Relations Journal*, 30(2): 101–17.

Tchobanian, R. (1995) 'France: from conflict to social dialogue?' in J. Rogers and W. Streeck (eds.), *Works Councils: Consultation, Representation and Cooperation in Industrial Relations*. Chicago: University of Chicago Press, pp. 115–52.

Telhaug, A. O. and Volckmar, N. (1999) 'Norwegian education policy rhetoric 1945–2000: education philosophy in the political party platforms', *Scandinavian Journal of Educational Research*, 43(3): 275–93.

Terry, M. (2003) 'Partnership and the future of trade unions in the UK', *Economic and Industrial Democracy*, 24(4): 485–507.

Thompson, P. (1983) *The Nature of Work: An Introduction to Debates on the Labour Process*. London: Macmillan.

Thompson, P. (1989) *The Nature of Work*. Basingstoke: Macmillan.

Thompson, P. (2013) 'Financialization and the workplace: extending and applying the disconnected capitalism thesis', *Work, Employment and Society*, 27(3): 472–88.

Thompson, P., Wallace, T., Flecker, J., and Ahlstrand, R. (1995) 'It ain't what you do, it's the way that you do it: production organisation and skill utilisation in commercial vehicles', *Work, Employment and Society*, 9(4): 719–42.

Thompson, P., Warhurst, C., and Callaghan, G. (2001) 'Ignorant theory and knowledgeable workers: interrogating the connections between knowledge, skills and services', *Journal of Management Studies*, 38(7): 923–42.

Thompson, S. and Hatfield, I. (2015) *Employee Progression in European Labour Markets*. London: IPPR.

Thurow, L. (1975) *Generating Inequality*. New York: Basic Books.

Tinker, T. (2002) 'Spectres of Marx and Braverman in the twilight of postmodernist labour process research', *Work, Employment and Society*, 16(2): 251–81.

Tjeldvoll, A. (2008) 'School management: Norwegian legacies bowing to new public management', *Managing Global Transitions*, 6(2): 177–205.

Torvatn, H. (2011) 'Cleaning in Norway: Between Professionalism and Junk Enterprises'. Work and Life Quality in New & Growing Jobs (WALQING) Social Partnership Series 2011.5, report for WP5 of the WALQING project.

Trist, E. and Bamforth, W. (1951) 'Some social and psychological consequences of the long-wall method of coal getting', *Human Relations*, 4: 3–38.

Troger, V. and Hörner, W. (2007) 'Teachers of technical and vocational education in France', in P. Grollmann and F. Rauner (eds.), *International Perspectives on Teachers and Lecturers in Technical and Vocational Education*. Dordrecht: Springer, pp. 1–26.

Trow, M. (2006) 'Reflections on the transition from elite to mass to universal access: forms and phases of higher education in modern societies since World War II', in

J. Forest and P. Altbach(eds.), *International Handbook on Higher Education*, vol. 18. New York: Springer, pp. 243–80.

UKCES (2009) *High Performance Working: A Synthesis of Key Literature*. Evidence Report 4. London: UKCES.

UKCES (2014) *UK Commission's Employer Skills Survey 2013: UK Results*. London: UKCES.

Ure, O. B. (2007) 'Lifelong learning in Norway: a deflating policy balloon or an act of piecemeal implementation?' Report 2007:30. Oslo: FAFO.

Utdanningsdirektoratet (2007) *The Education Mirror*. Oslo: Norwegian Directorate of Education and Training.

Valenduc, G. (2007) 'Occupational monograph: IT professionals in software services', in G. Valenduc, P. Vendramin, B. J. Krings, and L. Nierling (eds.), *How is Restructuring Changing Occupations? Case Study Evidence from Knowledge-Intensive Manufacturing and Service Occupations*. Final Report of WP 11 WORKS report. Leibniz Information Centre for Economics, pp. 73–97. <http://econstor.eu/bitstream/10419/67055/1/D11.1.pdf>.

Valenduc, G., Vendramin, P., Krings, B. J. and Nierling, L. (eds.) (2007) *How is Restructuring Changing Occupations? Case Study Evidence from Knowledge-Intensive Manufacturing and Service Occupations*. Final Report of WP 11 WORKS report. Leibniz Information Centre for Economics.

van Wanrooy, B., Bewley, H., Bryson, A., Forth, J., Freeth, S., Stokes, L., and Wood, S. (2013) *The 2011 Workplace Employment Relations Study: First Findings*. London: DBIS/ESRC Report.

Vanselow, A., Warhurst, C., Bernhardt, A., and Dresser, L. (2010) 'Working at the wage floor: hotel room attendants and labor market institutions in Europe and the United States', in J. Gautié and J. Schmitt (eds.), *Low-Wage Work in the Wealthy World*. New York: Russell Sage Foundation, pp. 269–319.

Viallon, R., Carny, J., and Collins, M. (2003) 'The European integration of a new occupation, the training and education strategies of national professional organizations: the case of the fitness sector in France and the United Kingdom', *Managing Leisure*, 8(2): 85–96.

Vickerstaff, S. (2003) 'Apprenticeship in the "golden age": were youth transitions really smooth and unproblematic back then?' *Work, Employment and Society*, 17(2): 269–87.

Vidal, M. (2013) 'Low-autonomy work and bad jobs in post-Fordist capitalism', *Human Relations*, 66(4): 587–612.

Voss-Dahm, D. (2008) 'Low-paid but committed to the industry: salespeople in the retail sector', in G. Bosch and C. Weinkopf (eds.), *Low Wage Work in Germany*. New York: Russell Sage Foundation, pp. 253–87.

Wald, S. (2004). 'The impact of overqualification on job search', *International Journal of Manpower*, 26: 140–56.

Warhurst, C. and Findlay, P. (2012) 'More effective skills utilisation: shifting the terrain of skills policy in Scotland'. Cardiff University, SKOPE Research Paper No. 107.

Warhurst, C. and Nickson, D. (2007) 'Employee experience of aesthetic labour in retail and hospitality', *Work, Employment and Society*, 21(1): 103–20.

Watson, I. (2008) 'Skills in use: labour market and workplace trends in skills use in Australia'. Paper presented to New Directions in Skills Policy and Practice NSW DET Conference, Sydney.

Bibliography

Weinkopf, C. (2008) 'Pay in customer services under pressure: call center agents', in G. Bosch and C. Weinkopf (eds.), *Low-Wage Work in Germany*. New York: Russell Sage Foundation, pp. 113–46.

Welsh Government (2014) *Skills Implementation Plan: Delivering the Policy Statement on Skills*. Bedwas: Welsh Government.

Wensley, R. (1999) 'Product strategies, managerial comprehension, and organizational performance', *Oxford Review of Economic Policy*, 15(1): 33–42.

Wiener, M. (1981) *English Culture and the Decline of the Industrial Spirit*. Cambridge, Cambridge University Press.

Wiggan, J. (2012) 'Telling stories of 21st century welfare: the UK Coalition Government and the neo-liberal discourse of worklessness and dependency', *Critical Social Policy*, 32(3): 384–405.

Williams, S. (2003) 'Conflict in the colleges: industrial relations in further education since incorporation', *Journal of Further and Higher Education*, 27(3): 307–15.

Wilson, R. and Hogarth, T. (2003) *Tackling the Low Skills Equilibrium*. London: DTI.

Wolf, A. (2011) *Review of Vocational Education: The Wolf Report*. London: Department for Education.

Wood, S. (ed.) (1982) *The Degradation of Work? Skill, Deskilling and the Labour Process*. London: Hutchinson.

Wood, S., Burridge, M., Green, W., Nolte, S., and Rudloff, D. (2013) *High Performance Working in the Employer Skills Surveys. Evidence Report 71*. London: UKCES.

Woolfson, C., Fudge, J., and Thörnqvist, C. (2014) 'Migrant precarity and future challenges to labour standards in Sweden', *Economic and Industrial Democracy*, 13(4): 695–715.

World Bank (2002) *Constructing Knowledge Societies: New Challenges for Tertiary Education*. Washington, DC: World Bank.

Wright, J. and Sissons, P. (2012) *The Skills Dilemma: Skills Under-Utilisation and Low-Wage Work*. London: Work Foundation.

Young, M. (1958) *The Rise of Meritocracy*. London: Thames and Hudson.

Index

aesthetic labour 38
age of employees 85, 86, 91
   café workers 159, 163, 164–5, 178, 183, 184, 199
   fitness instructors 136, 150, 199
   over-qualification 87
   vocational teachers 106
analytical framework 58–62
Anderson, P. 125
Andersson, T. 157
apprenticeships
   fitness instructors 151
   France 77
   Germany 45, 48, 59, 127, 158, 207
   intermediate jobs 127
   low-skilled service sector jobs 158
   national institutions 45, 48
   Norway 76, 79, 98
   skill, nature of 39
   UK 74, 75, 77
   upskilling 207
Arrowsmith, J. 53
Ashton, D. 32, 213
Auroux laws (France, 1982) 71, 83
austerity policies 2, 189, 212
   UK 2, 67, 75
Australia 17, 18, 25–6n2, 27, 30, 50
Austria 17, 18, 27, 55, 172
autonomy 4, 188, 190, 194
   café workers 166, 171, 173, 184, 191, 205
   defined 40
   fitness instructors 146, 148, 151, 191, 193, 205
   high-skilled service sector jobs 56
   knowledge work 2
   low-skilled service sector jobs 57, 157, 208
   national institutions 52
   new public management 24
   professional 203
   public sector 210
   vocational teachers 99, 105, 108–12, 121, 123, 190, 192, 195, 196, 200, 201, 205
   work organization improvement initiatives, Norway 83

Baccaro, L. 68
Bach, S. 94
Bailey, T. R. 157
Barroso, José Manuel 15–16
Bechter, B. 54, 61
Bélanger, J. 35
Belfield, C. 25
Belgium 27, 68
Bentham, J. 34
Bergene, A. N. 162
Berggren, C. 45
Bernhardt, A. D. 157
Bernstein, B. 213
Bieler, A. 68, 89
Blair, Tony 66
Bolton, S. 38
Bordogna, L. 94, 122
Bosch, G. 58
Boychuk, T. 6, 50, 61–2, 62, 151, 205
Braverman, H. 20, 41
Brinkley, I. 23
Briscoe, G. 29
Brown, G. 24
Brown, Gordon 17
Brynin, M. 25n2

café workers 9–10, 155–7, 182–4, 199
   autonomy 166, 171, 173, 184, 191, 205
   collective organization 162–4
   contracts and working time 176–7
   customization of product 167–8
   discretion 166, 173, 179, 181, 182, 184, 191, 194, 195–6, 204, 205
   employment regulations, labour supply, and workforce composition 198–9
   job design 191, 192, 193–4
   job quality 200–1
   managing staff 170–3
   pay 174–6
   performance outcomes 203–4
   progression 177–9
   service delivery 168–70
   training 165–6, 178, 197
   union organization and influence 198

Index

café workers (cont.)
  workforce 164–5
  work organization 166, 195–6
Canada 18, 25–6n2, 27, 50
capitalism
  convergence 64
  deskilling 20
  education and training 213
  globalized and financialized 189
  organized labour 212
  pressures 215
  upskilling 42
  see also varieties of capitalism
Carré, F. 7, 10, 58, 61, 198, 208
childcare 85, 91, 198
  café workers 177, 178, 179, 180
  vocational teachers 201
Clark, L. 38–9
Coalition government (UK, 2010–15) 67, 75, 102
Coates, D. 215
Cockburn, C. 39
Coffield, F. 117
collective bargaining 209
  analytical framework 59, 60, 61, 62
  café workers 162, 163
  employment regulations 60
  fitness instructors 131, 132, 133, 138, 146, 151, 152
  France 54, 70–1, 73, 84, 89, 133, 152, 163
  intermediate jobs 127
  low-skilled service sector jobs 157
  new sectors 62
  Norway 61, 68–9, 81, 133, 147
  sectoral focus 53–4
  UK 54, 61, 66, 67, 97, 131, 133, 147, 162
  vocational teachers 97, 101
  see also trade unions
competitive advantage
  'high road' strategy 208
  skills as source of 15, 32
competitive strategy 31–3
Conservative Party (UK)
  1979–97 administration 66, 74, 80, 89
  2015– administration 67, 75
  Coalition government (2010–15) 67, 75, 102
  skills policy 17
continuing professional development 147, 203
coordinated market economies (CMEs) 46–7, 48, 67
Crouch, C. 1, 213
customer-oriented bureaucracy 34–5
Cutler, T. 17
Czerniawski, G. 99, 119

Denmark 6, 17, 18, 24, 27, 49, 50, 51, 57, 94
  deskilling 20, 41–2, 188
  Digital Taylorism 24–5

employment regulations 60
fitness instructors 139, 140, 148, 152, 193
job design 209
service sector 21–3
discretion 4, 87–8
  café workers 166, 173, 179, 181, 182, 184, 191, 194, 195–6, 204, 205
  defined 40
  fitness instructors 125, 143, 151, 191, 205
  and health problems 200
  knowledge work 24
  low-skilled service sector jobs 156, 157, 208
  organized labour 207
  public sector 210
  Scandinavia 205
  trade unions' influence 8
  vocational teachers 108–12, 190, 192, 196, 201, 205
Dobbin, F. 6, 50, 51–2, 62, 151, 205
Doellgast, V. 57
Dølvik, J. 81

education and training 59, 209
  analytical framework 59
  café workers 165–6, 178, 197
  comparative view 73–80, 206
  fitness instructors 133–7, 147, 150–1, 196–7
  human capital theory 18, 19
  initial vocational (IVET), *see* vocational teachers
  low-skilled service sector jobs 158
  national institutions 44–8
  over-qualification 25
  policy 188
  qualification demands 87
  upskilling narrative 17–18
  vocational teachers 196
Edwards, P. 35
Elias, P. 29, 206
emotional labour 3–4, 35, 38, 190
  café workers 174
  fitness instructors 148
employment 85–6, 91
  regulations 202, 209
    analytical framework 60, 61–2
    café workers 176, 177, 180, 182, 198
    comparative view 65–73
    fitness instructors 148, 150, 152, 153, 198
    job quality 63
    low-skilled service sector jobs 158, 159
    vocational teachers 198
Ertl, H. 123
Esping-Andersen, G. 46
European Commission 15–16, 56
European Union (EU)
  France's labour market 72
  'more and better jobs' agenda 2, 189

256

Index

service sector work organization and skills 55
Social Chapter 66
European Working Conditions Survey (EWCS) 24, 87, 88

Fellesforbundet 162–3
Felstead, A. 139
financialization 89, 189, 211
Finegold, D. 32, 46
Finland 18, 24, 27, 50, 51, 56, 80
fitness instructors 9–10, 125–6, 151–4, 199
  better jobs? 146–8
  collective organization 131–3
  developments in the fitness industry 129–31
  education and training 133–7, 147, 150–1, 196–7
  employment regulations, labour supply, and workforce composition 198–9
  future 139–41
  job
    design 191, 192–3
    quality 200–1
    roles downwards 142
  monitoring and control 142–6
  performance outcomes 203
  skills, knowledge, and performance 148–51
  union organization and influence 198
  work organization 137–9, 195
fixed-term contracts 87
flexible specialization 20, 46
Fordism 21
foreign-born employees
  café workers 159, 164, 178, 180, 183, 198
  over-qualification 87
France
  café workers 183–4, 199
    collective organization 163–4
    contracts and working time 176–7
    customization of product 167–8
    education and training 197
    employment regulations, labour supply, and workforce composition 198, 199
    job design 191, 194
    job quality 174, 200, 201
    managing staff 170–3
    pay 174–6
    performance outcomes 203, 204
    progression 177–9
    service delivery 168–70
    training 165–6
    union organization and influence 198
    work organization, discretion, and autonomy 166, 195
    workforce 164–5
  collective bargaining 53–4, 70–1, 73, 84, 89, 133, 152, 163
  employment

  regulations 202
  unemployment and poverty 85–6, 91, 92
fitness instructors 126, 151–4, 199
  better jobs? 146–8
  collective organization 132–3
  developments in the fitness industry 129–30
  education and training 134, 136–7, 196
  future 139, 141
  job
    design 191, 192–3
    quality 200, 201
    roles 142
  monitoring and control 143–4, 146
  performance outcomes 203
  prospects for progress 210
  skills, knowledge, and performance 148–51
  union organization and influence 198
  work organization 137–9, 195
industrial relations, labour market regulation, and welfare 68, 70–3, 91
national institutions 9, 44–5, 64–5, 89–92
new public management 94, 96, 195
organization of work 51, 194, 205
  improvement initiatives 83–4
  service sector 55, 57
over-qualification 25–6n2, 26, 27
skill
  discretion and over-qualification 87–8
  formation systems 76, 77–80
  supply and usage 206
social model 70, 71
vocational teachers 94, 121–4, 199
  changing context of initial vocational education and training 96, 99–101
  discretion and autonomy 108–9, 111–12
  education 103–5, 196
  governance and management systems 115–17
  job
    design 190, 192
    quality 200, 201
  performance outcomes 202
  scope for teacher-led innovation and improvement 119–21
  union organization and influence 197
  work organization and skill requirements 194, 195

Gallie, D. 21, 39, 51, 52, 207
Gautié, J. 70
gender
  café workers 10, 160, 164–5, 178, 179, 180, 183, 199
  fitness instructors 10
  job quality 63

257

Index

gender (*cont.*)
  labour market participation 69, 85, 86, 91
  low-skilled service sector jobs 158
  pay gap 85
  polarization of skills 22
  skill, nature of 36, 37
  social skills 3–4
  vocational teachers 10, 106, 201
  welfare state 60
Germany
  apprenticeships 45, 48, 59, 127, 158, 207
  collective bargaining 53–4
  graduation rates 17, 18
  high skills equilibrium 32, 46
  intermediate service sector jobs 127, 181
  low-skilled service sector jobs 155, 157–8, 207
  minimum wage 212
  national institutions 44–5, 46, 48, 62
  occupational data 49, 50
  organization of work 51, 53
  over-qualification 25–6n2, 27
  service sector work organization and skills 55, 57
  skill
    nature of 39
    levels 6, 7, 8
  trade unions 212
  vocational teachers 123
  works councils 71
global companies 24
globalization 46, 89, 188, 189, 211
Goos, M. 22
graduate jobs 28–9, 127
Gramsci, Antonio 215
Green, F. 213
Grimshaw, D. 54
Grollmann, P. 102, 103
Groot, W. 25
Grugulis, I. 38, 39
Grumbrell-McCormick, R. 83

hairdresser teaching, *see* vocational teachers
Hall, P. 46, 47, 48–9
Heiret, J. 82
Helgøy, I. 56, 99
Henly, J. R. 177
higher education, *see* education and training
high performance working 30–1
high-skilled service sector jobs 23–5, 55–6, 57–8
Hochschild, A. 35, 38, 148
Hollingsworth, J. R. 52
Homme, A. 56, 99
Høst, H. 76
Houtsonen, J. 56
Howell, C. 68, 71

Høyrup, S. 203
human capital theory (HCT) 5, 18
  criticisms 18–20, 41
  influence 16
Hyman, R. 83, 189, 213, 215

income inequality, *see* pay, inequality
industrial relations
  comparative view 65–73
  over-qualification 25
  regulations 60
  sectoral focus 53
  varieties of capitalism 46
initial vocational education and training (IVET), *see* vocational teachers
intensification of work 88–90, 188, 201
intermediate service sector jobs 125–8
Ireland 18, 24, 27, 51, 129
Italy 18, 25–6n2, 26, 27

Japan 18, 26, 27, 46
Jellab, A. 100
job
  design
    café workers 191, 192, 193–4
    fitness instructors 191, 192–3
    organized labour 207, 208
    vocational teachers 190, 191–2
  quality 4–5, 200–2, 215
    analytical framework 58
    café workers 173–4, 182, 183–4
    intermediate jobs 127
    low-skilled service sector jobs 158–9
    national institutions 63
    prospects for progress 210
  satisfaction 25, 148
  titles 22–3, 50

Kasvio, A. 68
Keep, Ewart vi, 31, 33, 36, 37, 67, 73, 74, 75, 80, 82, 97, 156, 157, 206, 213
knowledge
  economy 20–1, 34, 188
  work 23–5
Korczynski, M. 34–5
Kosonen, T. 56
Kremer, H. 123
Krings, B.-J. 55

labour market regulation, *see* employment, regulations
Labour Party
  Norway 69
  UK 73
    1997–2010 (New Labour)
      administration 17, 66–7, 75, 80, 89, 95, 97

Index

labour supply 198–9
Lafer, G. 37
Lambert, S. J. 177
Lane, C. 54, 83
lean production 88
legislation, *see* employment, regulations
Lehndorff, S. 54, 58
liberal market economies (LMEs) 46–7, 48, 65
licence to practise, *see* occupational licensing
Lipowski, K. 117
Lloyd, C. 40
LO (Norway) 68, 77, 81, 99, 132, 162
Løken, E. 70
Lopes, H. 24
Lorenz, E. 51
low-skill service sector jobs 21–3, 57, 155–9

McDonaldization 21, 181
Maglen, L. 19
manufacturing
  cross-national perspective 6
  intermediate jobs 127
  job losses 34
  national institutions 44–9
  skill formation systems 206
  skills system research 4
  UK 66
  welfare state 60
Mason, G. 206
Mathers, A. 83
Maurice, M. 44
Mayhew, K. 26, 31, 33, 36, 67
Méhaut, P. 78
migrant workers, *see* foreign-born employees
Milner, S. 83
minimum wage 85, 209
  café workers 162, 163, 175, 182, 200
  employment regulations 60
  fitness instructors 146, 147, 152, 200
  France (SMIC) 71, 146, 152, 163, 175, 182, 202
  Germany 212
  Norway 68
  UK 66, 152, 175, 202, 211

national institutions 44–9, 62
national minimum wage, *see* minimum wage
National Vocational Qualifications (NVQs, UK) 74–5, 97
  café workers 165
  fitness instructors 134
  hairdressing 108, 110
neo-liberalism
  alternative to 213, 215
  austerity policies 2, 17
  economic performance 209
  education and training 17, 213

'employment logic' 6
entrenchment 189
EU 2
low-skill service sector jobs 155
new public management 5–6
opposition 212
over-qualification, under-utilization of skills, and work intensification 188
polarization of skills 22
resurgence 8, 211
rule-based management systems 151, 205
trade unions 163
UK 9, 65, 66, 73, 89, 211
utilization of skills 30
Neri, S. 122
Netherlands 18, 24, 27, 44-5, 51, 57
Newman, J. 95
new public management (NPM) 5–6, 24, 93–4
  France 94, 96, 195
  governance 210
  initial vocational education and training 95
  Norway 94, 96, 98, 114, 122, 195, 197
  UK 93–4, 95, 96, 121, 195, 211
NHO (Norway) 68, 99, 132, 162
Nordic countries
  collective bargaining 53–4
  education 214
  employment logic 6, 51–2, 155, 184
  intermediate service sector jobs 127
  national institutions 46, 210
  organization of work 51, 52, 62, 151
  skill levels 6, 8
  task discretion 207, 209
  utilization of skills 30
  works councils 53
  see also Denmark; Finland; Norway; Scandinavia; Sweden
Norway
  café workers 182–4, 199
  collective organization 162–4
  contracts and working time 176–7
  customization of product 167–8
  employment regulations, labour supply, and workforce composition 164–5, 198, 199
  job
    design 191, 194
    quality 173–4, 200, 201
  managing staff 170–3
  pay 174–6
  performance outcomes 203–4
  progression 177–9
  prospects for progress 210
  service delivery 168–70
  training 165–6, 197
  union organization and influence 198

259

Index

Norway (*cont.*)
  work organization, discretion, and autonomy 166, 195–6
  collective bargaining 61, 68–9, 81, 133, 147
  employment regulations 202
  employment, unemployment, and poverty 85–6, 91, 92
  fitness instructors 126, 151–3, 199
    better jobs? 146–8
    collective organization 132–3
    developments in the fitness industry 129–30
    education and training 134–7, 197
    employment regulations, labour supply, and workforce composition 199
    future 139–14
    job
      design 191, 193
      quality 200, 201
      roles 142
    monitoring and control 143–6
    performance outcomes 203
    skills, knowledge, and performance 148–50
    union organization and influence 198
    work organization 137–9, 195
  graduation rates 18
  income distribution 200
  industrial relations, labour market regulation, and welfare 67–70, 72, 73, 91
  intermediate service sector jobs 125–7
  low-skilled service sector jobs 158, 208
  national institutions 9, 64–5, 89
  new public management 94, 96, 98, 114, 122, 195, 197
  occupational data 50
  organization of work 50, 51, 52–3, 89–90, 194, 205
    improvement initiatives 80, 81–3, 84
    service sector 55, 56
  over-qualification 25–6n2, 26, 27
  performance outcomes 202
  polarization of skills 27
  productivity 68, 70
  skill, discretion, and over-qualification 87–8
  skill
    formation systems 75–7, 78–80
    levels 6
  skills supply and usage 206
  vocational teachers 94, 121–4, 199
    at work 105–7
    changing context of initial vocational education and training 96, 98–9, 101
    discretion and autonomy 108–12
    education 102–5, 196
    governance and management systems 114–15, 117
    job
      design 190, 192
      quality 200, 201
    performance outcomes 202, 203
    scope for teacher-led innovation and improvement 119–20
    union organization and influence 197
    work organization and skill requirements 194, 195
Norwegian Hospitality Association (NHO Reiseliv) 162, 166

Obama, Barack 16–17
occupational licensing
  fitness instructors 148, 203
  intermediate jobs 127
Ofsted 97, 110, 112, 113
Okay-Somervill, B. 25
Organisation for Economic Co-operation and Development (OECD) 14
  Adult Skills Survey (PIACC) 26
  France's labour market 72
  graduation rates 18
  higher education, returns to 76
  over-qualification and under-utilization of skill 30
  PISA tests of literacy and numeracy 76, 98
  Survey of Adult Skills (PIAAC) 87, 88
  utilization of skills 30
over-qualification 25–30, 87–8, 188, 193, 206, 214

part-time employees 85, 91
  café workers 160, 165, 172, 176–7, 183
  fitness instructors 132, 135, 137, 140, 141, 147
  France 72
  low-skilled service sector jobs 158
  UK 67
  vocational teachers 105, 107, 118, 201
  welfare state 60
pay 85, 86, 209
  café workers 162–3, 166, 170–1, 172–6, 178, 179, 182, 183–4, 185–7, 199
  employment regulations 202
  fitness instructors 131–3, 138, 140–2, 146–7, 150, 152, 199
  France 71
  human capital theory 18, 19
  inequality 19, 22, 85, 92, 156, 188
  job quality 200–1
  low-skilled service sector jobs 158
  Norway 69
  UK 67

vocational teachers 101, 115
see also minimum wage
Payne, J. 37, 40
people skills, *see* social skills
performance
  high performance working 30–1
  measures 5–6
  outcomes 202–4
Pocock, B. 174
Poland 17, 18, 27
polarization of skills 21–3, 26, 27, 41–2, 125
political economy of skills 60–1
Porter, M. 31
Portugal 18, 56
poverty 86, 92
product markets 58–9
public sector
  collective bargaining 61
  governance 208, 210
  knowledge work 24
  Norway 68, 69–70, 83
  performance
    measures 5–6
    outcomes 203
  polarization of skills 22
  trade unions 61
  UK 67
    fitness instructors 129–30, 131, 133, 138, 151, 152, 153, 195, 198, 201, 203
  work organization and skills 55–6
  see also new public management; vocational teachers
Purcell, K. 29, 206

quality, job, *see* job, quality

Rauner, F. 102, 103
Reay, D. 213
Regini, M. 59
Register of Exercise Professionals (REPs) 134, 147, 149
regulations, *see* employment, regulations
Reich, Robert 23
Ritzer, G. 21, 181
Rolfe, H. 127
Rosecrance, R. 15

Scandinavia
  low-skilled service sector jobs 157
  national institutions 210
  new public management 94
  occupational data 49
  organization of work 50, 51, 52, 82
  political economy of skills 60
  public sector, size 68
  service sector work organization and skills 56

skill levels 7
social model 17
task discretion 205
trade union density 68
work intensity 88
workplace development programmes 80
Scholarios, D. 25
sectoral focus 53–5, 62
service sector 3, 33–5
  welfare state 60
  work organization and skills 55–8
Simmons, R. 97, 98
Sissons, P. 29
skill
  -biased technical change (SBTC) 19, 22
  contested view of 39–40
  formation systems, *see* education and training
  nature of 36–40
Skinner, N. 174
Smith, Adam 21
social democracy, Norway 67–8, 69
social security, *see* welfare state
social skills 3–4, 36–7, 39; *see also* emotional labour
societal effects approach 6, 44, 48, 58
Soskice, D. 32, 46, 47, 48–9
Souto-Otero, M. 76
Spain 2, 18, 26, 27, 56
Stokke, T. 70
Stokland, D. 81
Streeck, W. 6, 45, 48, 49, 52, 59, 189, 208, 211, 212
student employees
  café workers 163, 164, 165, 176, 177, 178–9, 180, 183, 184, 199
  fitness instructors 135, 137, 147, 199
Sung, J. 32
Sweden 6, 18, 24, 27, 45–6, 50, 56, 61, 62, 69, 80, 89, 94, 99, 129, 155, 157, 164, 198
Switzerland 18

Tavistock Institute 80, 81
Taylorism 21, 24–5, 35, 51, 62, 83, 88
Tchobanian, R. 83
temporary employees 85, 91
  café workers 160, 178, 199
  fitness instructors 132, 141, 199
  France 72
  vocational teachers 105
Thompson, P. 23, 39, 41
Thompson, R. 97
Thurow, L. 28
Tilly, C. 7, 10, 58, 61, 198, 208
Trades Unions Congress (TUC) 65, 66

Index

trade unions 209
  analytical framework 59–60, 61, 62
  café workers 163, 179–80, 183, 184, 198
    France 163, 164, 171, 177, 179, 194
    Norway 162, 163, 164, 177, 179, 194
    UK 162, 164, 179
  fitness instructors 152–3, 198
    France 132, 133, 153
    Norway 132, 133, 151, 152–3
    UK 131, 133, 152–3
  France 70, 71, 72, 73, 90
    café workers 163, 164, 171, 177, 179, 194
    fitness instructors 132, 133, 153
    skill formation systems 78
    vocational teachers 100, 101, 116–17, 123
    work organization improvement initiatives 83, 84
  job design 207, 208
  low-skilled service sector jobs 157, 158
  Norway 68–70, 89
    café workers 162, 163, 164, 177, 179, 194
    fitness instructors 132, 133, 151, 152–3
    vocational teachers 99, 101, 115, 122
    work organization improvement initiatives 81, 83
  UK 60, 65–6, 67, 73, 90, 211
    café workers 162, 164, 179
    fitness instructors 131, 133, 152–3
    skill formation systems 74, 75
    vocational teachers 97, 101, 114, 116, 121–2
    work organization improvement initiatives 80, 81
  vocational teachers 197–8
    France 100, 101, 116–17, 123
    Norway 99, 101, 115, 122
    UK 97, 101, 114, 116, 121–2
  see also collective bargaining
training, *see* education and training
turnover
  café workers 160, 178
  fitness instructors 135, 141, 147, 149, 150, 152
  low-skilled service sector jobs 158

under-utilization of skills 25–30, 188, 214
unemployment 85–6, 91
  France 72
  Norway 69
  UK 67
Union of Education (Norway) 99, 102
unions, *see* trade unions
United Kingdom
  austerity policies 2, 67, 75
  café workers 183, 199
    collective organization 162–4
    contracts and working time 176–7
    customization of product 167–8
    employment regulations 198–9

  job
    design 191, 194
    quality 174, 200, 201
    labour supply 198–9
    managing staff 170, 172–3
    pay 174–6
    performance outcomes 203, 204
    progression 177–9
    prospects for progress 210
    service delivery 169–70
    training 165, 197
    union organization and influence 198
    workforce 164–5, 198–9
    work organization, discretion, and autonomy 166, 195
  collective bargaining 53–4, 61, 66, 67, 97, 131, 133, 147, 162
  deregulated labour market 156
  employment, unemployment, and poverty 85–6, 91, 92
  fitness instructors 126, 151–3, 199
    better jobs? 146–8
    collective organization 131–3
    developments in the fitness industry 129–31
    education and training 133–7, 196–7
    employment regulations 198
    future 139–40
    job
      design 191, 192–3
      quality 200, 201
      roles 142
    labour supply 198
    monitoring and control 143–6
    performance outcomes 203
    skill formation systems 196–7
    skills, knowledge, and performance 148–50
    union organization and influence 198
    workforce composition 198
    work organization 137–9, 195
  graduation rates 17, 18
  income inequality 156
  industrial relations, labour market regulation, and welfare 65–7, 73, 91, 198–9, 202
  intermediate service sector jobs 125–8
  low-skilled service sector jobs 157–8
  low skills equilibrium 32, 46
  National Institute of Economic and Social Research (NIESR) 44, 47
  national institutions 9, 44–5, 46, 47, 48, 64–5, 89–92
  new public management 93–4, 95, 96, 121, 195, 211
  occupational data 49–50
  organization of work 51, 53, 194, 205, 207
    improvement initiatives 80–1, 84
    service sector 56, 57

over-qualification 25–6n2, 26–8, 29
part-time working mothers 60
skills
  discretion, and over-qualification 87–8
  formation systems 73–5, 76, 77, 78–80, 213, 214
  nature of 36, 38–9
  polarization 22, 26, 27, 125
  survey 26–8, 29
  trade unions 60, 65–6, 67, 73, 89, 211
    café workers 162, 164, 179
    fitness instructors 131, 133, 152–3
    skill formation systems 74, 75
    vocational teachers 97, 101, 114, 116, 121–2
    work organization improvement initiatives 80, 81
  under-utilization of skills 28, 29–30
  utilization of skills 30, 81
  vocational teachers 94, 121–4, 199
    at work 106–7
    changing context of initial vocational education and training 95, 96–8, 101
    discretion and autonomy 108–12
    education 102–5, 196
    employment regulations, labour supply, and workforce composition 198
    governance and management systems 112–17
    job
      design 190, 192
      quality 200, 201
    performance outcomes 202, 203
    prospects for progress 210
    scope for teacher-led innovation and improvement 117–18, 120
    union organization and influence 197–8
    work organization 195
  work organization and skill requirements 194
United States of America 6, 16, 17, 18, 19, 20, 21, 22, 23, 25, 27, 28, 36, 45, 46, 47, 48, 50, 51, 57, 61, 68, 70, 94, 125, 127, 129, 156, 157–8, 177, 207, 212
upskilling 21, 41–2
  café workers 181, 183, 184
  economic argument 188
  fitness instructors 148
  job design 209
  low-skilled service sector jobs 158
  narrative 15–18
  research contribution 207–8
Ure, O.-B. 76

van den Brink, H. M. 25
varieties of capitalism (VOC) 6, 8, 46–8, 53, 61, 204
Viallon, R. 136

vocational education and training (VET), *see* education and training
vocational pedagogy 104–5, 109–12
vocational teachers 9–10, 93–5, 121–4, 199
  at work 105–7
  changing context of initial vocational education and training 95–101
  curriculum and assessment 108–9
  discretion and autonomy 108–12
  education 102–5
  employment regulations, labour supply, and workforce composition 198–9
  governance and management systems 112–17
  job
    design 190, 191–2
    quality 200–1
  pedagogy 109–12
  performance outcomes 202–3
  scope for teacher-led innovation and improvement 117–21
  skill formation systems 196
  union organization and influence 197–8
Voss-Dahm, D. 158

wages, *see* pay
Watson, I. 30
welfare state 85–6
  analytical framework 60, 61–2
  comparative view 65–73
  job quality 63
Winch, C. 38–9
women, *see* gender
Wood, G. 54
Work Environment Act (Norway, 1977) 69, 82
workforce composition
  café workers 198–9
  fitness instructors 198–9
  vocational teachers 198–9
working hours 85
  café workers 160, 172, 176–7, 178, 182
  employment regulations 60
  fitness instructors 140, 147–8, 150, 152
  France 71, 72
  vocational teachers 107, 118, 120, 123, 201
  see also part-time employees
work organization improvement initiatives 80–4
works councils
  analytical framework 60, 61, 62
  café workers 179
  France 71–2, 83
  job design 207
  new sectors 62
  Norway 68, 83
  sectoral focus 53–4
Wright, J. 29

zero hours contracts 67, 172